*Salvos Against
the New Deal*

BOOKS BY GARET GARRETT:

Where the Money Grows, 1911
The Blue Wound, 1921
The Driver, 1922
The Cinder Buggy, 1923
Satan's Bushel, 1924
*Ouroboros, Or the Mechanical Extension
    of Mankind,* 1926
Harangue, 1927
The American Omen, 1928
Other People's Money, 1931 (pamphlet)
The Bubble that Broke the World, 1932
A Time is Born, 1944
The People's Pottage, 1953, consisting of:
    "The Revolution Was" (1944)
    "Ex America" (1951)
    "Rise of Empire" (1952)
The Wild Wheel, 1952
The American Story, 1955

GARET GARRETT

U.S.

Salvos Against the New Deal

Selections from the *Saturday Evening Post*
1933-1940

Edited by Bruce Ramsey

CAXTON PRESS
2002

ISBN 0-87004-425-7

Library of Congress Cataloging-in-Publication Data

Garrett, Garet.
Salvos against the New Deal : selections from the
Saturday Evening
Post, 1933-1940 / Garet Garrett ; edited by Bruce Ramsey.
  p. cm.
ISBN 0-87004-425-7 (alk. paper)
1. New Deal, 1933-1939. 2. United States—Economic
conditions—1918-1945. I. Ramsey, Bruce. II. Saturday
evening post.
III. Title.
  HC106.3 .G254 2002
  330.973'0917—dc21

                                    2002000256

Printed in the United States of America
CAXTON PRESS
168300

Contents

Acknowledgements

Many thanks to Prof. Stephen Cox of the University of California at San Diego for lending a thoughtful eye to the introduction; to R.W. Bradford of *Liberty* for his encouragement; the staff of the Herbert Hoover Presidential Library, West Branch, Iowa; the Houghton Library at Harvard University; the Seeley G. Mudd Library at Princeton University; the Suzzalo Library at the University of Washington and the Seattle Public Library.

Introduction

By Bruce Ramsey

The New Deal, it is said, saved American capitalism. So I was taught in school. This book tells a different story. The New Deal had many enemies, but few with as sharp a pen as Garet Garrett. "He's a small man with alert blue eyes, an apparently inexhaustible supply of nervous energy and the most completely controlled and incisively logical mind we've ever come across," bragged the editors of the *Saturday Evening Post* in 1937. Garrett was their writer on political economy—reporter, essayist and advocate. While other critics mocked the politics of Franklin Roosevelt and his entourage, Garrett homed in on what the New Deal actually did to farmers, workers and industrial managers, and what that meant for the American political system.

At the end of his life, Garrett believed his cause, the old republic of limited government and free markets, had been lost. But at the dawn of the next century, that judgment is less certain. The contrary ideal, socialism, is dead. Americans once again celebrate the entrepreneur. Young Americans have hatched enterprises with astounding margins of profit, and have convinced themselves that nothing like them existed before. They could do well to read

Garrett, who might have written the following words about Bill Gates:

"You may take him to be the richest man . . . In twenty years, from nothing, he and his associates have created the largest one unit of industry in the world. It is the most celebrated instance of profit making. Where is the profit? In what form does it exist? A house to live in . . . and the cost . . . in proportion to the wealth he has created is trifling. The rest of the profit has been returned to its source. The more of it that was returned, the more of it that there was, until at last is ceases to have the meaning of money . . . He says himself, 'All anybody can get out of this is a job.' "

Garrett wrote that in 1928 about Henry Ford, who then ran an entrepreneurial, non-union company with the highest wages in the world.

Today's pioneers think they have created an economy that is fundamentally different. It isn't so different. It is new to them, but in its genetic code is the same wild DNA that spawned enterprises of a century ago, before they were domesticated by unions and government.

In Garrett's day, progressive thought considered government planning scientific and rational. Reformers had faith in the wisdom of bureaucrats. Today people know better. If they dared, many Americans would shuck off Social Security, farm subsidies, federal welfare and compulsory unionism. But they are held back, partly by the story they learned about the New Deal—that it saved capitalism and constitutional government.

That's one story. But there is another story, a story that has largely been lost, told by those who fought and were defeated. In the light of what we have now learned about markets and government, theirs is a more believable story than the one handed down by the court historians of Franklin Roosevelt.

And the one who told it best was Garet Garrett.

Edward Peter Garrett was born in the village of Pana, Ill, on February 19, 1878. The family soon moved to Iowa. He would refer many times to his upbringing on an unmechanized, self-sustaining farm. As an adult, he went back to living on a farm in Tuckahoe, N.J., near Atlantic City. Garrett was fascinated by the use and meaning of machines, but his personal ideal was rural self-sufficiency. In the 1930s he wrote of converting an old Model A Ford into the power source of a buzz saw.

His formal schooling ended at the third grade. He learned thereafter by reading books.

From fifteen to eighteen, Garrett experienced the depression of the 1890s. In his novel *The Driver*, he described Coxey's Army, a group of supplicants that marched on Washington in 1894 demanding cheap federal credit. Garrett also wrote of cold, ragged men in soup lines and of trains seized by men on strike.

That had been the *great* depression. People had toughed it out. Bad investments—stocks, bonds and mortgages—were washed away. Man and machine, freed of old debts and obligations, started over. They received no cheap federal credit. To have kept old obligations alive with credit would have been to hobble recovery with dead weight.

Nor did they cheapen money. There had been a great push in 1896 to throw off the gold standard, and the country had resisted it. And business recovered.

By 1898 good times had returned. Garrett, age twenty, hopped a freight for Chicago. He went on to Cleveland, where he started work as a printer, then as a newspaper reporter. Then to Washington, D.C., where he took the name Garet.

At twenty-five, Garrett became a financial reporter for the New York *Sun,* moving on to the *New York Times,* the *Wall Street Journal* and the *Evening Post.* In 1911 he published his first book, *Where the Money Grows*, a compendium of Wall Street sketches (reissued in 1993 by John Wiley & Sons). He wrote for muckraking magazines. Then, for most of the World War I decade, he went into newspaper management. In 1919, at age forty-one, he abandoned management to be a full-time writer.

He wrote fiction, all of it with an economic and political message. *The Driver* (1922) and *The Cinder Buggy* (1923)

11

were novels of nineteenth century entrepreneurs, telling the story of railroad reorganizations and of iron and steel. *Satan's Bushel* (1924) was an allegory of agriculture and its struggle with overproduction. ("Satan's bushel" was the bushel that broke the price.) *Harangue* (1927) was a fictionalization of the socialist takeover of North Dakota in 1919.

Garrett's first novel, *The Blue Wound* (1921), was hardly a novel at all, but a sort of animated essay. In it, Garrett imagined that by 1950, Germany had invented a super-weapon that could destroy everything within 300 miles. America did not have that weapon because it had relied on the German chemical industry instead of building its own.

Garrett was drawn to the idea of national self-sufficiency, especially at times of crisis. At the bottom of the Depression, in 1933, he wrote, "There is nothing—almost nothing—in Europe that we need." After the fall of France, in the *Saturday Evening Post* of July 20, 1940, he wrote, "We are the most nearly self-contained nation of modern times." To be self-reliant was to be strong.

At home, Garrett was a believer in laissez-faire; abroad he was a nationalist. Squaring this circle led him into an odd distinction between free trade and freedom of trade. "Free trade," he wrote, "means to abolish the protective tariffs, whereas freedom to trade means that people should be free to produce and exchange wealth with other people as they please, and make their own bargains at their own risk, with no direct intervention of government." He was for freedom *of* trade, but he thought that nations might protect their interests by imposing tariffs.

There is little here of Garrett's views on trade, because trade and international loans had more to do with the cause of the Depression than the curing of it, and this book is about the attempt to cure it. It is enough to say that Garrett rejected the free traders' argument that the Depression had been caused by the Smoot-Hawley tariff of 1930, which threw U.S. trade into a downward spiral. In Garrett's view, the share of international trade in the U.S. economy—about seven percent—was too small to take down the rest of industrial production. He argued in *The Bubble That Broke the World* (1932) that it was unpayable debt— much of it the World War I loans and postwar loans made by the U.S. government and banks—that seized up the world's financial engine.

As a nationalist, Garrett was a trumpeter of a uniquely American capitalism. At the high note of the Roaring Twenties, Garrett laid out his vision of the "new economy" in *The American Omen* (1928)—a largely non-union world of professional management, time-saving machines, just-in-time inventory control ("hand-to-mouth buying") and high wages. It was a world in which people accepted inequality of income and wealth. "There is no evidence that men want to be equal," Garrett wrote. "Here, if a man says the state owes him liberty, protection, equality of opportunity, that is already acknowledged. These are political benefits. But if he says the state owes him a living, he is ridiculed."

Then came the Great Depression.

In 1932, Garrett was fifty-four. For a decade, he had been economics essayist for the *Saturday Evening Post,* which in the days before television was the most influential magazine in the United States. It defined and reflected the American middle class.

Garrett was disturbed at the economic and political ideas then afoot, but not particularly by the two candidates for president. There was, thank God, no William Jennings Bryan. Hoover was no danger to the republic. Garrett had corresponded with Hoover, and would be invited to read and comment on the working manuscript of several Hoover books. Garrett did not know Roosevelt, but the aristocratic New York governor was no radical, and had affirmed that plank in the Democratic platform that called for "a sound currency to be preserved at all hazards."

But it was not to be. After his election but before taking office, Roosevelt started talking to the anti-gold people. Rumors swirled, and the president-elect did nothing to quell them. Bank depositors panicked. Roosevelt took office

March 4, 1933, at a moment of national nervous break-down, and made himself *de facto* dictator of the economy. Garrett was measured in his opposition. The situation *was* an emergency. Roosevelt had been given his powers by Congress, and by a people that was willing to try almost anything. Garrett allowed there was reason to experiment, though the repudiation of gold was anathema to him. By December 1933 he was ready to fight—as was his boss, *Post* editor George Lorimer. "Up until that time," wrote John Tebbel in *George Horace Lorimer and the Saturday Evening Post* (1948), "the *Post* had been primarily an organ of entertainment and enlightenment, notwithstanding its political campaigns. Now Lorimer frankly abandoned that concept of it in favor of an open and continued attack on the enemy."

His artillery piece was Garrett, who began firing at the New Deal's upside-down economics, its amorality and its threat to American liberty. Garrett called out to the America who knew and revered the old republic.

It was a losing battle. The most obvious beneficiaries of the old system—businessmen—were demoralized by the Depression. They wanted only to be saved. Roosevelt offered them the National Recovery Administration, which let them collude and fix prices—something that had been illegal for forty years—and to proudly post a Blue Eagle as a symbol of their patriotism. Instead of filing lawsuits and raising hell over the loss of their rights, they rushed to sign up.

An exception was Henry Ford, a man whose opinions followed no correct order. Ford went to see Roosevelt and NRA boss Hugh Johnson, and announced that he would have nothing to do with their illegal program. Wrote Garrett in *The Wild Wheel,* "But for the Ford Motor Company, it would have to be written that the surrender of American business to government was unanimous, complete and unconditional."

The contestant that vanquished the NRA was not some corporate giant, but a Brooklyn chicken dealer. The chicken dealer took his case to the Supreme Court and won a

14

unanimous decision. But it was one of the only ones. The court would fight the New Deal for two more years, and give up.

What business did, the farmers did and the recipients of relief did. "The people were willing," Garrett wrote in *The American Story*. "They were not coerced. They were writhing in economic pain. Many forgot and many seemed no longer to care that unless they absorbed their own troubles instead of unloading them on a paternalistic government they would never again be as free as their fathers were."

Did the people really want the Roosevelt program? Even after the mid-term elections of 1934, in which the New Dealers held their own, opponents argued that the people would not re-elect the president. But in November 1936, Roosevelt carried every state but Maine and Vermont. The Democrats held 76% of the seats in the House and 79% in the Senate.

Garrett wrote author Rose Wilder Lane, who was of similar political mind, that he was "sick with disappointment" in the timid campaign run by Republican Alf Landon. "All he has said is that he will go on doing as much for people as they expect the New Deal to do for them, only in a Constitutional manner, and it will cost less."

Nevertheless, Garrett had worked for the Republicans, and he took their defeat hard. "Our fighting base is gone," he wrote Lane. "Formerly we could say the people had never voted for the New Deal. That was a strong fighting position. Now they have voted for it in a positive, overwhelming manner. Then what? Shall one go on telling them they are wrong, or that they shall see, or that they have lost the world without knowing it, that they threw it away, and so on? Certainly not.

"Where is the new base? I don't see it. Where is the fighting position? I haven't any; no one else seems to have one. Hearst and Smith and Rockefeller embracing it. The Republicans saying they must reorganize the party on a liberal platform. As for me, I believed something. What I believed has been rejected. According to my own argument, what people reject they have a right to reject; what world they want they have a perfect right to bring to pass if they can."

Lorimer, who had run the *Saturday Evening Post* since the turn of the century, announced his retirement in December 1936. Terminally ill, he felt crushed by the American people's rejection of the *Post's* crusade. He was to be replaced by Wesley Stout. Garrett wondered if the crusade was over.

It was not. Early in 1937, Garrett wrote to Lane, "I was thinking to cut out, because apparently the *Post* was leaning away from the fight. But now Stout wants me to get into the labor story, and that changes my feeling about him and about the *Post*. Anyhow, I'm going to do it."

Garrett had always written favorably of the skilled worker, the "aristocrat of labor," who could "think with his hands." Of the unskilled worker, likely an immigrant from Eastern or Southern Europe, Garrett had little to say. Privately he considered the unskilled worker a drudge. But at least in America that worker was relatively well-paid. Wages had tripled in the previous fifty years, and were the highest in the world. The worker was also free to join a union, which in America existed to argue over the division of the output. That was all right. But when the unions went for control of the production line, Garrett was against them.

Garrett, who honored the strong, had to admit the vigor of the new union leaders. In early 1937, he interviewed John L. Lewis, who was organizing the steel industry. "It would take 5,000 words to tell you what I make of him," he wrote Rose Lane. "Powerful, intelligent, subtle, ruthless, remorseless, probably sinister, with amazing poise and self-control . . . During four hours of hard conversation he has been apparently spontaneous, unthinking, unguarded, almost naive. He listens. He never [admits] a weak position, but says, 'Well, what of it?'"

In Garrett's next letter, he wrote, "I ask myself what I should do if I worked on the assembly line. Would I join

16

Lewis? I wish I knew. I think I'd go with Lewis, even hating any kind of union. Why? I cannot be sure. Probably from seeing people go in and out of the Detroit Athletic Club. I know that gang and it's fine. But if my acquaintance with it were confined to seeing it go in and out, I'd go with Lewis. Worse still, if my acquaintance with it were confined to what it says or to what it knows about itself, I'd be for Lewis now. It's fine for reasons it does not know."

By that, Garrett meant that he understood the political implications of the capitalist system better than the capitalists themselves. In 1934 he had written to Hoover, "Almost I am persuaded that business itself has done more harm to capitalism and to its principles of liberty than all the demagogues."

In the midterm elections of 1938, the Republicans made a comeback, and the New Deal's momentum was stopped. Beginning in 1939, Garrett's attentions changed to the prospect of war. He had been forty-one when President Wilson convinced Congress to join World War I, a crusade Garrett would label "a total loss." In 1939, at sixty-one, he began his last great public fight, against war with Germany.

In the April 8, 1939, *Saturday Evening Post,* Garrett observed in an unsigned editorial "the steady onset of the idea that we shall have to save the world for democracy again . . . You can feel it . . . The American character is inhabited by a strong crusader spirit. Many voices, for different reasons, have been calling to it, and it responds."

In September 1939, Germany and Russia invaded Poland, starting World War II in Europe. In May 1940, Germany invaded France. Roosevelt declared a national emergency, and in June 1940 ordered military aid sent to England and France. Garrett opposed aid. He thought America might well have to fight Hitler, and that it might need those weapons for itself. Besides, he wrote in the Sept. 7, 1940, editorial, "For all we think and feel about Hitler, he has not attacked us."

In August 1940 Congress passed the first peacetime

17

conscription law in American history. Garrett accepted it. In the Sept. 24, 1940, editorial, he wrote, "In the extreme case, even freedom is subject to necessity, and one of its rights would be the right to conscript itself." Survival was a higher value than temporary freedom. But Garrett was uneasy about the purposes to which the new conscript army would be put—not defending America, but liberating some other country.

When Lend-Lease became law March 11, 1941, Garrett took it as a declaration of war. In the editorial of March 29, he wrote, "From now on there is for us no foreign war. Any war anywhere in the world is our war, provided only there is an aggressor to be destroyed, a democracy to be saved or an area of freedom to be defended." In June, Germany invaded the Soviet Union, and America was committed to defending a communist state as well. America had changed. "It is a strange land," he wrote, "and if it is ours we are strangers in it."

After the Dec. 7, 1941, attack on Pearl Harbor, the *Post* supported the war. It had little choice. It also ended its fight against the government's domestic policy. On March 12, Garrett and Stout resigned. In a letter to Hoover, Garrett wrote that the *Post* "has lifted up her garments to the New Deal."

Now that the war was on, Garrett wanted to be in it. He offered himself for a federal job, writing to the head of the U.S. Civil Service Commission, "I am entirely at the disposal of the government, for anything it may wish me to do, for the duration of the war." They didn't want him. Nor did mainstream journalism like *Harper's* and *Reader's Digest*. In 1942 he wrote, "There are ten or fifteen well-known writers who now find themselves marked, as if they were on a black list."

Garrett struggled for a platform. He lined up business backers for a series of pamphlets, then a new magazine, then an economic quarterly, but they either couldn't get a wartime paper ration or the publisher changed his plans. He had a few successes. In 1943 he had a stirring defense of "isolationism" printed in Colonel Robert McCormick's

18

Chicago Tribune. In 1944, he had published *A Time Is Born,* which is a reworking of *The Blue Wound.* That year the Caxton Printers in Caldwell, Idaho, published his most radical attack on the New Deal, the essay "The Revolution Was," which would remain in print in one form or another for most of the twentieth century.

At war's end in 1945, his friends at the National Industrial Conference Board installed him as editor of their publication, *American Affairs.* That lasted five years. Then, in the last four years of his life, he produced three books: *The Wild Wheel* (1953), a memoir of the world of laissez faire; *The American Story* (1954), his interpretation of American history; and his most popular work, *The People's Pottage* (1952), comprising his essays "The Revolution Was," "Ex America" and "Rise of Empire."

In "Rise of Empire" was the radical voice, listing the signs of empire that Garrett saw at the dawn of the Cold War. "War becomes an instrument of domestic policy," he wrote. Another sign was a system of satellite nations. "We use that word only for nations that have been captured in the Russian orbit, with some inflection of contempt," he wrote. "We speak of our own satellites as allies and friends or as freedom loving nations. Nevertheless, satellite is the right word. The meaning of it is the hired guard."

When I read these words in the late 1960s, I wasn't sure what to make of them. Was this a voice of the Right? As Justin Raimondo wrote in *Reclaiming the American Right* (1990), there was no room on the American political spectrum for a man like Garrett "for as long as the Cold War lasted." Today, because of his objections to war abroad and the administrative state at home, Garrett would be considered paleolibertarian or paleoconservative, the "paleo" meaning that he is rooted in American nationalist tradition.

Garrett was born into a self-reliant culture. "Let the people be; let them make their own mistakes and absorb their own troubles," he wrote in 1953. "Few Americans now

19

living have any idea how strong that conviction was." He died a pessimist, thinking his cause was lost.

But perhaps it is not. The adventurers of capitalism, dismissed in the the '30s, '40s and '50s as "rugged individualists" out of place in a social age, have returned. Garrett might be stunned by today's silicon wizardry, but he would have recognized the "New Economy" at once.

His work deserves to be read, particularly by those who value dynamism, change, the flux of the market, independence, self-reliance and the individual will. There are many who support those values but who have accepted the New Deal's view of itself—not because they should accept it, but because that is all they know. This book is for them.

The essays and excerpts in this volume recall a battle of ideas seven decades ago. Its view is not of the New Deal as filtered through sixty years of commentary and the inevitability of Big Government. Its links are with the America that went before, a time that today's Americans know nothing of at all.

Some of these essays are pure polemics. Some are journalism, which is to say, partial polemics. In pieces like "The Kohler Strike," for example, Garrett is a journalist—but he defines the contest in his way.

Prejudices are important in journalism. Reporting can unearth opinions and facts, but it is your values—your prejudices, in nomenclature less politically correct—that tell you what matters. Like H.L. Mencken, Garrett grew to cherish his prejudices, and to check every so often that he still had them on board. To Rose Wilder Lane, he wrote, "I wish you would do an essay on the importance of prejudice. I am building a series of wakes, one for each prejudice I have buried."

Without values, history cannot be made sense of, either.

My own values are similar to Garrett's. So is my line of work. I have been an editorialist or economic journalist for twenty-five years, in Seattle and Hong Kong. I can appreciate what he was able to accomplish—the amount of his reporting, and, more important, the amount of his thinking. It was in the course of researching a magazine article on Garrett that I looked up ten years of his writing in the *Saturday Evening Post,* and decided that it ought to be in a book.

There was too much for one book. And Garrett wrote his essays before television; by today's standards they are too long. Every essay here except "To Work" has been edited for length. "The Kohler Strike," "A Particular Kind of Money," "In the Name of Labor" and "Economic Royalism" have been edited only lightly. "We Are Building," however, was more nearly snipped in half. "Pharoahs" lost its final third. "A New Culture" and "The Perfect Closed-Shop Town" are excerpts, and chapters one, four and six are short items.

Only a handful of words have been added, and then only to smooth over a cut or to omit a long explanation of the non-essential. If that annoys scholars—well, this book is not primarily for them. They can look up the *Saturday Evening Post.*

This book is for those with an interest in Garrett's core belief, American liberty. That idea, which Garrett despaired of, has had a comeback. It is my hope that this book will contribute to its growth, and reconnect libertarians, classical liberals, liberty-loving conservatives and the entrepreneurs of the New Economy with the work of a man who battled for their values at the most discouraging time in the twentieth century.

By permission of the Houghton Library, Harvard University   bMS Am 1481 (68)

Garet Garrett, passport photo, 1925

CHAPTER ONE:
Premonitions

The New Deal did not come out of a void. It came out of ideas that had been percolating for a long time. Some of them—propping up cotton prices, and using federal credit to bail out railroads and banks—were implemented first by Hoover. A surprising amount of economic management had been tried by the Wilson administration in World War I. Other ideas, from academia, gained ground as the system's defenders conceded it. Garrett's first argument to the stunned supporters of capitalism was to cheer them up. Business was bound to get better; it always had. The system worked. It made sense. But as the Depression went on and on, deeper than anyone had foreseen, there were signs that this time, things would turn out differently.

'There Goes Mine'

From "Notes of These Times,"
October 8, 1932

An automobile dealer in New Castle, Pa.:

"That's a fine car you're driving. You won't see anything like that in this town. There are people here who could afford to buy fine cars. They have the money, they want the cars, and they won't buy them."

"Why not?"

"They are afraid."

"What are they afraid of?"

"Afraid to be seen driving them, for the feeling it might raise. This is no time to make a display of wealth. With so many people out of work, it is bound to excite resentment. There is now that restraint upon buying."

"Are you sure?"

"I know it. Don't I live here? And you can't blame them, either. I mean the people who might resent it. They know as well as we do one thing that's the matter with this country. Five per cent of the people have 90 percent of the wealth. That's the figure, isn't it?"

"Do you pay an income tax?"

"I do. Why?"

"Because if you do, then you belong to the 5 percent."

"I wouldn't think so myself. But what if I do?"

"Do you hear people richer than you are saying as you do that the concentration of wealth in the hands of a few is a bad condition?"

"I hear many people say it. Yes, and some who are richer than I am, a good deal."

"Well, they hear people richer than themselves saying the same thing, and those hear others saying it who are richer still, and so all the way up. There is a man whose wealth you would easily take to be a billion dollars who says the trouble with the country is that a few other men control all the wealth."

"What are you coming to?"

"Back to what your rich fellow townsmen are afraid of. Their fear of popular resentment is born in their own heads. This car you speak of—such a car as you say some people in this town would be afraid to drive—it has been driven in your streets and through your worst neighborhoods. It has been driven thousands of miles in every kind of road and street, through industrial cities where unemployment is much more visible than here, and never has there been a sign of resentment. It has been noticed, but not resentfully. As it passes, you hear murmurs of admiration, whistlings, ah's, sometimes a shout of, 'There goes mine.' And why is there no resentment? It is because those who do not have cars expect to have cars, and those who have cars expect to have better cars. People may be out of work, they may be sore and gloomy, but that is only for the time being—the bad time being. Nobody in this country—not even the man out of work—feels condemned to poverty. That would be the dangerous feeling. We have forgotten it. In the depression of the 90s—do you remember that?"

"I do."

"Well, then it was different. That really was an ugly time. There were cities and neighborhoods where a fine carriage had to pick its street not to raise a mob. You had then millions of people who never expected to own carriages of their own. They couldn't imagine it. Your customers who are afraid to be seen with fine cars are living in the 90s. Tell them so."

"I'll hire you to tell them, if you want a job. They wouldn't believe me."

"That's because you don't believe it yourself."

'If I Were King'

From "Notes of These Times," October 8, 1932

Lately, in one of the embarrassed Midwestern cities, a banker addressed the people by radio on the extravagant follies of government. The title was, 'If I Were King.'

Twenty years ago, speaking on the same subject, would this same banker or any banker have employed that title? In the first place, it would never have occurred to him; secondly, if it had occurred to him, he would have dismissed it at once for fear he would be misunderstood or ridiculed. And instead of saying what he would do if he were king, he would have told the people what they should do to mend their own government. Thus, unawares, a change has taken place. The nature of it is pervasive. How deep it goes, no one yet knows. It is a change touching both those who impart thought and those who receive it.

How often now one hears such expressions as, "What we need in Congress is a man who will tell Congress what to do, or send it home," or "What this country needs is a Mussolini."

The total mind is bewildered and harassed: thinking is in a state of extreme confusion. All prophets have failed. There are no barriers. That is not the difficulty. Unknown roads lie open in all directions. There is a medley of voices proposing this way and that way to go, just to see what will happen.

This milling round and round in a purgatory of doubt, fear and recrimination is an ordeal; the impulse to escape from it is strong. The banker who let his own world run wild to disaster, now telling what he would do if he were king, not about banking, but to settle the affairs of society—he makes a mental escape from the muddle of his banking world. The industrialist in whose hands the bubble of limitless profit exploded just at the moment when he thought it was indestructible, now proposing an economic dictatorship to manage prosperity hereafter—he makes a mental escape from the muddle of his industrial world. And people wishing for some power to descend upon them from above and make everything right by edict—that is a collective flight from responsibility. Something must be done.

And so about money. In a time of economic depression, the idea of Satanism in money rises to a pitch of obsession. One who writes about money will be immediately overwhelmed with letters from five hundred to ten thousand words long, telling how Satan may be cast out and what terrible things will otherwise happen. One who has written about money and who stops overnight in a hotel in any city will be waked on the telephone, or else taken unawares at breakfast, for fear he may escape without hearing a new formula of exorcism. With a little practice, one can tell by a glance at the handwriting or one look at the physiognomy whether the idea will be sound or unsound.

The Satanism of money consists in this—that if money is plentiful enough, it is not valuable enough; and if it is valuable enough, it is not plentiful enough. All schemes of reform, the mad and the sane together, propose that money shall be both constantly plentiful and constantly valuable at once and forever. Well might we wish for money like that—or wheat or cotton, gold or pig iron, potatoes or cabbages like that—both plentiful and valuable always. What is plentiful? Who shall measure and determine it? The debtor or the creditor? What is valuable, and who shall determine that?

To Control Change

From "Unemployment—What Is It?"
January 21, 1933

Leaders of industry themselves are proposing to do what only the antagonists proposed before—namely, to stabilize industry by coercion and restraint, to limit production by a plan beforehand, to control change. A planned economy hereafter. There is a passion for planning the economic future in a rational manner, so that prices, values, supply, demand, employment, production shall never be in this state of chaos again.

There is a saying that if industry had had only the vision to see the road a little way ahead and the chasm there, it need not have gone over the edge. It might have put on the brakes. But who is industry? Who shall personify it? Who shall see for the whole of it? Then we say that if industry is nobody in particular, or that nobody can be held responsible, it is time the state should do the seeing, keep its hand on the brakes and set them in time. Well, the state may have eyes. This Government's financial eye is the Federal Reserve Board. A year before we went over the cliff, it did have some glimpse of the danger and tried to throttle down the gas. The gas was credit. And with what result? Not industry alone, not business alone, not Wall Street alone, but popular opinion turned upon it with ani-

27

mal ferocity. By what right did it propose to hinder prosperity? Where was its certificate of wisdom?

An Unknown Road

From "Unemployment —In the Light of Happening," February 18, 1933

There is hardly a government in the world that has not in some way intervened to resist liquidation; but the American government, the only one with a strong tradition against it, has been the least restrained of all. Its first undertakings were in behalf of agriculture. Almost before we were aware of how it could be possible, the Government had its agents standing in the grain pit on the Chicago Board of Trade, buying all the wheat with public money, thinking to stabilize the price at $1.25 a bushel, because in its opinion that was a fair and right price. Note that two years later, when the price of wheat was under fifty cents and the money had been lost, there was no more talk of stabilization, because fifty-cent wheat could be trusted to stabilize itself; but whereas the Government, by acting on the price at all, had acknowledged its duty to uphold a fair price, and whereas it had failed, the argument was bound to follow—as it has—that the Government is further obliged to restore the price of wheat to what is fair.

If it had failed to solve the price structure, then, perhaps, all the more reason why it should try to save the capital structure. And so it did. Government itself assumed moral and financial responsibility for the solvency of the banking structure as a whole, and the further responsibility to protect the capital structure of the railroads as a whole. A private bank that was fairly book solvent and yet unable out of its own frozen assets to pay its depositors could borrow money for that purpose from the Government. A railroad unable to pay its creditors, and liable to pass into bankruptcy if it didn't, could borrow money for that purpose from the Government.

This is what is new in this depression, and wherein it departs from history. In previous depressions, a bank that was book solvent and unable to pay its depositors had no alternative. It was obliged to go into bankruptcy and liquidate. A railroad that could not pay its creditors simply went into receivership and was liquidated. And so on. Such a thing as the Government going into debt itself in order to assume and underwrite the debts of private enterprise was hitherto unimaginable.

It is an unknown road and one much easier to come into than out of. As it widens to the view, directional signs become visible, but they are in a language confused and half strange to this country.

Urging the Government to go on are, first, great classes of debtors who are thinking only of relief and not of what may be happening to public credit; secondly, those to whom any process of consuming public credit that raises taxes on the rich appears to be a way of leveling down wealth, whereas it may only be a way of devouring it, and, thirdly, all those now involved in the idea that a time has come for the people to surrender their economic responsibilities to the state and submit to a life that shall be planned for them.

The New Clients

From "Unemployment—What We Do About It,"
March 11, 1933

Hitherto, the condition of joblessness was an individual misfortune; now we take unemployment to be the misfortune of society as a whole.

Hitherto, poverty, the extreme and haggard accentuation of it, was the first aspect of depression, and the reaction of society was a call to charity. Now suddenly the word "charity" is forbidden. We speak instead of relief, and the idea underlying all forms of relief, private and public both, is that there shall be no sense of charity in it, no more on the part of those who receive it than on the part of those who provide it. Less and less do the social agencies speak of dependent people as dependents. They speak of them as their clients and take pride in the stability of a clientele—a very curious phrase.

"Brother, can you spare a dime?" belongs to balladry. The solicitation is almost certainly professional. Dr. Sidney Goldstein, executive chairman of the Joint Unemployment Committee, a body representing fifteen organizations dealing with the problems of unemployment, was speaking before a Senate committee for Federal relief. He said: "These men and women, I think we ought to understand, are entitled not to a charity dole from the hands of the communities in which they live. They are citizens of the United States and they are entitled to be maintained by the Government, in view of the fact that the primary function of the Government is to protect its citizens, not only against the danger of war but against the danger of disease, the danger of starvation and the danger of premature death. That to us, Mr. Chairman, is one of the primary functions of the Government of the United States . . ."

On the other side—if one may speak of sides—are all those who would regard emergency relief simply as such. They do not hold that relief funds are adequate, but they think a principle of local responsibility is at stake, together with principles very much deeper, touching the soul of American individualism and the free status of people in relation to the state. In the movement for Federal funds they detect, or it may be they only feel, what seems a confusion of thought and is, perhaps, not that at all but an object in disguise.

Before there was any clamor for Federal relief, why, for example, should a United States senator who sympathetically represents the social-work industry have sent telegrams at public expense to every city in the country asking whether, in its opinion, the time had not come for the Federal Government to act on unemployment relief? Why should the municipalities be thus solicited to unload their burdens on the Government? Or, in the same movement, why should miners be summoned before a committee of Congress to testify whether, in their opinion, it was not time for the Federal Government to come to the relief of the mining communities? What would a miner's opinion be worth as to that? The miners all said, of course, that the time had come; they described their distress. One complained that in his community, where there had been no work for two years, there was only bread and soup to eat. The soup had rice and barley in it, but wanted potatoes. But why no potatoes? Two years of idleness, land all around them, and no potatoes. Nobody asked them that question.

CHAPTER TWO

Revolution

From "The Hundred Days," August 12, 1933

Social revolutions are, by nature, sudden and more or less incredible in the time of taking place. The intended consequences are a transfer of power and a transfer of wealth. Formerly, the power to be transferred was political power; in the modern case it is economic power. But the essential design is in no way altered. Power for its own sake is not the popular object. People themselves cannot exercise it. They are obliged to delegate it to a dictator, reserving only the right to change dictators, even, if necessary, by another revolution. A redistribution of advantage and wealth—that is the popular object.

By this definition, the country is in a state of revolution. When Congress assembled on March ninth, under an emergency call, no one knew what it was going to do, nor did it know itself what it was going to do, either at the beginning or day by day thereafter. It went from one step to another, with that kind of uncertain certainty peculiar to sleepwalking. It received the demands of the revolution serially in the form of pre-prepared laws, and enacted them with practically no debate and no drama. In the early morning of June sixteenth it adjourned. The entire life of the session had been one hundred days. That was all the time it took to enact a complete temporary dictatorship in the person of the President, standing for the popular will.

Afterward, Louis McH. Howe, secretary to the President, said on the radio that Congress all the time realized it was enacting laws that were leading "where no one knew," the "most amazing legislation this country or any other country has ever seen," but it had the courage to go on and it "wasn't afraid of the dark."

The powers transferred to the President were such as these:

1. To control and administer all business and industry in the public interest;

2. To govern production, prices, profits, competition, wages and the hours of labor;

3. To determine the economic policy of the country; that is to say, whether it shall be national or international;

4. To debase money on behalf of the debtor class;

5. To produce inflation in the interest of certain classes;

6. To reapportion private wealth and income throughout the nation, in his own judgment;

7. The power specifically to reduce the gold value of the dollar by one-half—or, that is to say, the power, simply by proclamation, to double the price of everything that is priced in dollars, and to halve the value of every obligation payable in dollars, such as debts, bonds and mortgages, insurance policies, bank deposits.

It is true that these great powers expire under certain limits of time and circumstance, or when else the President himself may proclaim the emergency ended. But this is only to say it is imagined that the popular object may be achieved within the existing frame of government. A temporary dictatorship to effect the transfer of wealth. Then constitutional government again.

In a revolution it is not the rational mentality that acts. The fact of revolution, like the fact of war, is itself the evidence that reason has failed. Reason had not solved the crisis; and although the crisis might have solved itself, as had happened before, there would remain the liability to crisis, like a principle of evil in the economic affair; and the thought of this had become intolerable. Naturally, in these circumstances, there will arise an irresistible demand for action. Nobody knows what to do. Nevertheless, let something be done. Irrational as it seems, this appeal from thought to action may represent a kind of collective wisdom superior to reason. The source of it will be human faith in trial and error. Every new way has been so discovered; the reason afterward has verified it.

Therefore, a time will come when people will turn to a man not for his mentality, not for any plan he may have— since there is no plan—but for some quality of experimental boldness they feel in him, and give him an unlimited mandate to act. He is not to lead them really, for they as yet have no sense of direction; he is only to embody their will to act by method of trial and error. He will make many mistakes. And so it may be as the action proceeds that one will be torn between convictions of reason that are outraged in many particular ways, and a sense of respect for the historical process. For once, a social revolution could take place without the crashing of one wall, the gathering of one mob, the breaking of one human head. No force was needed where there was no resistance, nor anything rigid to be destroyed. The national mood was experimental. Almost anything could happen, except only a thing of violence.

In these reflections it must appear that use of the critical faculty is limited. For constructive criticism it is already too late. The facts are accomplished. For criticism of the dictatorship so created it is yet too soon. All that seems presently feasible is to name the conditions under which we arrived suddenly and almost unawares at a temporary dictatorship and then to define what it was that happened.

The first condition was a national neurosis. Fear was in control of behavior. It was fear of irretrievable loss, fear of sinking, fear of tomorrow, fear of people, and at last, fear of fear. This the President said in his inaugural address from

35

the Capitol steps, on the fourth of March: "The only thing to fear is fear itself, nameless, unreasoning, unjustified terror."

His first official act was to suspend banking operations throughout the whole country for a period of days, by decree, to everybody's instant relief. People were not afraid to be entirely without money in a land of plenty. Their common sense saved them at that point. But fear of losing their money before it was lost had cause them to behave as at the deluge.

Bank (Holiday)

Then immediately in this nightmare of fear two intentions began to move. One was the simple, direct intention by any means, legal or extra-legal, to deal with the crisis as a national emergency. The other might be called the ideal intention of an academic mentality that surrounded the President, pleasantly named the Brain Trust. This was a complex intention, not restoration, not prosperity again as it had been before, but a complete new order, scientifically planned and managed, the individual profit motive tamed by government wisdom, human happiness ascendant on a plotted curve. This complex intention had great fertility of ideas, and it overwhelmed the simple intention, which had no new ideas at all. The academic mentality wrote the laws and decrees, the President approved them, the Congress stamped them, and there was the spectacle of conservatives, liberals, radicals and demagogues walking in step toward something no one was sure of, moved by opposite reasons, some in the dark and some in a new light of their own making, invisible to the rest.

This kind of strange, unreal companionship in action is perfectly illustrated by a variety of conflicting motives that urged the idea of inflation, which came to be the central idea. Who wanted inflation, and why? All distressed debtors, naturally, because it would cheapen the money with which debts are paid, and that determined the attitude of the agricultural interest. The favorable attitude of business was similarly determined. If only prices could be restored to normal—normal being anybody's x—the sick economic body would begin to revive, and if the drug of

36

inflation would do this, why hesitate to administer it for fear the patient would become an addict?

It was amazing, too, what hold the idea of inflation gained in the world of finance. Inflation would make good again the deflated capital of corporations, the genial warmth of it would unfreeze the assets of troubled banks, it would restore to great financial institutions, such as life-insurance companies, the vanished value of their assets—always provided it went only so far as to produce these blessings and no farther.

But there were others who saw only and clearly the power of inflation as a social instrument, and how, once control of it was set in the popular hand, it could be employed to redistribute the nation's wealth and income. Even here was division. The demagogic mind was thinking only of transferring wealth by a primitive rule. The academic mentality, with its higher point of view, was thinking how the political power to regulate money and credit might be employed, not simply to take and give, not simply to ruin creditors for the happiness of debtors, but to control the distribution of the nation's wealth and income symphonically, for purposes of the new order. These wrote the law of inflation and took care to put plenty of power in it. Control belongs to the complex intention.

But all that was later; the embracement of inflation was something that happened. There is more to say of the conditions under which everything happened.

The first problem, of course, was to exorcise fear. The bank holiday, the gold embargo, the decree against hoarding—these were bold stokes. Fear as a national neurosis began at once to recede.

There was no program. There was no time to think one out. Yet action was imperative. Therefore, the materials of action, that is to say, the ideas, had to be assembled in haste. Most of them came from the one fertile and inexhaustible source, namely, the academic mentality. Prof. Raymond Moley,[1] Assistant Secretary of State, the President's most intimate adviser, commonly identified as

37

head of the Brain Trust, said at this time: "We are conscious of the danger that there is so little time to think."

It is thus explained why the legislation that ensued is so formless and unschematic, and why the most important acts represent simply grants of power to the President. Congress, too, had been seized with the fear of inaction. Many members, secretly groaning, supported measures they did not believe in because they were afraid to delay or obstruct action, afraid not to go along, afraid not to be afraid of the dark.

Even those members of Congress whose personal convictions were appalled by what they were doing were thinking and saying: "To change the nation's state of mind is desperately more important than the means we take to change it. Any means to do that. If not these means, what others? We do not know."

Such acquiescence reacted with a certain effect upon those who were writing the acts of the new order. Ideas more and more daring went into their conference tubs, and the crystals sent up the hill in haste were more and more astonishing. On the floor of the House one member exclaimed: "In some cases bills have been passed before they were printed, before any copies were available even for leaders of the house or members of the committees sponsoring them, without anyone knowing what they contained . . ."

There seemed to be nowhere any resistance. Finance, business, industry, agriculture, creditors and debtors, capital and labor, all on one millennium step. That was not quite so. The academic mentality, becoming aggressive as its authority increased, learned how to silence opposition. If a sound of protest came from any part of the old laissez faire world there was a voice in Washington to say: "Any opposition to this bill from you will only cause a worse one to pass in place of it. We who write these laws are neither radical nor conservative. We are doctors. We do not want Congress to go off the lot, for that would spill everything. But your opposition may easily provoke it beyond our control." Thus a great deal of protest was silenced in private.

And then as it appeared that to administer the laws would require a vast dictatorial bureaucracy, there arose in the world of business a fear of this bureaucracy-to-be and what it might do to those from whom offense had come beforehand. Thus, at last, a secret fear of dictatorial government. This intensified steadily as more and more arbitrary power passed to the executive arm and as the doctor spirit that would inhabit the administration began to reveal itself in print, on the radio and in private conversation. It was a lawless spirit, rising from a kind of exalted impatience toward any law that might be invoked to mar the good design. To anyone who said such an act was unconstitutional and would be so held by the Supreme Court, the answer was: "Those who imagine that the new order can be defeated by an appeal to the Supreme Court on the Constitution will be disappointed. Do they think the Government, having gone so far, would hesitate giving the Supreme Court a new mind?"

Such were the conditions under which this country embraced a dictatorship, with no conscious intention, no serious debate about it, by implied consent, all in one hundred days.

The first great crystal out of the conference tubs was the Agricultural Adjustment Act. It evolved from one imperative and many ideas. The imperative was that the purchasing power of the farmer must be restored to what it was in the last five years of the pre-war time, 1909-1914.

The law is as follows: the consumer shall be taxed on all such basic commodities as wheat, corn, rice, hogs, tobacco, dairy products and cotton, and the proceeds of the tax shall be paid over to the farmer provided he will agree to limit his production as the Department of Agriculture may suggest. The Secretary of Agriculture takes authority over all millers, packers, dealers in and processors of, agricultural commodities. The amount of the tax shall be whatever is necessary; it shall be fixed by the Secretary of Agriculture. His power over farmers is not dictatorial. The law says that he must engage them only in voluntary methods. But he has dictatorial power over all the means whereby agricultural commodities are converted for use and consumption. But now a new problem. If the plan works, agricultural commodities and all manufactures thereof, such even as cotton goods, will be so much higher in this country than anywhere else in the world that the existing tariffs will not prevent imports. It follows that the protective tariff against foreign agricultural commodities and all manufactures thereof must be increased by the amount of the tax.

What of our foreign trade? What of the idea that the future prosperity of agriculture, and of the country as a whole, lay in the revival of our export trade? Thus it was that into the Agricultural Adjustment Act, purporting to be a piece of emergency legislation, there came to be written an amazing money act, namely the Thomas amendment, investing the President with power, in his discretion, to devalue the dollar by one-half.

This amendment, purporting to transfer to the President the constitutional power of Congress to coin money and regulate the value thereof, authorizes the President, at his discretion, to (a) print $3,000,000,000 of paper money and exchange it for any outstanding interest-bearing obligation of the Government; (b) to fix the value of silver in relation to gold and print silver certificates; and (c) to reduce the gold value of the dollar by not more than one-half. This amendment represented the ultimate demand of the revolution. It was sponsored by the Administration and moved in Congress by the following statement from Senator Thomas:[2]

"Two hundred billion dollars of wealth and buying power now rests in the hands of those who own the bank deposits and fixed investments, bonds and mortgages . . . If the amendment carries and the powers are exercised in a reasonable degree, it must transfer that $200,000,000,000 in the hands of persons who now have it, who did not buy it, who did not earn it, who do not deserve it, who must not retain it, back to the other side—the debtor class of the Republic, the people who owe the mass debts of the nation."

Many thousands of bank depositors who had thought

their security was one of the new Government's principal anxieties might well have been dazed at this magnificently frank statement, even more by the fact that a law under which the value of their bank deposits could be destroyed was wanted by a Government that was supporting a law to guarantee bank deposits; but they were already numb, and, in any case, trapped. What could they do? Suppose they took the money out of the banks again. That would not save it. It is the peculiar terror of inflation that it devours the value of your money whether you leave it in the bank, carry it in your pocket or hide it in the cellar. The only money that is immune from destruction is gold money, but that door of escape was already locked by a law making it a crime to have gold in your possession.

A new problem appeared. All the outstanding obligations of the Government, bonds, certificates and so forth, were payable in "gold dollars of the present standard of value." It was thought absolutely necessary to repudiate this contract between the Government and all its bondholders, for else when the gold content of the dollar had been reduced there would be endless confusion. Two kinds of bonds—old dollar bonds and new dollar bonds. Two kinds of money—old dollar money payable by the Government according to the contract, and new dollar money current in the new order. Then the further problem: If the Government alone repudiated the contract, what of billions of private gold bonds existing—railroad and corporation bonds—payable in gold, by terms of the contract, in a country where it was forbidden to have gold in one's possession?

This entire problem was imaginary, really. Bondholders normally do not want gold in redemption: they want only gold-standard money. Nevertheless, the next act was a joint resolution of Congress declaring the gold clause in all cases to be a thing contrary to the public interest, because it obstructed the power of the Government to regulate the value of money; and on this ground it was made invalid and illegal, as to every kind of obligation, public or private.

The argument for the legality of this act fairly exhausted the kind of sophistry now current. In the Constitution it is written: "No state shall . . . pass any . . . law impairing the obligation of contracts." But the Constitution does not forbid the Federal Government to impair the obligation of contract; therefore, it may legally do so, though for a state to do so would be illegal and unconstitutional. Yet everyone must realize that when the framers of the Constitution forbade only the states to impair the obligation of contracts they did not mean to leave the Federal Government free to commit that offense; the only reason they did not forbid the Federal Government to do it was that they could not imagine the Federal Government wanting to do it.

Next was the National Industrial Recovery Act. This was also conceived in an unexpected manner. First, under the subject heading, Unemployment, was the simple imperative: Men must have jobs; therefore, somehow, work must be provided. The obvious thing was a great program of public works. But that would not be enough. Wages must rise, because now that the agricultural problem had been solved by taxing food, the cost of living is bound to rise. Then another problem: if industrial wages rise, industrial costs will rise; as this happens industry will add the increased costs to prices and so manufactured goods may rise so fast that the farmer's increased buying power will be absorbed. Obviously, therefore, the natural selfishness of industry must be controlled, and the only way to control it is for the Government itself to interfere, in the public interest.

Such was the train of ideas that led to the National Industrial Recovery Act to which the original public works act was attached as Title II. In effect, this act declares the President to be the managing partner in all industry. As the managing partner he demands, first, shorter hours, in order that employment may be increased; secondly, higher wages, in order that the relative purchasing power of labor may be increased; thirdly, that as costs rise with higher wages industry shall absorb them, for a while at least.

In return for all this the managing partner offers industry, first, the privilege by agreement to rationalize, pool and limit production, with immunity from the anti-trust laws; second, the right to suppress cut-throat competition, and, third, the expectation that with the buying power of both agriculture and labor established on a rising curve the volume of business will expand very rapidly.

To represent him as the managing partner, the President creates an Industrial Control Board, and delegates thereto the power to pet industry or to bite it. Good industry will write its own code of behavior and its own bill of undertaking as to hours and wages, and when these have been approved by the managing partner himself, which gives them the force of law, the industry may police itself to make itself keep the law, and that will be a happy partnership. Bad industry, unable to agree upon a proper code, will have one imposed upon it by the managing partner, and the Government will police it, and if that industry protests, the managing partner will say, "Very well. Since you are in spirit a noncooperating industry, contrary to the public interest, you are sentenced to go under a license system. Only those members of your industry who agree to accept this code will be licensed, and only such as are licensed may do business at all."

It is foreseen in the act that if it works then food, labor and merchandise will be so much more dearer here than anywhere else that the whole world will be trying to sell goods in this market. In that case the President is authorized to regulate imports and if necessary to forbid them.

In this arsenal of powers there is a weapon for every occasion. That was intended. Any idea of power that presented itself was liable to be seized and clothed with law, not that it was needed but only that it might be. That is why so many ideas are in conflict.

The idea of devaluing the dollar was to make American goods cheap to the foreign customer, if you were thinking of world trade; but it was to make American goods dear, if you were thinking of inflation within.

The idea of raising wages to increase the buying power of labor is inconsistent with the idea of raising prices by inflation, for the effect of raising prices is to reduce the buying power of wages.

To the academic mentality there is no confusion in contradiction. Everything shall be planned and controlled in the public interest, even discord. The economic machine is a vast organ. To change the curve of production, you press this key; to change the curve of consumption, that key; or to regulate the curve of stock-market speculation another one marked "money and credit control" and so on. They talk of overcurves and undercurves, as if they were musical tones. And they say that if some of the effects are startling at first, it is because the economic ear is accustomed only to primitive sounds.

There are yet other reasons why one who would speak of the effects must do it with some reserve. All the tones are in suspense. There are no finished effects. We are in the overture only, and the piece is strange. Moreover, it is true that some of the new sounds have been very pleasing.

The first and all-controlling fact was a change of feeling in the entire country, from worse to better. It began at once and grew steadily as in every direction signs multiplied of a real physical improvement in the state of economic being. How much of this was owing to any new cause and how much of it was but the deferred reaction form a state of abnormal depression, nobody was able to say. Nevertheless, the psychic relief was so tremendous that nobody really cared. Everybody said, "Whatever the cause, we are at last about to be delivered." As securities advanced, as common stocks doubled and trebled in value, hundreds of thousands of security holders—banks, institutions and individuals—who had been under water for three years, said or thought: "If this is inflation, more of it." In three months the quoted value of securities on the New York Stock Exchange increased $20,000,000,000. Agricultural commodities went up so fast that before the Department of Agriculture could organize its system of benefits and rentals the purchasing power of the farmer was well restored. Wheat that had been 42 1/8 cents in

December was a dollar a bushel by July. Cotton more than doubled in price.

The rise was in three phases. There was first the moderate phase that needed no explanation other than the change of feeling. After the passage of the Agricultural Adjustment Act, with its Thomas Amendment authorizing inflation, both securities and commodities began to rise immoderately. Speculators were anticipating the effects of inflation. For awhile conservative commentators warned: "Be careful. There is no inflation yet." These voices were suddenly silenced by the joint resolution of Congress repudiating the gold clause in Government bonds. After that there was no doubt that the President had committed himself to inflation. Definitely, the country was off the gold standard.

The American dollar began at once to fall. In terms of what did it fall? In terms of what the British would give for it in terms of their paper pound sterling, or what the French would give for it in terms of their gold-standard francs. That is to say, the American dollar was priced in terms of other people's money because it had no certain value of its own in terms of gold or anything else. As the dollar fell—to 90 cents, to 80 cents, to 70 cents—in terms of other people's money, everything speculatively priced in dollars—wheat, cotton, raw materials, stocks and bonds—advanced accordingly. This advance was very violent. Day after day the newspaper headline was: "The dollar falls. Commodities and securities rise. Wild rush to buy." Brokers' offices were suddenly crowded, as in the boom days of 1928 and 1929.

For several days there was the dramatic spectacle of the whole world in an uproar, trying to guess which way the President would make up his mind and at what point he would, by simple decree, arrest the fall of the dollar, and the President himself serenely navigating the Amberjack II off the New England coast, with the power in his oilskin pocket to fix the gold value of the dollar at any figure he might see fit, down to 50 cents.

His problem was very difficult. He did not know, nor

45

could anybody know, what the consequences would be of fixing the dollar at any value. If he made it too high, prices would fall, and that would be bad; if he fixed it too low, the speculators would make a great killing, and that also would be bad. What a strange anxiety for the President! Every speculator in the world trying to outguess him, and his the responsibility to outguess them—in the public interest.

Doctor Moley says: "One of the superb assurances that the President has given the country in connection with some of this legislation is that it is frankly experimental. He will inform the country if it fails with the same straightforwardness with which he asked the country to adopt it."

Suppose it does not fail. Then what? Doctor Tugwell, Assistant Secretary of Agriculture, one of the next lesser representatives of the academic mentality, says: "We possess every needful material for Utopia, and nearly everyone knows it; it is a quite simple conclusion in most minds that control ought to be taken out of the hands of people who cannot produce it from the excellent materials at their disposal."3

But is there a price to pay for Utopia? The money price may not be important. Whatever it is, it will be divided between the rich and that forgotten man who kept his private budget balanced, was never in debt and put something by in a savings account, or perhaps in a Government bond . . .

On April twenty-third the Government offered $500,000,000 three-year 2 7/8 per cent Treasury notes, recommended them particularly to small investors and explicitly said: "The principal and interest of the notes will be payable in United States gold coin of the present standard of value." Only thirty-three days later, by joint resolution of Congress, the Government repudiated this contract, declared the gold clause in this and all other Government obligations to be contrary to public interest and therefore invalid, and asserted its right to pay the notes in any kind of paper money it might see fit to print. There was no mon-

etary or economic necessity for doing this; the only real reason for doing it was that the gold clause stood in the way of
the Government's purpose to redistribute the wealth and
income of the country by inflation.

In the Securities Act the Government imposed upon the
private issuers of securities, for the protection of investors,
the law of seller beware. Then for its own purposes it acted
on the old law of jungle finance—the law of buyer beware.

Afterward the sophists said: "But you see, people still
have faith. Government bonds are very strong in the market place." True, the quotations were strong, but that was
because Government bonds were priced in dollars debased.
There was nothing else to price them in. A Wall Street
house doing exactly what the Government did with its
issue of $500,000,000 notes to small investors, would be
open to prosecution under the new Securities Act.

---

[1] Raymond Moley, 1886-1975, resigned shortly after and became a critic of
the New Deal.

[2] Elmer Thomas, 1876-1965, Democrat, was U.S. Senator from Oklahoma
1927-1951.

[3] Rexford Guy Tugwell, 1891-1979, professor of economics at Columbia,
advocate of national planning and one of the radicals of the New Deal. He
was co-author of the Agricultural Adjustment Act, which was declared
unconstitutional. In 1968 Tugwell admitted that the New Deal's policies
"were tortured interpretations of a document [the Constitution] intended to
prevent them."

CHAPTER THREE

We Are Building

The "news hook" for this piece was the Chicago World's Fair of 1933-34. Garrett used it as a take-off for what he wanted to say about building and the economy of building. The "hook" has been edited out, as have some of Garrett's digressions. What's left is an evocative piece of writing that recalls the 1920s boom, the depression and the uncertainty everyone felt. The New Deal is already started, but Garrett is not quite sure what to think of its ideas about building.

From "Since the Tower of Babel," October 14, 1933

To build is one of the grand human passions. When people are prosperous, then, naturally, they build, and the simple thought about it would be that building is an effect of prosperity. But it has been observed also that when people build they are prosperous, and we begin now to embrace the complicated idea that prosperity is an effect of building. Instead of building because they are prosperous, people are prosperous because they build. It is not altogether clear and we are not quite sure of it yet, since it belongs to a new way of thinking; but if we can say, as we have learned to say, that people have only to buy and consume more in order to be prosperous, then where is the difficulty of supposing that prosperity is an effect of building?

At any rate, this is the idea now moving the Government's program of public works. If only the building industry can be restored, prosperity will be obliged. Therefore, public buildings, such as post offices, where there is no immediate economic necessity for them. Simultaneously in many cities magnificent Federal structures to house Federal agencies and bureaus are rising in streets where towers, skyscrapers and common office buildings are falling into bankruptcy for want of tenants. Probably it would be cheaper—for the time being, at least—to continue housing Federal bureaus in rented space, but if it is true that prosperity is an effect of building, then these public works are not to be questioned on the ground of economic necessity. They are to be regarded from another point of view. It is something to be done with our surplus. Is it not better to be building with it, even though there is no immediate economic need for the building, than to destroy it by such means as to plow up cotton, to pension labor in idleness, to hire land out of production, to limit the power of machines and the hours of work, or, having produced the surplus in spite of ourselves, then to lend it away or to give it away merely in order to be rid of it?

You may take all the great monuments existing or that have ever existed in the world—temples, pyramids, cathedrals, castles, even the Tower of Babel—to represent what people did at that time and place with a surplus of food, materials and labor. They had to have a surplus above bare necessity to begin with. That is to say, they had to be in some measure prosperous in order to build. Nevertheless, the work of building excites them; as it grows it calls for more and more surplus to be produced, and it does seem— at least, for a while—that the more audaciously people build the more prosperous they are for that reason. Effect becomes cause, producing a further effect, which is cause again, and so it might go on and on forever if nothing happened.

What happens is something we do not clearly understand. We say the rhythm breaks, and spend the next two or three years blaming one another for letting it break. We have learned how to make towers stand in the sky. Yet we do not know exactly why we build them, or when to do it, or how many we can afford. First we built too many all at once and there is a great boom in materials, wages and real-estate values. Prosperity attends. Then because, as we say, building does not pay, we stop it all at once and there is a frightful depression in materials and wages and real-estate values, together with bank failures and the distress of unemployment. Each time we get started we think we shall be able for once to raise the tower of prosperity all the way to the sky and keep it there; as we raise it higher and higher, we keep saying, "See, it cannot fall!" And then, without warning, confusion overthrows it. The base was not right.

The truth probably is that both building is an effect of prosperity and that prosperity again is in certain measure an effect of building; but in any case there must be a first cause, and that is the human passion to build. It is a passion to externalize the ego, collective or individual. The Tower of Babel was pure ego. The sons of Noah said: "Go to, let us build a city and a tower, whose top may reach to heaven; and let us make us a name." The collective ego of the Greeks expressed itself in beautiful architectural forms that had no economic meaning. The conquering ego and the building ego are much alike. All great conquerors have been at the same time mighty builders. Never did one destroy a city but he felt the impulse to raise a grander one in its place. Building is a kind of conquest, and, as a curious fact, consumes the same things—that is to say, a surplus of food, materials and labor. With what a skyscraper represents you could prepare a battle, provided you had not made a skyscraper first. All that has gone into the making of a skyscraper is irrevocably converted to that one form. You can no more eat or wear a skyscraper than you can eat or wear a battle, and no more recover the energy that has been spent upon it than you can recover the energy of high explosives. There is the further interesting fact that a building mania and a war produce similar economic phenomena—namely, all the entails of boom and depression.

It was in Chicago that the building passion of our time came to a peak. The ego it expressed was both collective and individual, with the individual impulse dominant. Thirty years ago in Chicago the people's Sunday recreation was to line the Michigan Boulevard and watch the parade of fine carriages. Proud horses in silver-mounted harness, liveried servants outriding, the owners of this magnificently inefficient transportation all with one air pretending to be a little bit bored, whereas they were delighted with the "Ah's" and the "Oh's" that swirled behind them, and returned to their lakeside mansions with their egos uplifted. The automobile destroyed that scene. At a little distance the difference between a rich man's car and anybody's car is so slight, and the movement of traffic is so imperative, that there is no longer any ego distinction to speak of in the means of private transportation. And what the motor car did to the carriage parade the increase of wealth did even to the lakeside mansions. They multiplied so fast that they became quite common, and it was first naive and then a little gauche for the rich to give themselves airs about their housing. Besides, the Sunday crowds, moving in low-priced pleasure cars, sweetly ignored them.

The form of everything changed; the parade, nevertheless, continued. It became a parade of tall buildings, appearing in the guise of economic motive, to adorn a name or to advertise the sudden way of a man in the world. As, at night, you drive south on the shore boulevard and come to the noiseless, weightless bridge that divides the new city from the old, you are blinded by a battery of canted electric lights. They illuminate a tower, stunningly beautiful as it rears its ivory magnificence in the spotlight. If it were the only object of its kind in the world, people would come for thousands of miles to look at it. What tower is that? You hear a name. And who was he? The chewing-gum king. So chewing gum did it. Such a monument to chewing gum. No. A monument to success. A monument to the fact that success is not in the thing, but to what one brings to it, to anything, even chewing gum.

Beauty is debatable, but height is measurable. Hence the passion to build higher and higher, out of the world into the clouds. The ground is only to start from.

Then suddenly it stopped. Not only in Chicago. All over this country, all over the world, building all at once stopped, and the construction industry collapsed, with terrific economic consequences. Why did it stop? We say it stopped because there was no longer any profit in it. But why did the profit cease? The reason we commonly give is that the profit ceased because building had been overdone and there was more than enough of it; specifically, there was an excess of office space in high buildings. Yet here we are creating more space of that kind, in the way of a public-works program, with the idea that prosperity is an effect of building. Even though we shall thereby create a further surplus of office space, still, nevertheless, we shall be consuming our surplus of food, materials and labor. By consuming our surplus, even though in works economically unnecessary, we shall regain our prosperity. But if that is true, why did building stop at all? Why, all at once, did we stop consuming our surplus?

The profit motive in building is calculable; the ego motive that complicates it is not. The profit motive alone could never explain Radio City in New York that went on rising steadily all through the depression—almost the only thing in the world that was rising except the curve of unemployment—at the expense of a private fortune already so large and so notoriously conservative that no thought of profit at 6 or 8 per cent could possibly have involved it in a showman's dream. Can you imagine that the individual ego has fits of lethargy and grows weary of building, whereupon it becomes necessary, perhaps, for the collective ego to take up the work? Or can you imagine that the individual ego, having expressed itself, would rest upon its achievement and be loath to perceive that the tower finished yesterday is already a little obsolete?

When we say, for example, that a time comes when from the private passion to build there is more than enough, wherefore the profit departs and the building stops—when we say this, we are thinking only of what was or is. More of the same thing. True, there may be enough of that, or too much. But there is not yet enough of the new thing. Forty years ago in New York, in Chicago, in any great city, one might have said there was enough of what was, a surplus of it. That also was a time of depression. But see how much of what was has vanished to make room for what had not yet been imagined and now is, and how obsolete is the remainder! What is will vanish in the same way, and what will appear in place of it is either not yet imagined or imagined dimly.

Technical knowledge is already far ahead of what we possess in the shape of buildings. With our knowledge of raw materials, of lighting and air conditioning, not only is the newest building already old; it is likely that this knowledge will increase in a manner to make obsolescence one of the staggering problems of the near future.

One of the great show pieces in Chicago's parade of tall buildings is about to undergo an internal surgical operation for the purpose of an experiment with air conditioning on a scale never before attempted. And thus windowless architecture begins to be indicated. The word "window" is from the old Norse word "windauga," meaning "wind eye." The glass window to let in the light and keep the weather out was an important event in the history of human culture. It was a notable and luxurious possession, and this not so long ago but that window taxes still survive in Europe. A movable window, sliding or hinged, was a wonderful refinement. Almost we forget that there are millions of habitations in the world still without windows. A generation hence there may be millions more for the reason that for the first time it is possible to make the interior of a building what it ought to be—namely, a perfect artificial environment, soundproof, flooded with a soft, cold light; the air washed and conditioned for humidity and temperature. Luxurious caves of any size for the modern troglodyte.

The sons of Noah, raising the Tower of Babel to make them a name, were confounded in a mysterious way. A moment came in the heat of the day when they found themselves speaking to one another unintelligibly, in strange tongues; and no one could make his ideas understood. Confusion stopped them. And there was probably a very serious depression thereafter in the whole post-diluvian world.

It is a curious fact, may it be cause, effect or coincidence, that even in modern times every notable collapse of the building passion has occurred in association with a sudden confusion of social, political and economic ideas; it has occurred, moreover, on the threshold of great change. It is possible, therefore, that what stops building is not that we run out of credit, since works, as we know, tend to create their own credit; not that we use up our surplus, since it is not consuming the surplus that seems to cause the depression afterward; it is possible that what stops it is that we are all at once struck with an intuition of deep change wherein one order will end and another begin.

Taking change in the least of its meanings, who is it now that can say what the new architectural forms will be? Yet everyone knows that they may be radically different.

Who can say that towers will not be made of glass? Who can say what the future of a tower city is? Twenty-five years ago, one could have said that any city here would grow higher and bigger, and say it with certainty. Now powerful forces are acting to limit the self-aggrandizement of cities, to alter their functions, to decentralize life. The idea of regions appears. This refers to one aspect only of physical change.

What we call the economic structure, the building of buildings—that structure all at once is wide open to change. And who is it, again, that can say what will come of so many new ideas touching the manner of changing it, or what at last will crystallize out of so many ways of thinking? The very forms of wealth, the means of security, the terms and rewards of success, the relations of a citizen to his government, the latitudes of individualism—which of these parts of the economic structure are not undergoing change, not by any thought-out design but by trial and error in the building?

The shapeless shadows of oncoming change may freeze the private building passion even among people who are not afraid of change, really. People who believe in progress are not; and though they should say they are afraid to build, afraid to do this, afraid to do that, it would mean only that they were unable to see what next to build. If they believe in progress they will accommodate their enterprise to any change. What stops them is confusion, the turmoil of ideas, the running together of many theories. Much of what is they see to be passing; the sands are running out from under; but that which will be in place of this is not yet visible.

CHAPTER FOUR

The Blue Eagle

The centerpiece of the early New Deal was the National Recovery Admininstration—NRA— a new bureaucracy that set out to administer minimum wages and minimum prices on American industry. The actual wages and prices were to be set by the industries themselves meeting in collusion, with approval of government. It was to be voluntary; cooperating companies could post the image of a blue eagle, with a gear in one claw and lightning bolts in the other, and the motto, "NRA. We Do Our Part."

A Change So Radical

From "Since the Tower of Babel,"
October 14, 1933

The astonishing initial response to NRA, with almost no critical resistance to a change so radical in the relationship between business and Government, has been interpreted as a reaction against rugged American individualism. It has been so interpreted even by those who know the peculiar susceptibility of the American people to slogans and phrases, and by those at Washington whose quarrel with the doctrine of laissez faire had long been one of passionate conviction and who, therefore, find deep satisfaction in thinking they have performed the obsequies. Yet all these might well be deceived by temporary appearances. There is, for example, this striking contradiction that the act of embracing NRA and the experiment of Government dictation in business, which seems a negation of individualism, is parallel to the act of repealing the prohibition amendment, and that is a triumph of obstinate individualism. It is possible that only people who are very sure of it would be so willing to submerge their individualism for purposes of an economic experiment. That is a thought with which one will return from going to and fro in the country and up and down in it. What else? Well, such else as three observations, in the following order:

First, a sense of chagrin, amounting to a sense of guilt, at the spectacle of unemployment. It happens often that a hard-headed banker, merchant or industrialist is brought to the midday board to air his mind to the visitor. He believes in the system he grew up with—rationally he believes in it. He holds in all matters for the natural principle. He believes in competition, struggle, survival and success. The Government is mad. You cannot restore prosperity by decree nor by passing a law commanding it to return. He gets rid of all that. Then a strange thing happens. In a moment he turns heretic. "But my God!" he says. "Look at this unemployment. You cannot bear to look at it. People willing to work and yet unable to exchange their labor for the necessities of life in a land of surplus. Millions of them. We cannot say there is nothing wrong with a system that leaves a result like that."

No one feels personally responsible, of course; yet there is again and again this sense of guilt about it, especially on the part of those who know how to take care of themselves, and do, whatever happens.

Second, an observation on the great strength of the experimental spirit, together with the complete native assurance that, come what may, we shall be able to control the circumstances. In a thousand different ways men in doubt, men who cannot be rationally convinced, are saying to the President: "You want to jibe her in the wind? All right. You are the new captain. We should think it was risky. The rig may carry away. But all right, try it." Certainly never before so easily and with so little mutinous feeling aboard was a great ship of state jibed in the wind and put upon a strange, uncharted course. Faith in the ship, faith in any boldness of action, faith in our own resourcefulness.

And third, an observation on thinking. If the energy now spending itself in the process of thought were a quantity, like the output of pig iron or electric power, and a curve were made of it, you would see that it had risen to an amazing peak. Plans for tinkering the economic mechanism, plans for making it over, plans for making a new one, only those that get printed, are by the thousands. Those that get written to editors are by the tens of thousands, and those that exist happily only as thought are by the millions.

A Law for Buttons

From "Washington Miscellany,"
December 9, 1933

If now there is not a law about everything, it is only because something has been forgotten.

Agriculture, in collaboration with Government, wrote its own basic law, which Congress passed as the Agricultural Adjustment Act; rising out of that basic act are all the innumerable laws of decree and regulation that now govern the production, distribution, manufacture and consumption of agricultural commodities and food products. There is, for example, a law of milk. A dairyman, except he bootlegs it, may not sell his milk in his own community for any price he likes; he must sell it only at the lawful price. There is a law obliging those who wear cotton and who eat meat and bread to pay a tax that shall be handed over to the farmers according to a law of benefits, and the benefits are distributed by various laws of benefit, such as a law of holocaust upon hogs, to make a scarceness of them; a law of destruction upon cotton; a law of wheat and corn acres hired out of production to the Government; and so on; and all of this, done by decree, is according to a basic act that says the national income shall be redistributed by law in order that the farmers shall have more.

Labor, in collaboration with the Government, wrote its own law into the National Industrial Recovery Act—Section 7(a)—and proceeding from this are the laws of decree that now govern every mode of behavior between employee and employer.

Under the National Industrial Recovery Act, every trade and every industry is commanded, in collaboration with the Government, to write a code for itself. Hence a law of wages in every department of trade and industry, a law of hours, a law of machines to limit their use and output, a law upon oil gushing out of the ground, and laws against selling below cost, or, that is, laws against losing one's own money except in ways permitted or required by the Government. There are laws of minimum and maximum, laws of exception, laws of quota, laws of tolerance and intolerance, touching things both great and small. There is a law for buttons. There is a law for men's garters and suspenders. There is a law for waxed paper. There is a law for used automobiles, concerning how they shall be valued and sold.

All this exercise of the legal mentality in the Government's service notwithstanding, there is everywhere some doubt. The United States Supreme Court has yet to be heard from. Ultimately it must pass upon the laws. Many of those imposed by decree and regulation, even great parts of the emergency acts of Congress, may turn out to be unconstitutional. That is why the Government has all the time been loath to hale anyone to court or to be haled there itself. However in the two cases

in could not avoid—one being sued and one obliged itself to
sue—it has won. The law of milk was upheld in Chicago.
The law of peaches was upheld in San Francisco.

A peach canner in California refused to let the AAA tell
him how much he should pay for peaches and what he
should sell them for, and how many he could can. Thus the
AAA was challenged and had to act. It went to Federal
District Court in San Francisco and asked for an injunction
to shut this canner up. Appearing in the defense, the canner stood upon constitutional grounds, two among others,
that he bought and canned and sold peaches entirely within the confines of the state of California, wherefore the
Government had no right to touch him under pretense of
regulating interstate commerce, and secondly, that in
touching him by decree and regulation it would deprive
him of his property without that "due process of law" guaranteed to him in the Constitution.

The court held for the AAA against the canner, on the
ground that the peach industry in California was affected
with the national public interest, wherefore Congress had
a right to regulate it. The court said: "The Congress made
a legislative finding that a national emergency exists. This
court, upon that finding and upon its own judicial notice of
the economic distress throughout the nation, here arrives
at a similar conclusion. In the cling-peach industry and in
other industries, due to great overproduction and ruinous
competition, the members of that industry and the trade
and commerce thereof have been near the point of ruina-
tion . . . It is needless to point out that the welfare of the
nation has been seriously handicapped by these conditions
and the country's trade and commerce have been vitally
affected. Under conditions such as these, the court is bound
to arrive at the conclusion that the peach industry is affected with a national public interest and that the Congress
has the constitutional power to adopt appropriate legislation to cure these evils. The due-process clause in such a
situation cannot properly be construed to obstruct the
national policy."

So now the mind of the United States Supreme Court,

61

as it may be revealed in the body and spirit of past decisions, became a subject of intense and anxious study. Its mind may be moved, or may already have been moved unawares, by a sense of the national emergency. And if the court itself is immortal, the nine members of it are not; and since the President appoints them, subject to the approval of the Senate, two or three places made vacant by death or retirement might enable him to change the ruling mind of the court. That is, he could appoint a liberal or a radical in place of a conservative, if it had been a conservative seat that fell vacant; and even one such shift might make an important difference. As it now sits, the court is three liberal, two in the middle and four conservative. Three of the four conservatives are past seventy.

The Supreme Court was intended to be a judicial power entirely free from interference by the President or the Congress. Nevertheless, there is an opening in its armor of independence. The Constitution omitted to say how many judges should constitute the court. Congress may determine the number. By an act of legislation, Congress may increase it at will or reduce it by a process of attrition, simply forbidding vacancies to be filled until the number is less. It has been so long since anything of this kind happened that almost we forget how simple it is.

In 1866, to prevent President Johnson from acting on the personnel of the court by appointment, Congress passed a law saying no vacancy should be filled until the number of judges had been reduced from ten to seven. The number had declined to eight when General Grant succeeded Johnson. Congress by another act then increased the number to nine, and the court of nine immediately reversed a decision on greenback money that had been given by a court of eight.

A Lost Eagle

From "The Great Moral Disaster," August 18, 1934

Government in its natural principle can have no sense of right or wrong in the means, only a sense of expediency. The less restraint there is upon its power, the sooner it will go wrong. That is why the founders of our political system took so much thought and pains not only to limit the powers of government but to make them self-limiting.

Nevertheless, a way has been found to achieve government by decree, and to do it by sanction of law. The way is for the Congress to delegate law-making powers to the President; and he is authorized to delegate them again to others, called administrators; and then suddenly there is a great body of extemporaneous law, issuing from the White House and from innumerable administrative bureaus, in the form of decrees and regulations—law that people must obey under pain of fine and imprisonment, though it is written in no statute book, was never debated and may be superseded by another decree or another regulation in the pleasure of the Government, with or without notice.

There are many present beneficiaries; so long as that can continue to be true, it will be popular government. All those to whom the father idea of government is a passion, are delighted. If they see they do not care—and as yet, almost nobody seems to care—that from government by decree, no matter how benevolent it may be, the way is short and smooth to the point at which people who knew only how to ask, "What is the law?" begin to ask, "Who is the law?"

We arrive unawares. The National Recovery Administration deprived a Tennessee hosiery mill of its Blue Eagle, alleging that it had violated the code, and referred the case to the Department of Justice for criminal prosecution. In this scheme, observe, there are two penalties for violating the code—first, the loss of the Blue Eagle, which kills the business, and then fine or imprisonment. One penalty is inflicted by the National Recovery Administration; the other by a court. Without its Blue Eagle, the Tennessee hosiery mill was unable to obtain any new orders, since automatically it came under a nation-wide boycott, and for that reason it closed, throwing several hundred workers into unemployment. As it did this it protested that it had not violated the law and demanded its Blue Eagle back; the National Recovery Administration insisted that it had violated the law and refused to give the Blue Eagle back.

A high quarrel was running when the Department of Justice returned the case to the NRA with a letter from the Attorney General saying: "The available evidence is not sufficient to warrant a criminal prosecution. I do not see that this conclusion has any necessary relationship to any administrative action you may take . . . It is entirely conceivable that proper ground might exist for the withdrawal of the Blue Eagle . . ."

Which is to say that in the opinion of the Department of Justice, the National Recovery Administrator possesses the right and the power to inflict a capital economic penalty for alleged violation of the law, in a case where it would be impossible to prove to a court or a jury that the law has been violated. On his personal judgment he may do it. "In determining whether the Blue Eagle should be withdrawn or restored," said the Attorney General to the National Recovery Administrator, "you will naturally be governed by the facts within your knowledge which bear upon the proper exercise of your administrative discretion."

Who, then, is the law?

By 1934, NRA codes covered twenty-two million workers, which accounted for eighty percent of private nonfarm employment, imposing minimum prices, minimum wages and sometimes detailed wage classifications. Industrial wages and prices rose strongly in 1934, though production was stagnant.

CHAPTER FIVE

The Kohler Strike

One part of NRA that survived was Section 7(a)—at least, organized labor's interpretation of it—which rewrote the rules of union organizing and set off a war between labor and capital. One of the most famous battles in this war was at the Kohler Co., near Sheboygan, Wis.

From "Section 7(a) at Sheboygan," October 27, 1934

In the struggle of union labor to extend its power over industry, no one episode can have been more simply tragic than the Kohler strike. Its implications are universal; therefore it deserves to be impartially examined for the sake of truth, if there is truth; and yet the first difficulty is that so few noncontroversial statements may be made about it. At least two. There was a strike. There was a riot. As to why there was a strike, or why it came to a frightful head, or who was to blame for the killing of two and the wounding of forty, the testimony is, on one side, distorted by a complication of passions and, on the other side, simplified by convictions of principle.

Families are divided—father against son, brother

against brother, wife against husband. One finds in one's working notes this: "To be verified: Did loyal Kohler worker lose his mind on seeing his own daughter in the picket line?" The note is scratched. It turned out to be not exactly true. Yet it was by no means improbable; in a local newspaper office it is believed. Even the children are involved emotionally. A ten-year-old boy whose father was in the picket line and whose uncle was inside climbed to the top of the iron gate and shouted at his uncle, "I'd like to smash your head if I could." The uncle tells it, hardly without tears, for he is fond of the boy; he thinks he shall never be on speaking terms with his brother again.

What was the background? What were the conditions antecedent? What were the materials of discontent and what were the chemistries of idea and suggestion that acted upon them?

The general scene is Sheboygan, an industrial town of 40,000 on the lake side of Wisconsin. Its virtues are thrift, industry and love of order. More than four-fifths of the houses are owned by the resident family. There is neither a bad street nor a shanty dwelling. The true fiber is German. The Lake Michigan shore from Milwaukee north was heavily settled by Germans seventy-five years ago. The principal industries are furniture, enamel ware, shoes, toys, machines, not any of them big—and then Kohler.

In 1873 an Austrian, John M. Kohler, began making plowshares, windmills, the cast-iron pillar that was a common architectural feature of the period. From the art of manufacture that were founded in these things came the modern products that now bear the name of Kohler, such as bathtubs and sinks, plumbing fixtures in brass, radiators and boilers.

In 1899 the Kohler works were rebuilt on a farm-land site four miles out. Then the founder died and the elder son, Walter J. Kohler, was president. He had the idea of an ideal village environment for the employees. Hence the Village of Kohler, population 1800, where executives, foremen, artisans and Kohlers of the third generation lived side by side in lovely vine-clad homes.

In any housing scheme related to a single dynastic industry, it is difficult to avoid the inflection of paternalism. Some wage earners do not mind it; others hate it. Here the idea was to assist employees to create for themselves a preferred environment, free of company interference. Thus, the land was turned over to the Kohler Improvement Company, a nonprofit corporation, to be resold to employees at its original cost as farm land plus the cost of converting it into home sites. There are no company houses; there is no renting. The Village of Kohler is not company-managed; it is autonomous and self-governing. If it is possible for a social-minded industry to create an ideal living environment for its employees without involving itself in paternalism, it has been done here.

By no means all Kohler employees live in the Village of Kohler. They are free to live where they like. When the pay roll was at its peak in 1928, fewer than one-third lived in the Village; the rest lived in near-by towns, most of them in Sheboygan. There is no evidence that those who live in the Village constitute a preferred employee group, except that as the depression deepened, some employees, unable out of their wages to meet their building-and-loan payments in the Village, were allotted a few extra hours and their wages were assigned to the building and loan association.

All of this is important as background because, when the strike came, the strikers bitterly denounced Kohler paternalism, in the temper of one who said: "Once you go to live in Kohler Village you belong to Kohler body and soul." That sentiment was common among them, and may be related to the fact that only 2 per cent of the employees living in the Village joined the strike.

Kohler belongs to the durable-goods industry. Only when people are prosperous and building new homes is there a good demand for fine bathtubs, kitchen sinks and brass plumbing fixtures. During the six or eight years that preceded the depression the immense activity of building

67

caused the Kohler company to be very prosperous. It expanded its payroll and its works; it built the largest pottery in the world for making porcelain bathtubs and bathroom fixtures. The depression, when it came, was particularly disastrous to all industry of the Kohler kind. New building practically ceased. Residence construction in the whole country declined to one-tenth of what it had been in 1928.

Continuity of employment had been for years the darling thesis of Walter J. Kohler; he had written and talked a great deal about it; he believed he knew how to guarantee it.[1] Like everyone else, he greatly underestimated the depression. During the first year, even into the second year, the Kohler Company continued to work full time at full wages, piling up its output in warehouses that had been built beforehand with just such an emergency in view. In the third year its warehouses were full and its working capital was running low. Then wage rates began to be reduced and the policy of spreading the work on short time, earnestly recommended by the Government, was adopted. Everybody still had some work; nobody had enough. In the fourth year workers actually began to be cut off; but unless or until the disemployed found other jobs, the company continued them in their group insurance and they were continued also in their rights in the employees' benefit association. So it happened that hundreds who had been dropped from the payroll still regarded themselves as Kohler employees. Later they were organized as such by American Federation of Labor agents and were militant in the strike. A very curious fact, this. Strikers who were no longer employees in fact, many of them having been off the payroll for a year, yet asserting the right to vote as employees on who should represent them in collective bargaining with the company.

In July, 1933, the plumbing-fixtures industry met the NRA with a code that stipulated a minimum wage of forty cents an hour and a maximum week of forty hours. This code was not approved until January of the next year. But the Kohler Company did not wait. It applied the code to itself on August 1, 1933—four months before it covered the plumbing-fixtures industry as a whole—and the case at Kohler then was that the minimum wage rate was what it had been before the depression and that 95 per cent of Kohler employees were receiving wages in excess of the minimum. But nobody was making full time. Work had to be spread thinner and thinner, until at last, the 1929 minimum wage rate per hour notwithstanding, no employee was able to live decently out of his pay envelope. That was because the building industry did not revive; until it revived, the Kohler Company could not sell more bathtubs, sinks and brass plumbing.

To keep going at all, it had to begin borrowing money at the bank, since its own working capital was exhausted; and with the thought of keeping its credit good, it was paying the preferred-stock dividend out of capital. It was losing money at the rate of $1,000,000 a year. The Kohler Company could no more go on forever doing this—borrowing money at the bank, paying dividends out of capital and losing a million a year—than the employees could go on forever living out of their very thin pay envelopes. They were both in the same fix. Kohler stockholders and Kohler employees were both devouring Kohler capital, like one great patriarchal family living on its fat.

Here may be witnessed the fallacy in the idea of spreading work. For a short time, it affords some relief, even though it is only a way of obliging wage earners to share their wages with one another in the guise of sharing their jobs. But when it has long continued it raises the bleak question whether horizontal misery is preferable to inequality of circumstance.

At this point the Kohler Company carried at least 1000 entirely superfluous employees, working only a few hours at a time. For all the production it could possibly sell, the Kohler Company might very easily have relied upon those living in the Village of Kohler alone, and these would have been only too glad to work full time at lower rates per hour. The cost of production would be reduced by increased efficiency of operation, wherefore the selling price of bathtubs, sinks, plumbing fixtures, radiators and boilers, could be reduced, with the effect of increasing the demand, this in turn creating more jobs, and so on. Such measures were inhibited at first by the policy of continuity of employment and then forbidden by the code that fixed minimum wages and maximum hours. After that, everybody was helpless.

However, bad as it was, still there was no wretched poverty in Sheboygan, at least none that was visible. Many people were on relief, but everybody was still well clothed, well nourished and well housed. One who had been seeing many industrial towns of comparable size, forty to sixty thousand, would have said on the look of the people, the look of the shops and movies, by the air of unusual tidiness and order, that it was the least likely one in a hundred to suffer an eruption of violence. If one had stopped at the Kohler plant this wrong impression would have been confirmed. There would have been the general manager, Herbert Kohler, brother of the president, sitting at his desk in overalls or going about the works calling men by their given names, they answering in the same manner.

Then of a sudden what happened to Sheboygan was Section 7-A. That is the now most famous section of the National Industrial Recovery Act, and it reads as follows:

Section 7 (a). Every code of fair competition, agreement, and license approved, prescribed, or issued under this title shall contain the following conditions:

(1) That employees shall have the right to organize and bargain collectively through representatives of their own choosing, and shall be free from the interference, restraint, or coercion of employers of labor, or their agents, in the designation of such representatives or in self-organization or in other concerted activities for the purpose of collective bargaining or other mutual aid or protection;

(2) that no employee and no one seeking employment shall be required as a condition of employment to join any company union or to refrain from joining, organizing, or assisting a labor organization of his own choosing.

It sounds quite simple. Senator Wagner,[2] as a member

of the first National Labor Board set up under the National Recovery Administration, said any child could understand it. Yet it has been from the beginning the most slippery, unmanageable piece of writing that, perhaps, ever went into a law. The NRA officially construed it one way. The National Labor Relations Board has construed it in an opposite way. The President has construed it in ways that had afterward to be construed again. Only organized labor has been entirely consistent.

On the face of the law one reads that employees, free of any coercion or restraint by the employer, shall have the right to organize and to bargain collectively through representatives of their own choosing. That is all it says. But if that is all it means, then there was no point in putting it there, because that right was already fully established in the law. No one would have thought to challenge it. The strife, the rioting and bloodshed, nearly every strike that has occurred since the enactment of Section 7-A—the whole controversy, in fact—is about something that is not in the law. And it is this:

Shall the majority of the employees have the sole bargaining power—that is, the power to bargain not only for themselves but for the minority, too, and for the individual, and make binding terms for all?

If the answer is yes, then it remains only for the American Federation of Labor by aggressive enrollment to gain a bare majority of employees, and its power over industry will be supreme. If the answer is no, the situation is left much as it was.

The answer of the NRA was no. On February 4, 1934, it issued an official interpretation, saying: "Section 7-A affirms the right of employees to organize and to bargain collectively through representatives of their own choosing; and such concerted activities can be lawfully carried out by either majority or minority groups, organizing and meeting such representatives in such manner as they see fit. Also in affirming this right of collective action, the law lays no limitation upon individual action."

When the President intervened in February to avert a

71

general strike of automobile workers, the following statement was issued from the White House: "Reduced to plain language, Section 7-A means employees have the right to organize in to a group or groups."

Certainly. They had already that right; they had possessed it for a long time. Nobody was disputing it.

But then the new National Labor Relations Board, which had been leaning toward the answer yes, in September said it in an unequivocal manner. In a case of the Houde Engineering Corporation of Buffalo, where 1105 employees elected to be represented by the United Automobile Workers union, 647 elected not to be, and 400 did not vote, the National Labor Relations Board ruled that the chosen representatives of the 1105 should have sole power to bargain for the entire 2152, whether the entire 2152 wished it or not; and the ground for this ruling was that collective bargaining with majority and minority groups both, "resulted, whether intentionally or not, in defeating the object of the statute." And then it proceeded to define the object of the statute as, "to encourage collective bargaining."

This decision exactly squares with what the American Federation of Labor read into the law from the beginning. It had been asserted in every strike during the preceding twelve months. From the day Section 7-A was enacted, the American Federation of Labor took it to be a weapon to destroy the two barriers by which, hitherto, it had been frustrated in its quest of supreme power—namely, the principle of the open shop and the company union. One would go down with the other.

An open shop is a place where members of an A.F. of L union, members of a company union and members of no union at all work side by side. A closed shop is a place where all the terms—hours, wages and conditions of labor—are settled between the A.F. of L union and the company, and only those holding union cards and paying union dues may work. Theoretically, it may not absolutely follow that where a majority of the employees as A.F. of L.

members have the sole power to bargain for all employees there will be a closed shop; but, in fact, this is bound to follow, and always does, and no union-labor enthusiast has any doubt about it. And this, therefore, is what union labor is fighting for really—the closed shop against the open shop.

Pursuing that object, and beginning upon the enactment of Section 7-A, the American Federation of Labor put on a terrific campaign to write up its membership. The answer to this throughout industry was the appearance of many new company unions. One appeared at Kohler named the Kohler Workers' Association.

The only way union labor can think of a company union is that it is a device of the employer, by coercion in some degree, to create a specious appearance of employee contentment and loyalty and as a barbed-wire entanglement to collective bargaining. It may be that there was never such a thing as a company union that was entirely spontaneous in origin. It has first to be suggested, it must receive some impulse, generally from above; its form, its constitution and by-laws, are provided. But it may be equally true that an A.F. of L. union does not create itself in a spontaneous manner. Its form, its constitution and by-laws are provided; and this is the work of professional organizers who get so much a head for enrolling members. In either case, the employee has only a very simple thing to do— namely, to sign. In one case he pays an initiation fee and dues, but membership in the company union, as a rule, costs him nothing; and this fact alone is proof to the A.F. of L. union man of the unnatural character of the company union.

There is always some pressure. If the employer exerts only so much pressure as to say he would be pleased to see his employees in a company union, that, in the eyes of union labor, is coercion. The professional organizer, on the other hand, may employ as much pressure as he can command—group pressure, even mob pressure—and that is all right. That is not coercion. Even legally it is not, for the only kind of coercion regarded by the law is coercion by the employer.

At Kohler, when the employees were being invited to join the Kohler Workers' Association, Walter J. Kohler made several speeches from which everybody would know that he liked the idea. Yet he was careful to say that the employees were free to do as they pleased. If they preferred to join the A.F. of L. union outside, that was all right, too, and nobody should be penalized for doing so. It was an open shop. Members of outside labor unions had worked there for years. Everybody knew that. The president of the new A.F. of L. union lived in the village of Kohler. Everybody knew that, too, and knew him, and knew that two of his sons were at Wisconsin University on Kohler endowments.

Walter J. Kohler stood on the official NRA interpretation of Section 7-A, which was that employees were guaranteed the free right to organize in any such groupings as they might prefer. Let such as wished to join an A.F. of L. union do so and send their representatives to bargain collectively for them. The Kohler Company would recognize them, receive them, bargain with them. The point he would not yield was that these should have the sole power to bargain, not only for themselves, but for the whole body of Kohler employees, whether the others should wish it or not. And that at last was the crucial point: Whether or not one group—the A.F. of L. union—should have the supreme bargaining power.

The opposite scene was on the lake front, where the professional American Federation of Labor organizers were holding out to Kohler workers, both employed and disemployed, the promise of higher wages, shorter hours, redress on their own terms for every grievance they might think of, if only they would sign up in the A.F. of L. union.

Sheboygan is an hour and a half from Milwaukee, and Milwaukee is one of the great seas of militant labor unionism. Sheboygan was an open-shop town. There were unions, ten or twelve, but they were old-fashioned craft unions, very conservative—printers, carpenters, bakers and such—who did nothing but hire a band and go on parade once a year, on Labor Day, with embroidered blue banners on gold eagle sticks, and hold a picnic. Strikes were almost unknown.

Secondly, there was submerged in the population of Sheboygan a sultry element, temperamentally unstable, with a low ignition point. Long after the Germans there had come to Sheboygan a people styled Russians. They were not Russians really; they were descendants of Germans who had once colonized in Russia. The Sheboygan Germans had never recognized them as kin.

The Chamber of Commerce, in its analysis of the population, sets them down as Russians and notes that they are one-tenth of the total. They were known to be difficult, easily moved to a sense of injury, and, on the whole, a little trouble—some, but that was all. They represented a rather low grade of labor; the industries of the city had absorbed them, but they were never quite assimilated. Such was the element that would be responsive to harangue. For the agitator, perfect material.

Thirdly, there was Kohler, deeply hated for two reasons—namely, first that he had attached his labor in bonds of subservient loyalty, and acquired international fame as a grand employer; and second, that he was an inflexible defender of the open shop. To put upon him the power of union labor would be a triumph of the first class.

One of the lawyers on the union side was asked: "Why, in fact, did you pick on Kohler, who is such a good employer, and why was there so much feeling in it?"

His answer was: "You put your own finger on it. Kohler is not an ordinary employer. That is why. Suppose you have on one side labor and on the other side a typical employer whose attitude is impersonal. There is a quarrel, then a settlement of some kind, with no deep feeling about it. But suppose the employer has a great name for his sympathetic attitude toward labor. In that case, a quarrel will be worse—in feeling, I mean. Grievances will look different. Then, of course, Kohler had a tradition to defend—the tradition of happy and contented labor in an open shop. I dare say he has been sincere in his own way. You know that Father Maguire, of the Chicago Regional Labor Board, came here to settle the strike and failed. He said to us, 'This is my first failure. In every other case I've been able to beat the table with my fist and say to the employer, "Here, now, settle this thing. Sign and be done with it." I couldn't do that to Kohler.' The trouble Kohler has with his labor reminds me of the trouble my mother has with her maids. I tell her so. When she gets a new maid she begins right off to take a personal interest in her, thinking of her comfort, and her diet, and making her presents, and all that."

And so it was that the American Federation of Labor sent its best-trained and best-paid organizers to Sheboygan. With them came a group from Milwaukee to start a weekly labor organ. They named it *The New Deal*. The name was a shrewd choice. At every mass meeting conducted by the organizers it was emphasized that all this was in keeping with the New Deal at Washington, a direct and essential part of it. The Government had delivered into the hands of labor a new charter of rights; and now the Government expected labor to organize, to bargain collectively, to embrace its own power.

Roosevelt banners were carried in the picket lines. There was probably not a striker in Sheboygan who did not earnestly believe that he was supporting the New Deal against the old profit system and the selfish employer. Had not the Government been acting to raise wages and shorten hours? Had not the Government been saying that was the way back to prosperity? Wages had been increased, the hours of the week had been shortened, but not yet enough. The employer was obstructing prosperity. And how could the employer say he was unable to increase wages while he was still taking profits for himself, with labor unable to live on its share, if, indeed, it were employed at all? A cartoon printed in *The New Deal* represented capitalism sinking in a sea of depression and saying, "Don't throw them! I'll drown before using them!" to the Government above with two life preservers in hand, one marked Higher Wages and the other Shorter Hours. All the arguments were plausible; and below the level of argument was what the least intelligent could translate to themselves in the words of one who said: "I pay my fee and my dues, and now I tell my boss to go to hell!"

Besides the ardent labor unionists, there were Socialists saying the state ought to commandeer the Kohler works, put everybody back to work at high wages and make bathtubs and plumbing for the people; and Communists caring not what else happened so long as there was trouble. After a mass meeting on the lake front, Communist literature would be found scattered about—the *Moscow Weekly*, printed in Moscow, the *Daily Worker*, organ of the Communist Party in the United States, printed in New York, and the gospel according to Lenin in pamphlets. *The New Deal* was probably for a while self-supporting, even a source of revenue. It made a very lively show of advertising from local merchants who were afraid of a boycott.

The work of the organizers was systematic and well done. First it was to organize new unions by industries, with aggressive men at the top, and then to enroll and egotize members. The people on relief were organized and taught how to strike. They struck several times on Federal Emergency Relief Administration jobs because compensation insurance had not been provided. That was all auxiliary; the organized unemployed, trained in the exercise, could be relied upon to march with trouble when the strikes started. In a very short time a militant A.F. of L. union had been established in every Sheboygan industry. For the professional organizer it was a clean-up.

Then the strikes began. Not with Kohler first. That would have been stupid. The program was for the unions to demonstrate and build their power, and so work up to Kohler. There was a series of strikes. There was a bakers' strike, at which one of the old employing bakers was so aghast that he dropped dead. There was a strike in the

77

shoe industry, then several in the furniture industry, then a machinists' strike, all with progressive success, and then a bad one at the toy works, where 65 voted to strike and 401 voted not to strike, and the 65 carried it. The 401 marched in a body to the city authorities and demanded to be protected in their right to work. The police tried to make way for these through the picket line and there was trouble—a small riot. Tear gas was used against the pickets; twenty were arrested, fingerprinted and photographed. Nevertheless, the strikers won, and the city, on demand, surrendered all records of the twenty arrests, the fingerprints, the photographs, and these were burned in public.

At this point apparently the morale of public authority broke. The law of peaceful picketing was in contempt. It might as well have been forgotten.

The next strike was in the shoe industry again. The total number of employees involved was 130, but the picketing mob was 3000 strong. The police were overwhelmed and did nothing about it, except to divert traffic. That strike was won. Kohler came next.

The demands made by the A.F. of L. Union of Kohler Workers No. 18,545 upon the Kohler Company were fourteen. Eleven were of a minor character; the essential demands were three: (1) a 62 1/2 per cent increase in wage rates, (2) a 25 per cent reduction in hours, and (3) the A.F. of L. union to have the supreme bargaining power. The last demand was the only one that really mattered. All the rest could go by the board, even the demand for a 62 1/2 per cent raise. This the A.F. of L. union admitted in its appeal to the National Labor Relations Board. The one issue, it said, was that of sole bargaining power—the A.F. of L. union to bargain not only for itself but for all the employees. If that point was won, everything else, of course, would come.

On July sixth, Walter J. Kohler received the representatives of the A.F. of L. union to entertain its fourteen demands. On July eleventh he replied in writing, to say that the company could not pay a minimum wage rate of sixty-five cents an hour with its competitors in the North paying forty cents and in the South thirty-five cents, according to the code; that the company did recognize the right of its employees to bargain collectively, or individually, in majority groups or minority groups, in full observance of the official NRA interpretation of Section 7-A, and that it would continue to recognize that right; but that it would not concede the right of the A.F. of L. union or any other group to exercise sole and supreme bargaining power. This reply never was acknowledged. On the morning of July sixteenth the strike began.

The number of pickets was several thousand, supported by the organized unemployed from Sheboygan. Many came in their own motor cars, which were parked all over the landscape. They established a camp and a commissariat. The rope technic of picketing was adopted. The rope was hundreds of feet long, held by strikers in close formation. They would carry it so far in one direction, at a command halt and reverse, and thus back and forth. The works were entirely surrounded and cut off.

The evening before, on a rumor, more than 200 employees, men and women, had rushed from the Village of Kohler into the works. It is said they were not ordered or expected to do this. They had passed the night there, and now they were inside. They could not get back to the Village. Anyone who tried it either way was roughly handled. It was a state of siege.

There was at once a problem of food. Through an underground chute to the Village, small parcels could be dragged by rope, but the quantity was nothing for 200 people. Then someone thought of the parcel post. The strikers would probably not dare to stop a U.S. mail. The postmaster was in doubt. He asked for instructions. The answer was that the mail must pass, and that the parcel post was mail. So by mail thereafter the besieged employees received their food, cots to sleep on, blankets, and so forth.

Next there was a problem of fuel. The strikers had cut the works off from coal by derailing the cars as fast as they arrived. If the Kohler power plant had to shut down the

79

whole Village of Kohler would be without water, sewerage and fire protection. Certainly coal could not be shipped by parcel post. Then Father Maguire of the Chicago Regional Labor Board appeared. He persuaded the strikers to pass one car of coal every other day—just enough to keep the power plant going.

Such were the conditions of siege; it settled down that way and continued for ten days, with only now and then the diversion of someone trying to pass the picket line and getting bruised up for it. The pickets, carrying on that ceaseless drill with the rope, began to get sore feet. Now and then one would drop out, go to the Kohler medical department for relief, and return to the line. They did this quite as a matter of course, being used to do it; and the Kohlers kept saying the strike, after all, was not very serious. They had only to let it wear itself out.

But the hotheads were getting restless. With nothing else to do, they turned back a car of coal. Thus the fuel problem was raised again.

When the strike began, the whole police force of the Village of Kohler consisted of two deputies. But during these last ten days a considerable body of deputies had been formed, some shotguns had been acquired, and six or eight motor trucks had been wrapped around with sheet iron, so that no one could easily climb aboard. These were the armored cars afterward spoken of.

So now a message was sent to the railroad, saying, "Send us back that car of coal," and the Kohler village deputies, armed, went down to the gate to receive it. The strikers were unprepared; they let the car pass. Then the deputies decided to go on and clear the outlying premises. They abated what were called picket nests in the small woods on the fringe of Kohler Company land. In doing this they disburdened the strikers of a half-truck load of clubs, blackjacks, sling shots and such weapons. The strikers submitted to be disarmed. For the rest of the day the deputies patrolled the main street of the Village of Kohler in their sheet-iron trucks. The picket lines were not disturbed. But all nerves by this time were tired and taut.

That night the riot occurred. A great mob of men, women and children attacked the works on two sides at once. The line of attack was more than a mile long. The missiles were bricks and stones and ball bearings, brought in trucks. Women carried them about in their skirts. Some of the inventive strikers had rigged stone-throwing machines, but most of the throwing was by hand.

No attempt was made to defend the works. The deputies were ready to act; the Kohlers kept saying that windows, if that were all, could be replaced. It was not until the mob began to converge on the general offices, where the 200 besieged men and women were in refuge, and then not until stones began to crash through the glass, that any resistance was offered. The deputies began to use gas bombs. The wind happened to be just right and the mob retreated with gas in its face. Up to this point it seems certain that no shot had been fired by the deputies. Suddenly the wind changed, turning the gas on the deputies; and the infuriated mob advanced, exhorting itself with wild cries not only to destroy the works but to tear the Village of Kohler to the ground. When the Village was attacked, the deputies fired.

Two were killed, thirty-four were hurt, seven of them seriously. Of these, twenty were not Kohler employees. Nevertheless, in that frightful way, old bench friends, the two parts of more than one family, brothers, kin, had faced one another with intent to kill. All had seen something they might pray to forget. The sequel was that both sides welcomed the National Guard. The rope disappeared. Picketing continued, but only in a peaceable, lawful manner.

The two dead were buried with dazed ceremony. The president of the Wisconsin State Federation of Labor referred to them as "men whose lives have been sacrificed in a class struggle that has been waged through the ages," and to the riot as "a massacre, with human life on one side and profits on the other." "Profits Slew Them," said *The New Deal*. Wells of deep bitterness remained, but violence was spent.

The police having failed, the citizens privately organized a law-and-order league and took 11,000 signatures in one week—more than a quarter of the entire population. The effect of this was very quieting. The work of the law-and-order league consisted mainly in apprehending those who went about at night throwing paint on the houses of the union's enemies.

The next scene is a room in the very modern courthouse at Sheboygan, where through counsel, the Kohler Company and the Union of Kohler Workers No. 18,545 are placing evidence before a referee from the National Labor Relations Board. The evidence bears on two questions: Does the A.F. of L. union represent a majority of the Kohler employees? If so, shall it possess and exercise the sole power of collective bargaining? The riot is not mentioned. What had that to do with either of these questions? Nothing. What did it yield toward a solution to the labor problem? Two graves, some people maimed, a very large glazier's job, hatreds that will never die, and no meaning whatever.

Then the evidence all goes to Washington, and the National Labor Relations Board decides that the Kohler Company was very wrong to let its employees see that it liked the idea of a Kohler Workers' Association, a company union; that this wrong may be remedied by an election with secret ballots, and that if a majority of the employees vote for the A.F. of L. union, than that union shall possess the sole power of collective bargaining for all the employees.

On Labor Day at Sheboygan was a parade of union labor; afterward a picnic on the lake shore. The largest single body in the parade was that under a banner inscribed, Kohler Workers. Some walked there who were not Kohler employees and never had been; others who had been off the pay roll for more than a year and would still assert their right to vote that the A.F. of L. union should represent them. As this group marched through the gate at the picnic grounds, it was eagerly applauded by children.

It was a rainy day. The picnic was half ruined. But there

had been no possibility of great joy in it. Hearts were heavy. The oratory was flat. The largest banners were those of men who had put themselves up to run for the office of county sheriff; the candidates went about wearing union buttons, buying refreshments, shaking hands, soliciting votes. *The New Deal* had a closed wagon there, like a ticket wagon at the circus. A young man at the window sold five-cent tickets in dollar strips; the tickets were currency for beer, coffee, ginger ale and hot sandwiches.

The employees vote, the employees pay, the employees buy. And for all the solicitude, what do they get? If they are exploited by the employer and rise against it, they pass only to others who do not work with their hands—the politician, the organizer, the lawyer. You could not walk among them, listen, talk to them, without coming to certain reflections. They are wishful; they have an immemorial sense of injury, and they are bewildered. Because they are bewildered, all the more do they hold fast to what they know. To a halfway point they have been aggressively, one-sidedly educated in the material of modern economic theory and wonderfully simplify it. Within the limitation they are logical, resourceful, in argument even reasonable. They ask you a question, sure that they know the whole answer beforehand; and as you begin to answer it you realize you cannot answer it satisfactorily even to yourself but by going beyond their depth. Therefore, you answer it badly.

They are not deceived. The answer is weak. They know it and you know it. What then? It is impasse.

They ask you to read from *The New Deal,* not anything a labor leader says—you might suppose a labor leader to be biased—but what Father McGowan of the National Catholic Welfare Council is there quoted as having said about industry because in March it was deaf to President Roosevelt's plea for giving recovery another boost by yet shorter hours and higher wage rates: "When you dread the coming of Communism remember last March. When you wonder why recovery is slow, remember that if recovery is to come and stay, incomes from work have to grow and incomes from property ownership have to decline." Then they read you a quotation from the Wall Street Journal saying that the profits of 50 corporations were 174.6 percent higher in the first half of 1934 than in the first half of 1933. What do you say to that?

Must profits come first?

Must prosperity return before labor can be reemployed at a living wage or must labor be reemployed at a living wage before prosperity can return? Which way does it make sense? If you say it is confidence that must return first, that capital is wanting a sense of security, they have expected you to say that, and they say labor is also wanting security. Does the security of capital come before the security of labor?

With all these essentials present in surplus, does it make sense to say that in order to be prosperous people shall first have to save and do without and work for less?

If it is the profit system that produces the enigma, why not try production for use, not for profit?

Consider that on such questions academic intelligence is divided. Consider also that they are compound questions and belong to three worlds at once—the social, the political and the economic. There is in no case a perfect answer. There is in every case a simplified answer. It is the one provided. It is the one they wish were true and prefer to believe; and now it is supported by much eminent opinion, including opinion of the government itself.

What is it that they want? More, of course—better living, higher social status, security. Yet deeper still they want something near kin to revenge. They know their history by heart. Not so very long ago it was unlawful for labor to organize at all. A labor union was treated as a conspiracy. There was no bargaining. The employer had arbitrary power. He made the terms. That was bad. It worked badly. Capital can no more be trusted with arbitrary power to dictate the conditions of labor than labor alone could be trusted with it. That is now admitted. But it was organized labor that forced that arbitrary power to be divided. For fifty years it has been, on the whole, reasonably divided, in a way to produce a state of working tension, and that is what works best. But now labor itself demands the supreme power, and the chief of its claims to possess it is emotional. The boss once had it.

There is yet one minor scene. It is the home of Walter J. Kohler. It is a beautiful new home, not a grand one, a mile from the works. He is on the terrace, talking. "This is not important," he says, "this house, the grounds, the little waterfall, not even to me. I am not important. Only the works are important. As for myself, I have the feeling that whatever happens, I can always go out and make a living for Mrs. Kohler with my own hands." Probably he could. It is one of the traditions of the Kohler family that everyone shall know how to use his hands.

The principle of union representation by majority vote began in the New Deal and has remained U.S. law ever since.

On Sept. 27, 1934, the Kohler Workers Association beat the A.F. of L. union 1,063 to 643 in a representation election. The A.F. of L. kept a small picket at the company until 1941.

In 1951, the Kohler Workers Association beat the United Auto Workers-C.I.O. in a representation election 2,064-1,575. The next year the union rejected a contract offer. About that time, the company demanded that workers in the enamel shop, an environment with a lot of fumes, work eight-hour shifts instead of six, and when twelve workers refused, they were fired. This brought on a referendum for the company union to affiliate with the U.A.W.-C.I.O, which passed, 2,248-1,129.

Walter Kohler had died in 1940. The company was led by Herbert Kohler, the man Garrett had met as general manager. Herbert Kohler refused to recognize the U.A.W. as sole bargaining agent for the Kohler workers, and in 1954 there began the second Kohler strike. This was the longest in U.S. labor history, lasting until 1965, when the company lost at the U.S. Supreme Court. It then recognized the U.A.W.—and Herbert Kohler retired.

As of 2002, the company is still independent. It is head-

ed by Herbert V. Kohler Jr. and remains organized by the United Auto Workers, AFL-CIO.

---

[1]Walter Kohler, 1875-1940, had been elected governor of Wisconsin in 1928, but lost the Republican nomination in 1930 to Philip LaFollette. Kohler won back the nomination in 1932 but lost to the Democratic candidate, ending his career in state politics.

[2]Robert F. Wagner, 1877-1953, Democrat of New York. Called "The legislative pilot of the New Deal," Wagner helped write the National Industrial Recovery Act of 1933 and the National Labor Relations Act of 1935, which is also called the Wagner Act. He was a senator from 1926 to 1949.

CHAPTER SIX

Taming the Machine

Garrett was fascinated by machines. In 1926 he had written a book, Ouroboros, or the Mechanical Extension of Mankind, *on the meaning of the machine for human civilization. Then came the New Deal, which tended to see the machine as antisocial, an enemy of labor, a thing to be tied down and regulated.*

The Infallible Sign

From "Washington Miscellany,"
December 16, 1933

Hitherto, one of the infallible signs of recovery from a state of economic depression has been a rising demand for new machinery. The machine industry, therefore, was the first really to get started again out of the slough. What this meant was that the mills and factories were laying out capital on more and better equipment in order to reduce their costs of manufacture. The necessity to reduce their costs was from the fact that at depression prices there was no longer any profit. Those that were able to reduce their costs could go on; those that were unable to do it, wanting either the capital or the courage, or wanting both, would have to quit. The strong and adventurous units of industry, making themselves over to get back their profit, and succeeding with it, made it very hard, of course, for the weak, whose destruction was thereby hastened. Those who got their costs down and their profits back immediately swept the field. The high-cost producers with their old equipment were ruined. But that is how industry, when governed by a law of ruthless competition, got rid of its obsolescence. In every depression the forward part of industry was made over new. It got started again by so reducing its costs that it could afford to produce and sell at low prices. Then when and if prices did rise again, profits might run very high because costs were low.

Such a thing now is forbidden. That infallible sign in the revival of the machine industry, therefore, may not appear in the same way; and in case it does not, it will be well to know why. The new idea is that prices must rise first. Production must be limited until they do. In order to limit production, not only must industry get along with the machinery it has but machines themselves, even these, must be hindered for the sake of limiting production. The logic is simple. If the trouble was overproduction by machines that displaced human labor, and if the problem is how to reemploy labor, then obviously the thing to do is to limit machines.

This conclusion now is running in the NRA codes. Those industries in which the ratio of machine power to human labor is very high pledge themselves under the codes to install no new machinery unless a new machine is needed to replace one that quite wears out—at least, not until the capacity of existing machines is fully required and the NRA for that reason shall license new equipment to be installed. It is so written in the code of the textile industry and again in the code of the iron-and-steel industry. The provision in the iron-and-steel code reads, "that until such time as the demand for its products cannot be adequately met by the fullest possible use of existing capacities for producing pig iron and steel ingots, such capacities should not be increased. Accordingly, unless and until the code shall have been amended as hereinafter provided so as to permit it, none of the member of the code shall initiate the construction of any new blast furnace or open hearth or Bessemer steel capacity . . ."

Suppose there had been such a code in the iron-and-steel industry fifty years ago when the Bessemer process for cheapening the cost of steel was coming in and the price of steel was falling from eighty dollars to less than twenty dollars a ton, with the result that transportation and construction were revolutionized. Or suppose today there was a new machine by use of which the cost of producing cotton textiles could be halved. What could one do with it?

The idea of limiting machine power has gone deep. In various codes it is required that the work hours of machines shall be limited. In the public works section of the National Industrial Recovery Act it is stipulated "that the maximum human labor shall be used in lieu of machinery;" and then, as if the thought had occurred to the legislators that there might be some hidden absurdity in going back to the wheelbarrow, the pick and the shovel, they added—"wherever practicable and consistent with sound economy and public advantage." But if the maximum use of human labor in lieu of machinery can be consistent at all with sound economy, there is nothing in the machine age, and never was, and everything we have been doing for a century and a half is absurd.

Nobody has yet proposed seriously to destroy machines—at least, not in an overt manner. The restraint at that point lies not in the logic of limitation but in some recess of the common sense. However, to wear them out or to replace them in kind only as they wear out is a kind of destruction of the seed. Competition of the old order did junk and destroy machines in a wholesale manner, but only machines for which better and more efficient ones could be substituted in the struggle to reduce costs. Thus machines were pruned away, but the seeds of mechanism at the same time were stimulated.

Nor has anybody yet seriously proposed to destroy the

fabricated products of machines. There again is some restraint of common sense. Logically, there is very little difference between plowing under ten million acres of growing cotton and throwing bales of cotton cloth on a bonfire. So far, only what we call natural products, such as raw cotton and hogs, have been destroyed in the undertaking to reduce supply and raise prices; but even raw cotton and hogs are, indirectly, products of the machine, and there is an intuition of that fact on the part of those farmers who are now trying to pledge themselves and one another to stop using tractors and other forms of mechanization in agriculture. All with the one idea of limiting production and causing prices to rise.

Hitherto, recovery has never been an effect of rising prices; on the contrary, rising prices have been an effect of recovery. The two primary conditions of recovery have been, first, heroic and competitive reorganization of industry to rid it of obsolete method and equipment, and, second, a reduction of costs. The methods are now to be reversed. Let obsolescence alone. Wear out the machines we have. First, increase wages, costs and prices. To do this, limit production, limit the machine, limit labor. Produce less and consume more. The law of necessity hitherto acting was a law of nightmare. For that it is proposed to substitute a law of the disciplined event. To say this has never happened before is not to say it cannot happen. But certainly it was by the other way that the world grew as rich as it is, which is richer than it ever was before. And the risks of the new way are apparent. One of them is that we shall start uphill again with a tremendous load of physical obsolescence— specifically, a load of worn-out or wearing-out machinery— instead of having under us, as always before at starting-up, a new and much more efficient mechanical equipment.

Birth Control for Machines

From "Machine Crisis,"
November 12, 1938

The machine is always upsetting the equilibrium, menacing the stability of the price structure, devouring jobs and displacing labor. It leaves destruction in its wake. It destroys the present in order to bring the future to pass. This is true not only of the machines we see now, not only of the machines since the beginning of what we call the industrial era; it has been true since man first discovered, one by one, the six mechanical powers of which all machines are compounded. The wheel turning on an axle was a machine that must have destroyed whole primitive cultures. The pessimist understands this of the past, intellectually; he will admit that the lot of mankind on earth has been greatly benefited. He cannot imagine it will go on happening.

It is not his idea to destroy the machine that is. Even sit-down strikers now know better than to do that. He accepts the machine. But he says it is already big and powerful and cunning enough. What he wants of it is good without evil. Therefore, tame it, chain it down, control it for the greater benefit of those who now live.

This was the meaning of NRA, with its pessimistic Blue Eagle and its codes to regulate the speed of machines, to limit their hours and output, to forbid more machines but on certificate of need from the Government.

"We've got to have a showdown with the machine," says the governor of Pennsylvania.

It is debated in the United States Senate. The senator from Washington rises to say: "If we are to become more efficient in our industrial machinery, we shall narrow the field of activity and the possibilities for employment for all our young people. I would not repel the machinery, but I cannot escape the honest conviction that it will become part of the duty of this body which we call the Congress to meet that issue head on."

Whereupon the senator from Illinois rises to say: "I suggest that one of the principal sources of revenue this Government has overlooked is a tax on patents . . . Taxes upon the benefit of the patent, the value of the patent and the proceeds of the patent financially, would do a great deal to stay the course for a while of other new patents bringing forth new machinery."

That is the thought of birth control applied to machines; and it goes even further. A bill has been introduced in Congress forbidding patents to be granted on labor-saving machinery. There are many proposals to tax existing machines in some manner proportional to the amount of labor they are supposed to save—so much for one that displaces one man, twenty times more for one that displaces twenty men, and so on.

When the Government provides jobs at manual labor in the name of work relief it does not by decree shorten the handle of the shovel. That would be too absurd. But it avoids as far as possible the use of machinery, to make the work last longer.

A British scientist made more reverberation in this country than in his own by suggesting that science take a holiday. No more inventions for a while. Well, the pessimists were making that suggestion more than a century ago, with science still in its cradle. And they were suggesting then what else they are suggesting now, namely, that no more new machines be permitted without proof of need, or until there was a demand beforehand for what they were trying to produce. Fancy the great sailing-ship industry consenting to the need for a steamship; or fancy, five thousand years ago, the Egyptian water carriers consenting to the need for a water wheel that took away their jobs.

Men are writing books to prove that the world is complete and that the free competitive system is dying, because new inventions, though they may be more and more wonderful, will be, at the same time, more and more footling. But you do not need books to say what a distinguished economist of his time, Emile de Laveleye, said in one paragraph, more than fifty years ago:

"The industrial activity of the greater part of the century has been devoted to fully equipping the civilized countries of the world with economic tools; the work of the future must necessarily be that of repair and replacement rather than new construction. This mechanical equipment having at last been made ready, the work of using it for production has, in turn, begun and has been prosecuted so efficiently that the world has, within recent years, and for the first time, been saturated, as it were, with the results of these modern improvements."

A saturated world before motor cars, aviation and radio! You may prefer to have lived in that world, with coal-oil lamps and no plumbing unless you were rich, but that has nothing to do with it.

It sounds very reasonable to say, "Let us tame the machine." We have learned to subdue and control the elemental forces of nature. Why not control the machine, instead of letting it run wild?

The elemental forces of nature are fixed and constant. Man does not create them. He has to take them as they are. His will and imagination do not enter into them; he must act upon them from without. The machine he does create. This will and imagination are inside of it. So when you speak of taming the machine, what you are really suggesting is that the creative power of man shall be restrained. Whether it should be or not is another question; only, let us be sure that we know what we are saying.

Of all the New Deal ideas, the notion of economic recovery through limiting output, raising prices and restoring the capital structure is least remembered. When the booming economies of Southeast Asia and South Korea collapsed in 1997, the advice from U.S. economists was to deregulate, cut the ties to political cronies and sweep away the dead capital. About that time, I spoke with Martin Baily, the chairman of President Clinton's Council of Economic Advisers. I asked him whether the administration's advice

93

to Asia was an admission by a Democratic president that the New Deal's economic strategy had been wrong. He looked at me quizzically. Such a strange question. I asked it again, explaining it. "Roosevelt is one of my heroes," he said, carefully. "He created bank deposit insurance."

And Roosevelt's strategy of propping up capital values by limiting the output of labor and machines?

"Policy errors," he said.

CHAPTER SEVEN:
A Particular Kind of Money

Not all the early Supreme Court rulings went against the New Deal. On February 18, 1935, the high court upheld the government's repudiation of private and public contracts to pay in gold money. The next day's headlines on the Seattle Post-Intelligencer *read, "Government upheld on gold; markets in frantic rise; victory delights Roosevelt. Buying waves send shares up $2 to $9. Grains climb. U.S. bonds with gold clause show decline. Supreme Court gold ruling big victory for government. Justice McReynolds sees unbridled chaos as result of gold decision. 'The Constitution as we have known it is gone.' Dissenting opinion scathing in denouncement of 'counterfeit profits' realized by government in dollar devaluation."*

"From 'Pieces of Money,' April 20, 1935"

When the Chief Justice of the United States Supreme Court had finished giving down the law in the gold-clause cases, Mr. Justice McReynolds, representing an overwhelmed minority of four, rose in his place, not to read the minority opinion but to put forth his opinions nakedly. He went on, stressing more and more the moral implications of what had been done, to the very last sentence, which was: "And the shame and humiliation of it all no one of us can foresee."

In an average thousand of intelligent persons, how many would you expect to have read more of the gold-clause decisions than the newspaper headlines? Mr. Justice McReynolds rightly supposed the number would be very few. And of these who wished to take the trouble, how many not already familiar with the difficult language of money would be able to entertain a clear idea of devaluation, or say for sure what fiat money is, or to define money at all? Ask at dinner, at lunch, in the streets, ask them what their interest in money is, and you will find that their interest is that of the woman who said: "All that money means to me is a piece of paper you have to have in order to live." And she was a very intelligent woman.

Seldom does anyone read what is engraved on that piece of paper. On the floor of the Senate, a few weeks ago, in a colloquy with a defender of money debasement, Senator Glass, of Virginia,[1] drew from his pocket a piece of paper money, saying, "I agree that the Government should have dominion over money. But I hope that the senator will agree that when the Government has dominion over money it will keep its word and not swindle people, and not write a lie on every bill it issues. Let me read the senator what the Government says. The Government says that this twenty-dollar note that I have is redeemable in gold on demand at the United States Treasury, or in gold or lawful money at any Federal Reserve Bank. And the senator knows that is not true. He knows it is a lie, printed right on the face of the bill. He knows that it will not be redeemed except with another piece of paper . . . We are on a fiat currency basis, and under the decision of the United States Supreme Court, we are on a fiat bond basis."

The senator had held up a Federal Reserve Note, the commonest kind of money now in circulation. Every senator present had identical pieces of it. And yet senators who had voted the laws to falsify the promise engraved on the face of it were scandalized at what Mr. Glass said—as if they themselves had never before seen the words he read, and some of them certainly never had.

That piece of paper you have to have in order to live has in itself no value. It is money only in a fictional sense. It is a sign of value, and nothing more. Intrinsically, it has no more value than the piece of paper on which you write a check. Your check also is a sign of value. Why does one hesitate to cash a check for a stranger? Because a sign of value may be bad. To make sure, one calls up the bank and asks, "Is this check good?"

It is a crime to write a bad check. For the same reason it is a crime for an individual to counterfeit paper money. The engraving and printing may be just as good as the Government's own; the counterfeit bill may pass from hand to hand undetected and serve every purpose of money. Nevertheless, it is a false sign of value. When it is found out, the one who innocently has it in hand will bear the loss; the bill will be destroyed and those who engraved it will be tracked down and sent to jail.

The laws forbidding private persons to create false signs of value are, indeed, strict, and for obvious reasons. No money fanatic has yet proposed to repeal them. How absurd it would be to propose that everyone should be free to write and print his own money, and that such money should be legal tender. That would be madness. And yet how plausibly may it be proposed, always in words of clothed meaning, that Government shall write and print false signs of value, declare them to be money and force people to accept them as such.

The reason why it is necessary for the Government, as Senator Glass says, to have dominion over money, is clear. This dominion is a tremendous power, second only to the military power; it is a power of life and death over economic society, and one that may be exercised subtly and in subversive ways to any political end, even to the end of revolution. That is why it cannot be trusted to lie in private hands. The temptation to abuse it is too great.

But all human experience since the invention of money

testifies that neither may a government be trusted not to abuse it. This is a very old truth. Aristotle discussed it in his *Economics*, the first scientific treatise ever written on that subject, more than 300 years B.C. He perceived that where a state possessed omnipotent power over money, there was nothing to prevent it from practicing gross fraud upon its citizens; also that such frauds acted so indirectly that democracies were slow to realize what was happening to them. In time it was learned, even by democracies, that although the government must have dominion over money, it must be restrained in the power to abuse it; and so all civilized governments have been restrained by constitutional law, by imperious customs and by fear of the consequences.

This Government was. It no longer is. Every act of monetary legislation since March, 1933, has been with one intent—namely, to strike down the restraints—and one by one they were struck down, until only the fear of legal damages under the Constitution remained. On February eighteenth, last, the United States Supreme Court, reviewing those acts of monetary legislation by which restraints had been done away with, the court said—a majority of the court said—that some of them were legal and some of them were not, yet, nevertheless, wherein they were illegal there was no redress for such as might fancy they had been defrauded. The entire court, majority and minority together, agreed that the Government had been guilty of repudiation; and yet, to the petitioners who had come before the court with the repudiated promises of the Government in their hands, a majority of the court said: "There is nothing to be done about it." And that became the law.

On the floor of the United States Senate, three days later, Senator Glass made this bitter comment: "The Supreme Court has said that what Congress did was a cheat and a repudiation, and then it further said that those who had been cheated and those upon whom repudiation had been practiced, if they undertake to recover what the Government had agreed to give them, can go to hell." And the Senate reporter, having closed the quotation, added in brackets: "Laughter."

Thus, omnipotent power over money passed to the Government—that is, to the Congress and the President. The Government now is free to write and print what signs of value it will, either false or true, or both, in utter confusion.

Given this absolute power, together with a writ of legal immunity, the Government may reduce the value of money to any point. If it can reduce the value of the standard dollar two-fifths, as it has already done, then, said the four members of the Supreme Court in their dissenting opinion, "The destruction of all obligations by reducing the standard gold dollar to one grain of gold or brass or nickel or copper or lead will become an easy possibility."

In the extreme event, the consequences would be appalling. Yet as the value of the dollar might be falling to ten cents, to five cents, to one cent, those pieces of paper we have to have in order to live would not visibly change. The value of the dollar might be reduced to the vanishing point and those pieces of paper would not shrink or fade or lose their beautiful texture, nor would their numerals be altered. Why? Because they are not value in themselves. They are but the signs of value. That is the whole point of debasing the dollar—to abstract the value and leave the sign intact.

The first moral lesson is here. Those who trust the Government not to print false signs of value, who trust it to mean what it says and to uphold the integrity of money—they are victimized. Those who are cynical and believe nothing, will find ways to save themselves. Faith is folly and cunning is wise. But how ugly!

When Senator Glass, holding up his piece of paper, said, "We are on a fiat-currency basis," what did he mean? What is fiat money? The word "fiat" means, "be it done." Fiat money is a piece of paper on which the Government puts its stamp and says, "That is money." If people decline to accept it, the Government passes a law, saying, "This money is legal tender for all purposes, and it is forbidden for anyone to refuse to accept it."

The phrase, "legal tender," means that the money may be used at its face value in settlement of debt. If the creditor refuses to accept it, nevertheless the debtor, by reason of having tendered it, is legally acquitted of his debt. Thus, if the Government should reduce the dollar to the value of one grain of gold, which would be roughly four cents, and then declare, "That is the standard legal dollar and full legal tender," a debtor who had borrowed dollars when they had a value of 100 cents, could tender in full payment of his debt the same number of four-cent dollars. The Government has already reduced the dollar from a value of 25 8/10 grains of gold to the value of 15 5/21 grains—that is, roughly from 100 cents to 60 cents, and the 60-cent dollar is full legal tender in payment of debts contracted in 100-cent dollars.

If the 60-cent paper dollar is redeemable in 60 cents' worth of gold, it is not strictly fiat money. What gives fiat money its character is that it is not redeemable in anything. That is what Senator Glass was talking about. You may take from your pocket a green ten-dollar bill and read, "Federal Reserve Note. The United States of America. Redeemable in gold on demand at the United States Treasury," but if you take it to the United States Treasury and ask for the gold, you will not get it. If you got it you would have to hand it back, because, with cunning beforehand, the Government passed a law saying it is illegal for a citizen to have gold in his possession.

Here you are almost certain to ask: "But why should paper dollars be redeemable?" The one imperative reason is to limit the quantity. Dwell upon this. It is the one constant and controlling fact about money. No kind of money—not even gold and silver—will retain its value unless the quantity be limited. Gold and silver are limited by nature and by the quantity of labor required to produce them. If by any discovery gold became as plentiful as pig iron, its monetary value would cease. Silver is worth much less than gold because it is more plentiful, and for no other reason.

A Particular Kind of Money

Then you come to paper money. It is created to serve as a convenient and necessary substitute for gold and silver because there is not enough gold and silver to pass from hand to hand and transact the daily business of the world. But if it is true of gold and silver that they retain their value only because the quantity is limited, so, also, is it true in a very acute sense of paper money. The quantity of paper money is limited neither by nature or by the labor of producing it. In one week the United States Bureau of Engraving and Printing might produce a million dollars for each man, woman and child in the country, and it might be exactly the same to all appearances as the paper money we have now in our pockets, but what would it be worth? The necessity, therefore, to limit the quantity of paper money is absolute. How, then, is it limited? By making it redeemable on demand, dollar for dollar, in something of customary value, preferably gold and silver, that are limited by nature.

It is true that the quantity of paper money in the hands of the people may be many times more than all the gold and silver in the country, so that, in fact, it could not all be redeemed in gold and silver; redeemability, therefore, is a relative fact. But as a relative fact it is understood and as a relative fact it works, so long as the amount of paper money is no more than is needed to pass from hand to hand. If it is no more than is needed, it will keep its value, and so long as it keeps its value, people will not think of trying to redeem it in actual gold and silver. They want only to know that they could redeem it.

The perfect illustration is that of a solvent bank. It does not keep its depositors' money all in cash; it keeps only about one-tenth of it in cash and lends out the rest at interest, because it knows from experience that so long as the depositors have faith in the bank they will not ask for cash. But let them begin to doubt the solvency of the bank. Then they will demand their deposits back in cash, just to see if they can get it.

To same is true of a monetary system. So long as people believe in the integrity of their Government and trust it not to issue more paper money than is needed as a substitute for gold and silver, they are content. But let anything happen to shock that faith, let it be even rumored that the Government is untrue to the understanding of paper money, or let the Congress begin to talk of repudiation and devaluation, and what happens? Then paper money begins all at once to be presented for redemption.

Senator Glass said also, " . . . and under the decision of the Supreme Court we are on a fiat-bond basis." What is a fiat bond? Consider what a Government bond is. It is a beautifully engraved promissory note, signed by the Government, interest payable annually and principal payable in full on a certain date. One who buys it is lending the United States Government money on its promissory note.

When an individual comes to you wanting to borrow money on his promissory note, what do you do? First, you take steps to satisfy yourself as to the security. Will the man be able to pay the interest annually, and then the principal in full when the note is due, or is he likely to ask you to receive payment in another promissory note? Has he ever broken his word?

But now it is the Government that comes wanting to borrow. Is the word of the government good? Fancy having to ask a question like that! The Government does not expect you to ask it, resents it if you do; yet you have a reason to ask it; and the reason you have to ask it is what makes the Government resent it—namely, that for the first time in its history it has broken its word.

In every note or bond on which the Government borrowed money from its citizens it had engraved this pledge: "Payable principal and interest in United States gold coin of the present standard of value."

That was the gold clause.

By long custom it had ceased ever to be insisted upon literally. The Government did not in fact pay principal and interest in gold coin. Nobody wanted gold coin. All that anybody wanted really was money of a certain value. This had been so for so long that nobody could remember when it was otherwise. There was no gold coin in general circulation, yet our money was gold-standard money. It might have continued so for generations more; it did continue so until, in 1932, a Democratic Congress began to debate repudiation and devaluation as a political experiment. Then, for the first time, people began to think of gold, and gold hoarding began.

But the gold clause—what happened to it? On June 5, 1933, the Congress, pursuing a political obsession, repudiated it utterly. It did not say the Government might repay its creditors with 60-cent gold dollars. It repudiated the obligation to pay them in gold dollars at all or in dollars of any specific value. It said, in effect, that the Government's notes and bonds were payable in any kind of money the Government might deem fit to print.

Well, now you may look again at the promissory note, called a bond. The word of the borrower is doubtful. It is doubtful because it has been broken. If the Government may with impunity repudiate the redemption clause, so also it may repudiate the interest clause or the repayment clause. You cannot imagine it. Nevertheless, the difference between partial and total repudiation is not a difference in either power or morals; it is a difference of degree only.

However, these may be, after all, political considerations. What you want to know is very simple. Is the Government's note good? Suppose, as you might have done with an individual borrower, you go to the Government's bank—the United States Treasury, that is—and ask, "Is the Government's note good?"

The Treasury will say, "Certainly."

You may say: "What I mean is, will it be paid?"

The Treasury will say, "Certainly."

You may ask: "In what will it be paid?"

The Treasury will say, "In money."

You may ask: "In money such as what?"

The Treasury will not answer that question, perhaps, but if it does, it will be obliged to say, "In money such as there is at the time."

And now you may begin to see what repudiation of the gold clause meant.

The gold clause imposed a limitation upon the quantity of bonds the Government could sell, just as the necessity to keep the value of paper dollars at a parity with gold dollars was a limitation upon the amount of paper money it could issue. You will be asked to believe that these two limitations, both imperative in any sound monetary system, laid the Government under a disability in the exercise of its power to raise extraordinary revenue for emergency purposes, such as unemployment relief. But that was not so.

All the ways by which a government may raise revenue come at last to be two—namely, that the government borrows or the government takes. There may be a limit to borrowing. There is no limit to taking so long as there is anything left to take. To tax is to take. But to levy taxes any popular government may be tempted to avoid. Therefore, such a government will resort to monetary anesthetics such as devaluation, inflation or legalized repudiation. And yet, any of these measures, guaranteed at the moment to be painless, will turn out to represent taking. Ultimately, those pay who might honestly have been taxed in the first place. If food were laid under a sales tax of 30 per cent for unemployment relief, everyone would know it and the why of it, and relief expenditures, you may be sure, would be confined to relief. Well, but food has risen 30 per cent in price because of what has happened unawares to the pieces of money that one must have to buy food—because of the cheapening of money by devaluation and inflation and repudiation—and this cheapening of money was a device adopted in lieu of heroic direct taxation.

The answer the United States Treasury might have made to you, that a promissory note is payable only in "money such as there is at the time," would be strictly accurate. In fact, any other answer would be illegal.

The law of June 5, 1933, repudiating the gold clause in all Government obligations, at the same time annulled the similar redemption clause in all private notes and bonds

104

and mortgages. But it did much more than that. It made it unlawful for the Government, or for any corporation or private person, when writing a promissory note, a bond, a mortgage, to promise that repayment shall be made in any particular kind of money. The exact language deserves examination.

The law reads: "That every provision contained in or made with respect to any obligation which purports to give the obligee a right to require payment in gold, or a particular kind of coin or currency, or in an amount of money of the United States measured thereby, is declared to be against public policy; and no such provision shall be contained in or made with respect to any obligation hereinafter incurred."

It follows, literally, that it is now unlawful in this country for a borrower, be it the Government, a corporation or a private person, to promise that the value of what is to be paid back shall equal the value of what was borrowed. The ostensible reason for this amazing prohibition is that the Government shall be free by fiat to fix the dollar at any value it may deem expedient; that it shall have the power to say of a 50-cent dollar, a 25-cent dollar or a 5-cent dollar, as it has already said of a 60-cent dollar, "This is the standard dollar and full legal tender in settlement of all obligations." It follows again, literally, that no one knows today what the value of the dollar will be tomorrow, or a month hence or a year from now. The Government itself does not know. And that now is the state of the currency.

Currency is the money current. Suppose that you take a check for $100 to the bank and say, "Cash, please." You will get some ten-dollar bills, some five-dollar bills and maybe five one-dollar bills. Now examine this currency. You will find four kinds, all gray on one side and green on the other. There had been five; now one is missing.

The missing piece is what was known as the yellowback, or the gold certificate, beginning with the ten-dollar denomination and rising in multiples up to $1000, or even higher in rare examples. On the face of this gold certificate had been engraved these words: "This certifies that there have been deposited in the Treasury of the United States of America ten dollars in gold coin, payable to the bearer on demand." This yellow gold certificate was a unique piece of money in the world. It was, said the Secretary of the Treasury in 1926, in fact "a mere warehouse receipt for gold deposited." Around the world, from New York to Hong Kong and back, it was treated, not as a piece of paper money as good as gold, but as gold itself, because no one could imagine that the United States Treasury could ever refuse to honor a warehouse receipt for actual gold left with it for safekeeping.

Yet that happened. When, in 1933, the Government seized all the gold, it seized also these gold certificates, because they were the same as gold, and made it a crime punishable by fine and imprisonment for a citizen to have one in his possession. One citizens possessing gold certificates made a case of his rights and went to the United States Supreme Court, demanding either his gold or the equivalent of it in 60-cent paper dollars, which would be $1.69 in paper money for every $1.00 of the gold certificate. The Supreme Court decided that along with the gold-clause cases. It said in its majority opinion, first, that when the plaintiff demanded his gold, the dollar had not yet been legally devalued, wherefore he could not have calculated his loss; secondly, that if he had got the gold, it would have been illegal for him to keep it, because he was required by law to hand it back to the Government. Wherefore he was adjudged not to be damaged and sent away.

So much for the piece that is missing.[2]

Taking now, as they come, the four kinds you have, the first is a one-dollar bill. On the face of it was engraved: "Silver Certificate. This certifies that there has been deposited in the Treasury of the United States of America one silver dollar payable to the bearer on demand." In small letters at the left: "This certificate is receivable for all public dues and when so received may be reissued." That means the Government will receive it for taxes and then issue it again. It is signed in the lower right corner by the

Secretary of the Treasury. In the center is a portrait of Washington.

On the face of it, this piece of money is the same as silver in the hand. If you were thinking to hoard silver, it might occur to you to collect and hoard these certificates. But observe that the engraved promise is the same as the promise that appeared on the face of the missing gold certificate that was seized by the Government.[3]

The next piece is a five-dollar bill. On the face of it is engraved: "United States Note. The United States will pay to the bearer on demand five dollars." In small letters: "This note is legal tender at face value for all debts public and private, except duties on imports and interest on the public debt." In the center is a portrait of Lincoln and in the lower right corner there is the signature of the Secretary of the Treasury.

This is the famous greenback. It appeared during the Civil War, frankly as fiat money, redeemable in nothing, secured by nothing; simply, the United States of America will pay bearer five dollars on demand. The Government was in desperate need of money; its borrowing power had been dangerously stretched and it had been obliged to suspend gold payments. Hence the resort to this piece of fiat money, which was issued to upward of $400,000,000 in face value. Its gold value was very much less. There were two sets of prices in the country—gold prices and paper-money prices. But consider the difference between honorable default and repudiation. The Government had suspended gold payments of necessity; it was off gold. Yet in this extremity it repudiated nothing, and the understanding was that this fiat money, the greenback, was temporary and would sometime be redeemable at its face value in gold.

Ten years after the close of the Civil War, the Congress passed the Specie Resumption Act, providing that the greenbacks, beginning in 1879, should be redeemed in gold coin; owing, however, to the clamor of a Greenback Party and a Silver Party, both demanding that in no case should the currency be contracted, the law provided also that as the greenbacks were redeemed in gold coin at the Treasury they should be reissued. This very awkward stipulation twice nearly wrecked the Treasury, for the greenbacks, as fast as they were redeemed in gold and then reissued, kept coming back to be redeemed again. The Government was obliged, therefore, to sell bonds and buy gold from Europe. Yet it never faltered, thanks at last to Grover Cleveland. Then, in a little while, as the business of the country grew, the troublesome greenbacks were absorbed in the activities of trade so that they stopped coming back for redemption. They became as good as gold, because they could be redeemed, wherefore at length nobody wanted the gold. More than $300,000,000 of these greenbacks are still suspended in the stream of money current.[4]

The third piece, next, is a ten-dollar bill. Engraved upon it: "National Currency. Secured by United States bonds deposited with the Treasurer of the United States of America." At the left: "First National Bank of Baltimore will pay to the bearer on demand ten dollars." At the right in small letters: "Redeemable in lawful money of the United States at United States Treasury or at the bank of issue." Signed by the president of the First National Bank of Baltimore. It might be any national bank.

This is the old and honorable national bank currency, secured dollar for dollar by Government bonds, which, after the Civil War, displaced all forms of paper money theretofore issued by state banks acting under state charters. The Congress laid a prohibitive tax upon paper money issued by any other than a national bank and then authorized national banks to issue paper money against Government bonds pledged at the United States Treasury. After that nobody had to look at the paper money in his pocket or read the newspaper every morning to see what state bank had failed, leaving its paper money worthless. But this National Bank Note will presently disappear. The particular bonds that were employed to secure it have all been called by the Treasury for redemption.

It is the fourth kind that is now the paramount piece of

108

paper money, and also the most expansible. It is another ten-dollar bill.

It might be a twenty, fifty or one hundred. On the face of it is engraved: "Federal Reserve Note. The United States of America will pay to the bearer on demand ten dollars." In small letters at the left: "Redeemable in gold on demand at the United States Treasury, or in gold or lawful money at any Federal Reserve Bank." In the center is a portrait of Alexander Hamilton. In the lower right corner is the signature of the Secretary of the Treasury.

This was to have been the scientific, panic-proof kind of paper money. It was designed to expand and contract in a sensitive relation to the volume of business. In the original plan it was to be secured both by a gold reserve and by what is called commercial paper, meaning the short-term promissory notes of merchants and manufacturers. There could be no better security for paper money. It was issued by the twelve Federal Reserve Banks, and first appeared with the foundation of the Federal Reserve Bank System in 1914. Gradually the limitations upon its issue were relaxed; it began to be issued against the security of Government bonds, contrary to the first scientific idea, and the limitations having been greatly relaxed, it is proposed, in a bill now pending in Congress, to relax them much more, in order to facilitate inflation.

This is the piece of paper money Senator Glass held up in the Senate, saying that what was engraved upon it was a lie. It is no longer redeemable in gold at the United States Treasury, or anywhere.

Prior to the laws of devaluation and repudiation enacted in 1933, all four kinds of this paper money (a) the silver certificate, (b) the fiat greenback, (c) the old and honorable National Bank Note, and (d) the Federal Reserve Note— were, in fact, redeemable in gold dollars, and the gold dollar contained 25 8/10 grains of gold. Now the law is that the gold dollar, if you could see one, would contain only 15 5/21 grains of gold. But you cannot see one. There is no such dollar in existence. None of this paper money is redeemable in gold. The silver certificate is redeemable in silver only by

109

present consent of the Government; it has the legal right to say no. The three other pieces—the greenback, the National Bank Note and the Federal Reserve Note—are redeemable only in other pieces of paper.

The steps in devaluation were these:

FIRST, all citizens were commanded to bring forth their gold and deliver it to the nearest bank in exchange for paper money. They had been taking their gold out of the banks and hoarding it, partly because they were afraid of the banks, yet also because the Congress was debating devaluation and repudiation. Besides threatening them with fine and imprisonment, the Government appealed to them on the grounds of duty, patriotism and self-interest, saying they were obliged to bring back the gold in order to save the banking structure of the country from collapse. The banks had to have the gold back, or else they could not make loans. Moreover, the country was still on a gold basis and the paper money they would receive for their gold was still the gold-standard money they had always known.

SECOND STEP. When the gold was safely back in the banks, the Government declared itself to be off the gold standard, and to pay or receive gold was universally forbidden. That put the gold beyond reach. Nobody could touch it.

THIRD STEP. Then the Congress passed the devaluation law. This law authorized the President, in his own discretion, to restamp the dollar.

FOURTH STEP. Then the Congress passed a law to repudiate the gold-redemption clause in all Government obligations and all private obligations, so that nothing anywhere should be payable in gold.

FIFTH STEP. The President by proclamation declared that a dollar should be worth only 15 5/21 grains of gold where it had been worth 25 8/10 grains before, thereby reducing the value of the dollar two-fifths.

SIXTH STEP. All the gold in the banks of the country was seized by the Government and taken into the United States Treasury. Now observe what happens. The

110

Government takes a gold dollar and says, "Here is what was a gold dollar. It is no longer a dollar. It is simply 25 8/10 grains of gold. The law says that 15 5/21 grains of gold shall be a dollar. Therefore the Government takes 10 1/2 grains, or the least trifle more, and puts that to one side."

When this operation was finished, the gold was in two piles. Three-fifths of it was in the pile to the right side. But in the pile to the right was precisely the same number of dollars that had been brought into the Treasury. Out of that pile the Government counted back to the banks from which it had seized the gold exactly the same number of dollars that had been seized, saying, "We shall keep them for you. We shall give you credit for them on our books."

And what of the other pile? The Government said, "That pile is mine." And in that pile, built up of 10 1/2 grains of gold abstracted from each gold dollar that had been brought in, there were 2,800,000,000 new dollars of 15 5/21 grains each.

This is the pile of gold that was referred to by the Secretary of the Treasury in a radio speech, August 28, 1934, on the good fortune of the Government in its financial accounts, saying, "But we have another cash drawer in the Treasury . . . I will call our gold drawer. In it is the very large sum of $2,800,000,000, representing profit resulting from the change in gold value of the dollar . . . For the present, this $2,800,000,000 is under lock and key . . . But I call attention to the fact that ultimately we expect this profit to flow back into the stream of our other revenues and thereby reduce the national debt."

And it was to that speech to which the overwhelmed minority of the Untied States Supreme Court referred in these words: "It is said the United States have realized profits amounting to $2,800,000,000. But this assumes that gain may be generated by legislative fiat. To such counterfeit profits there would be no limit; with each new debasement of the dollar they might expand. Two billions might be ballooned indefinitely—to twenty, thirty, or what you will. Loss or reputation for honorable dealing will bring us unending humiliation; the impending legal and moral chaos is appalling."

There was no profit. All that happened was that the Government restamped the gold, and that the value of the country's gold was increased by $2,800,000,000, by the trick of pricing it in debased paper money, at the expense of the citizen whose money the Government had borrowed.

If there be such a thing in morals as the law of necessity, the necessity itself must be clear; and then a sin will be twice a sin that does not work. Was it, in fact, necessary to demoralize the monetary system? Secondly, has it worked?

We present the only modern instance of a great nation debasing its currency and repudiating its obligations to its own citizens in a gratuitous manner, unless it be Germany after the war. Great Britain suspended gold payments in 1931 only after the Bank of England could see the bottom of the gold bin. She had to do it. Even then she did not confiscate her citizens' gold nor forbid them to possess it.

The American Government not only suspended gold payments; it abandoned the gold standard, with more than one-third of the visible monetary gold of the whole world in its possession. There was neither a scarcity of gold nor a scarcity of money. There was a panic and there was private hoarding of gold. But largely because the Congress began talking of a managed currency, of commodity dollars, of rubber dollars, in place of gold-standard money. Even if the Government had been obliged during a panic to stop paying gold, that would not have been to abandon the gold standard. There was no necessity to devalue the dollar, to debase the currency, to repudiate anything.

What obsessed the Government was the idea of getting rid of the gold standard in order to be free to manipulate money for purposes of a great political and social experiment. The theory was that as the Government cheapened money by devaluation—one, the blessing that debtors would be eased of their debts; second, the blessing that prices would rise in a manner to produce a kind of economic ecstasy, and so prosperity would be restored.

112

A PARTICULAR KIND OF MONEY

Has it worked? It is true that a great many debtors have been eased of their debts, but mainly this has been accomplished by a transfer of their mortgages from the hands of private creditors to those of the Government.

It is true that prices have risen, but it has not produced the psychic effect that was imagined. The reason is clear. Rising prices produce economic good feeling only when there may be at least the delusion that values are rising. When everybody knows that the rise in prices itself is the delusion, that prices are rising in terms of paper money only because the value of paper money is falling, then a state of economic good feeling is not experienced.

In the world of private enterprise the borrowing and lending of capital tends to cease. Why is that? You need to think of only one reason. It is unlawful in any note or bond or obligation to write a promise that the value of what is paid back shall equal the value of what was borrowed. Who, therefore, will be anxious to lend?

The saving of capital tends to cease. Why? Because capital must be saved in terms of paper money and nobody knows what that paper money will be worth.

There comes a saying in Wall Street, seriously and literally meant, "Do not save what you cannot afford to lose." Then appears, as you would expect, a reckless feeling toward money. Since nobody can say what it will be worth tomorrow, why not spend it now? Evidence of this feeling is wherever you look for it. Observe how people—not the rich only, but all kinds of people—are spending their money in a time of depression, at the race tracks, in betting and sports, in the play places, all in a spirit of tomorrow be damned. That is one of the moral effects of breaking down faith in the integrity of money.

There begins to be statistical evidence. It appears that for the first time in our history our saving is below zero. We are consuming each day more than we add. What does that mean?

If you should see a family on a farm eating its seed corn, butchering its brood sow, burning its front porch in the parlor stove, you would know what it meant and it would

113

make you shudder. It is not so easy to see the wearing out of machines and the alarming rise in obsolescence throughout industry. It is hard to realize that we may be devouring our tools. If we are, it is disastrous. If we are not, we are coming to it. Even the Government now begins to see that. Yet seeing it obliquely, not as a consequence of what it has done to the integrity of money and the inviolability of contract, it turns its mind to another problem, which is how now artificially to stimulate what it calls the durable-goods industries, such as are active only when people are saving capital and have it to lend and when others are willing to borrow and adventure it for a profit that may be calculated beforehand in some particular kind of money.

The devaluation of the dollar did not affect people's willingness to accept the government's bonds. In June 1933 the yield on thirty-year Treasuries was 3.21 percent. By February 1935, when the Court upheld repudiation, it was 2.79 percent. Financial journalist James Grant noted in Money of the Mind *(1992) that the bond yield "would keep right on dropping, the second, third, and fourth Roosevelt terms notwithstanding, until it reached 2.03 percent in April 1946." And offering $35 an ounce, the Federal Reserve vacuumed up gold from around the world. When America entered World War II, its share of the world's gold reserves had risen to 60 percent, compared with 38 percent in 1929.*

It would seem that Garrett had been totally wrong.

But by the 1960s the gold was flowing out to foreign central banks. On August 15, 1971, President Nixon stopped selling gold at $35 per ounce. On that day the dollar truly became fiat money. There followed the worst decade of peacetime inflation in U.S. history.

Shorn of its monetary role, gold became available for U.S. residents to own. On Jan. 1, 1975, the remaining restrictions on ownership were lifted. On Oct. 27, 1977, gold clauses were allowed in private contracts. A few remained; in Seattle, the landlord of the city's most prominent department store cited a 1929 gold clause to a federal court, winning permission to break a ninety-nine-year fixed-price

114

lease. In 1996, federal law made pre-1977 gold contracts unenforceable.

By 2000 the dollar's purchasing power measured in 1933 dollars had fallen to less than eight cents.

---

[1]Carter Glass, 1858-1946, Democratic congressman 1902-1918, and chief author of the Federal Reserve Act; Treasury Secretary for President Wilson, 1918-1920, U.S. senator 1920-1946. He was offered the job of Treasury Secretary by Roosevelt, but turned it down when Roosevelt refused to promise to keep the gold standard.

[2]Gold certificates were illegal to own until April 24, 1964.

[3] Yes, and they repudiated that, too. The Treasury stopped redemption of silver certificates on June 24, 1968, under President Johnson. Almost all the one-dollar bills had been silver certificates until 1963, when the government issued one-dollar Federal Reserve notes. The last 90% silver coins were minted in 1964.

[4]For years, the most reliable way to get a United States Note was to ask for a two-dollar bill. The last United States Notes were printed in 1969, but they were $100 bills and never issued. The law mandating them was repealed, and the Treasury destroyed its entire stock in 1996.

CHAPTER EIGHT:

That Old Straitjacket

On May 27, 1935, the U.S. Supreme Court found the National Recovery Administration unconstitutional. In the famous "sick chicken" case, the A.L.A. Schechter Poultry Corp. of Brooklyn, New York, won a unanimous decision that Congress had impermissibly delegated its power. The NRA had penalized Schechter for violating the wage and hour code, for allowing buyers to make "selections of individual chickens" from coops and for the sale of an "unfit chicken." The government argued that all this was justified by the economic emergency, but Chief Justice Charles Evans Hughes didn't accept that. "Extraordinary conditions do not create or enlarge constitutional power," he ruled.

It was not a precedent that would be followed. But for the moment it was "Black Monday" for the New Dealers, who responded with a torrent of suggestions for constitutional amendments and even for ending judicial review. This was Garrett's defense of the constitutional order.

From "The House We Live In," August 3, 1935

Now many voices are heard to be saying of the house of liberty in which this nation was born that it is very old-fashioned, wanting all the modern conveniences, and too strait for new ideas.

This means only that a sleepless struggle as old as the house itself has come again to a crisis. The occasion was the unanimous decision of the United States Supreme Court declaring the primary grand device of the New Deal to be unconstitutional.

It is not a party struggle. The dominant political parties have several times changed sides. It was a Democratic president[1] who, in 1887, vetoed a bill appropriating $10,000 for free seed to be distributed among drought-distressed farmers in Texas, on the ground that one could find no warrant in the Constitution for such an appropriation and believed the tendency to stretch the powers and duties of the Government, even though with benevolent intent, should be resisted, "to the end that the lesson should be constantly enforced that, though the people support the government, the government should not support the people." And now it is a Democratic president who stands at the extreme opposite sign, committing the government to guarantee every unemployed person a job at public expense.

The conflict is between two ideas of government so deep and so antagonistic that never have they ever been quite reconciled. One is the idea of a powerful, unlimited central government, acting directly upon the people in a providential manner, minding everything they do, and originally imperious only to do good to them. The other is the idea of representative, constitutional government, possessing only such powers as have been jealously surrendered to it by a free people—therefore, a limited government. And this conflict has its source in the first problem of political science— how to reconcile government with liberty. Government tends to devour liberty; and yet government is so necessary that people must surrender some liberty for it. How much? That is the arguable question.

What the NRA represented was an extreme extension of one idea—not in the historical sense extreme, but in the American scheme extreme indeed. What the unanimous

118

decision of the United States Supreme Court represented was a vehement counter-assertion of the other idea. That was all. But it was enough to raise a storm of political passions.

There is conviction on both sides. Where there is conviction there will be prejudice. All of that may be respected. Only, as we may respect it, so it is all the more important to keep sight of the fact that what we are dealing with is a collision of ideas and not, as the voice of frustration would suggest, a struggle between the powers of light and darkness, those in the light wanting only to make new laws to secure social justice and promote human welfare, those in the darkness defending the old law for such guilty and reactionary reasons as they may be able to justify to themselves.

Shall nine men, not elected by the people, holding office for life, tell the people what they may and may not do?

Shall this country remain in a straitjacket of a Constitution that was written for thirteen little seaboard colonies before anybody had imagined railroads?

A member of the House of Representatives rhetorically asked: "Shall Congress be permitted to enact legislation to protect the destitute, the aged and all others who are victims of capitalistic cruelty? Shall an academic body, unreachable by the people, appointed for life, and largely schooled in an atmosphere of wealth and exclusiveness, succeed in throttling such legislation practically every time it is passed?"

The mayor of New York City[2] said: "You cannot leave the destinies of the American people in the hands of a tribunal, no matter how well meaning they may be." In what hands they should be left, he did not say. But the tribunal to which he was referring said something apparently he could not understand. It said the destinies of the American people should be left in the hands of the American people, and it said this because it is so written in the Constitution.

The style of criticism toward both the United States Supreme Court and the Constitution was set by the President. On the Friday following the Court's decision

119

declaring the NRA to be unconstitutional, he assembled the newspaper correspondents at the White House and talked to them for an hour and a half. That clause in the Constitution granting Congress the power to regulate commerce among the states—the interstate commerce clause—had been written, he said, in the horse-and-buggy days, when there was no interstate commerce to speak of. That was the clause, liberally construed by himself and his advisers, under which the Government had been extending the power to act directly on social and economic conditions, both to reform them and to promote recovery, as, for example, through the mechanism of the NRA; and just when both he and his advisers were happily thinking they had found solutions to various national problems, then suddenly their solutions had been thrown back in their faces by the Supreme Court.

Such a literal and narrow interpretation of the interstate commerce clause would mean that it was the only national government on earth without power to enact laws in control of social and economic conditions. He deplored the decision. It would mean the Federal Government was stripped of all authority to act on behalf of human welfare. And with what the reporters described as feeling, the President suggested that the Supreme Court not long before had construed the same clause broadly when it was for the benefit of the coal-mine owners, wanting an injunction against strikers, only to narrow it again when the government needed the broad construction in order to improve the living and working conditions of miners.

In the *New York Times* report of that extraordinary interview (June 1, 1935), this paragraph occurs: "He compared it with the decision in 1857 in the Dred Scott case, an important factor in the events that precipitated the Civil War. Mr. Roosevelt did not make the latter reference, but later in the conference nodded when an interviewer cited the results of the older decision."

The use of these open reflections, the President said, was to clarify the public mind. What he wished people to see clearly was that in what a disastrous way the New Deal had collided with the judicial power and that something would have to be done about it. He was not yet prepared to say what ought to be done. But at the Capitol, on the floor of the Senate and in the well of the House, voices were saying rashly what ought to be done about it. They were saying this dictatorial judicial power ought to be abated, and resolutions to accomplish its downfall were in writing, one to forbid the Supreme Court to declare an act of Congress unconstitutional, another to limit the tenure of judges, so that it should be a changing court, more responsive to the popular will.

And rising at the same time was the absurd argument that this dictatorial judicial power, telling Congress what it could and could not do, was nonexistent—that for the Supreme Court to declare an act of Congress unconstitutional is in itself an unconstitutional act, because there in nothing in the Constitution about it; that John Marshall, the great Chief Justice of the United States, invented the power and put it over on the country; that in England such a thing never happens, and there a judge was once hanged for declaring an act of Parliament void.

Those who take this position, if they take it sincerely, must be ignorant of what made the American system unique, ignorant of the nature of the judicial function therein, and unable, besides, to distinguish in principle between the parliamentary government as in England, and representative constitutional government in the American form. It is true John Marshall developed the judicial power, just as the early Presidents developed the executive power and the early senators and representatives developed the legislative power. But the judicial power does not invalidate an act of Congress. Only the Constitution does that.

What was it the Supreme Court did?

In the first place, it did nothing on its own initiative; it never does. Two disputants came before it. One was the government in its executive aspect. The other was a poultry dealer in Brooklyn. This poultry dealer had refused to obey certain NRA laws laid upon him by the national government—laws such as one saying in what manner the buyer of a live chicken should abstract the chicken from the dealer's coop and another saying what wages should be paid in the chicken yard, and how many persons should work there, and what should be the length of their working day.

The reason the poultry dealer gave for disobeying these laws was that the national government had no right to regulate his business, since it was a local business in Brooklyn, and not in any reasonable sense interstate commerce. For his disobedience the national government, acting through the enforcement bureau of NRA, haled the poultry dealer to court, and from the decision of the inferior court there was an appeal to the Supreme Court, whose decisions are final.

Observe now what is taking place.

Who are these two before the Supreme Court? One is the Brooklyn poultry dealer, as a corporate person. But who is the other? For convenience, we say it is the government. That is not so. The government consists of three powers—namely, the legislative power, the executive power and the judicial power. This trinity of powers does not appear against the poultry dealer; therefore, it is not the government. It is the executive power only that appears against him; the poultry dealer is appealing to the judicial power, saying his individual rights and immunities have been invaded in an unconstitutional manner by the executive power.

The executive power now argues its case against the poultry dealer. It says the government cannot confer upon people the national blessing of minimum wages and maximum hours of labor, it cannot reform social and economic conditions and abate the evils of sweating and chiseling, it cannot, in brief, act upon human welfare at large, and the whole NRA scheme will fall—unless those seven words in the Constitution granting to Congress the power "to regulate commerce . . . among the several states" be construed to the point that the manner of abstracting chickens from a coop in a Brooklyn chicken yard are deemed to be matters

122

that affect interstate commerce, and, therefore, become subject to regulation by the national government.

The Supreme Court answers, in effect, that the contention of the executive power is absurd. If that could be done to the sense of words, then there would be no meaning to writing and no use whatever in having a written Constitution. It said, moreover, as to NRA, that in principle it was wrong. The law under which it had been created was wrong. Congress passed the law, but it was not a law really. It was an act delegating to the President the power to make laws. And so it was that there came to be a system of bureaus making and imposing laws upon the country, many of these laws having the force of criminal statutes. Thus the spectacle, very repugnant to the Constitution, of a bureaucratic system making its own laws, which is a legislative function, and then enforcing its own laws, which is an executive function, besides most of the time judging its own laws, which is a judicial function.

The principle here involved is at the very base of political liberty. The axioms concerning it are famous in the great essays on government. This one is from the Blackstone Commentaries: "Wherever the power of making and that of enforcing the laws are united together, there can be no public liberty . . . Where the legislative and executive authority are in distinct hands the former will take care not to entrust the latter with so large a power as may tend to the subversion of its own independence, and therewith the liberty of the subject."

This truth the Congress forgot, or disregarded, when it passed the NRA act. It surrendered its own lawmaking power to the executive power. The Constitution does not permit it to do that. And that is what the Supreme Court said. The judicial power, besides upholding the Brooklyn poultry dealer in his right not to be minded in his chicken yard by the executive power of the national government, was at the same time defending the lawmaking power of Congress, even against the impulse of Congress to surrender it.

In this case did the Supreme Court say there shall not be an NRA, even one like the one that was? No. It said that if people want an NRA like that, it will be necessary to change the rules, according to the rule for changing them, which means to amend the Constitution. There is nothing that people may not do that they really want to do, nor does the Supreme Court say there is; it says only there is a constitutional way to do it, and it is bound to say that because it is itself bound by the Constitution.

Congress cannot abolish itself. That is what the Supreme Court means when it says the Congress may not surrender the legislative power to the executive power. It is not permitted by the Constitution. But the people may abolish Congress by writing a new set of rules and leaving Congress out; they may abolish the judicial power, if they want to do that, and impose upon themselves a personal government—all in a constitutional manner.

In the famous Dred Scott decision, which President Roosevelt has associated the NRA decision, the Supreme Court said a slave was a slave, under the Constitution as it was then; and it added the opinion that Congress had not the constitutional power to abolish slavery in any territory in the United States. It took a war to abolish the fact of slavery; and still slavery was not illegal until the Constitution was amended to forbid its existence in any part of the United States.

In the '90s the Congress passed an income-tax law, and the Supreme Court held it to be unconstitutional, because the Constitution then read that federal taxes should be uniform and apportioned among the states according to population. In this matter the Court had strong opinions. It foresaw that an income-tax law, giving the Federal Government direct and unlimited access to the wealth of its citizens, might become an instrument for taking wealth from one class and giving it to another, agreeable to any sudden social theory that might arise; besides, that it would enormously extend the power and resources of the Federal Government.

Nevertheless, an income tax was wanted, and the

Constitution was amended; and then the same Supreme Court, maybe of the same opinion still as to the political unwisdom of an income-tax law, was obliged to uphold it.

Such are the procedures under a representative constitutional government in the American form.

The reason why an act of the British Parliament is never declared unconstitutional is that there is no way to do it. It cannot happen under the parliamentary form of government. An act of the British Parliament is the supreme law of the land, whereas here the Constitution is the supreme law. All that an English court can do is interpret the meaning of the act itself.

Observe the difference. If the British Parliament should surrender its lawmaking power to the king, as it once did, the people could either submit or rise against it. Here, if Congress surrenders its lawmaking powers to the President, as it did in the NRA act, the Supreme Court says the Constitution forbids it. Then, if the people really want it done, they may have it done, or if they want parliamentary government in place of representative constitutional government, they may have that, by changing the supreme rules according to the rule provided in the Constitution for changing them.

The rule allows amendments to be proposed by a two-thirds vote of Congress or by a national constitutional convention to be called on petition of two-thirds of the state legislatures. Amendments may be ratified by three-fourths of the state legislatures or by conventions in three-fourths of the states.

There has been no national constitutional convention since the one that wrote the original Constitution in Philadelphia in 1787. All the twenty-one amendments have been proposed by Congress and ratified by the states.

The first ten, ever since known as the Bill of Rights, were submitted to the states all at one time by the first Congress. This was by agreement. A majority of the states had been willing to ratify the original Constitution only on the understanding that Congress would immediately propose a set of amendments to define individual rights and immunities and the limits of Federal power over the states—one forbidding the Federal Government to establish any religion, or to abridge the freedom of speech and the right of assembly; one to regulate seizure and search; one to guarantee the right of trial by jury; one saying a citizen should not be deprived of life, liberty or property without due process of law; and so on, and then one to say: "The powers not delegated to the United States by the Constitution, nor prohibited by it to the states, are reserved to the states respectively, or to the people."

Remember that each of the thirteen original states was a sovereign political entity in itself. Some of them might have dreamed of a separate empire. All of them had to surrender a measure of sovereignty for the idea of a United States of America; and, naturally, they were very jealous to make the original compact clear, especially to limit what they were giving up. There was no absolute necessity for union, unless you suppose it was the necessity of destiny acting. We can see now what was going to happen, since it has happened, but at the time it had all to be imagined.

One thing, however, was clearly foreseen. The premonition of it appears vividly in the first ten amendments. It was foreseen that there would be a ceaseless tension between the states, defending all the sovereignty they did not surrender, and the federal government, always seeking to extend its own power. And it has been so to this day. The irrepressible question of state rights. The Civil War was fought upon it and still it rises.

All the other amendments have been proposed and ratified in obedience to unmistakable movements of public opinion. There have been eleven, such as, one to abolish slavery, one to enfranchise the Negro, one to empower Congress to levy a progressive income tax, one providing for the popular election of senators, one to enfranchise women, one for prohibition, and one to repeal that one. The only reason why a national constitutional convention has never been invoked is that there never yet has been a time when the people were willing to throw the original

126

Constitution into the crucible, melt it down and mold it over.

Such is the rule for changing the supreme law of the land. Only part of it has ever been employed, and that part seldom, though several times to effect deep change. The criticism of it is that the process is slow and cumbersome; that the sovereign power—namely, the people—is unable to act swiftly. But the process is slow and cumbersome only when it is obstructed; and when it is obstructed, you may be sure that public opinion is inert or divided. Let it be really aroused and the process is not slow. The amendment to abolish slavery was proposed to the state legislatures in February, 1865, and in December of that same year the Secretary of State proclaimed that it had been ratified by three-fourths of the states. The amendment to repeal prohibition was proposed to the states, ratified and written into the Constitution, all in one year.

Public opinion has as many movements as the wind, sudden, unreasonable, cyclonic, erratic, going to and fro, and then the great trade winds of thought and conviction, rising slowly, moving deliberately, knowing their way and how to go. Which of these would be preferred to act upon the supreme law of the land to change it?

It happens in the world of political action that a man with power to command the wind suddenly changes his mind, and would direct it today contrary to his judgment only yesterday.

The instance is present.

President Roosevelt now represents the idea of an all-seeing, all-doing central government, one that shall have power to regulate social and economic conditions by one national plan—wages, hours, prices, production, distribution, the petty practices of trade—and the authority to go into the states to do this, on the ground that such a government can do it for them much better than they can ever hope to do it for themselves. He advocates such changes in the supreme law as may be necessary to give free scope to that idea. This was the thesis he developed in that extraordinary interview with the newspaper correspondents. The crucial question before the country, he said, was this: Shall the Federal Government possess that power, or shall it be left in the hands of the several states, where it was put in horse-and-buggy days, and where is will now produce only disastrous sectionalism, each state intent on its own problems, and competition among them causing human welfare to sink?

But only five years ago, when he was governor of New York, Mr. Roosevelt said, on March 2, 1930, in a broadcast speech: "It was clear to the framers of our Constitution that the greatest possible liberty of self-government must be given to each state, and that any national administration attempting to make all laws for the whole nation, such as was wholly practicable in Great Britain, would inevitably result at some future time in a dissolution of the union itself . . . The doctrine of regulation and legislation by master minds, in whose judgment and will all the people may gladly acquiesce, has been too glaringly apparent at Washington during these last ten years . . . It is obvious that almost every new or old problem of government must be solved, if it is to be solved to the satisfaction of the people in the whole country, by each state in its own way."

If there are barriers, even cumbersome barriers, between the winds of doctrine and changes in the supreme law, it is because the framers, besides knowing much that we have forgotten about the philosophy of government, knew something, too, about human nature and the startling effects that may be produced upon it by the fondness of the heart for power.

In the case of the executive power vs. a Brooklyn poultry dealer, the Supreme Court did not consider whether it was good or bad for the dealer to permit his customers "to make selections of individual chickens taken from particular coops," nor whether it would be good or bad for the national government to possess the power to mind the manner of taking chickens out of a coop. The only question it considered was whether the government rightly possessed the power. Was it permitted by the Constitution? If not, it was a power that had been seized. The Congress had no right to delegate it because the Congress itself did not possess it. The only way the government could get it was to ask the people for it.

The founders could not have foreseen that the fundamental principles of the government they were setting up would ever come before the Supreme Court in a chicken coop. But this would not have astonished them at all; they might have been delighted. They knew how easily a government is persuaded to exalt its executive power, all the more easily if the intent is to do good, and yet how destructive this may be of individual rights and immunities; and they would have been pleased to know that after a century and a half even a chicken coop might serve as a formidable barricade.

Their problem was to write a Constitution under which it would be impossible for the government in a constitutional manner ever to deprive people of their liberties. People should be free to surrender them if they wished to do so; that, too, was provided for; but by no means should their liberties ever be taken away without their consent. And they discovered that government, in that case, must be founded on two principles—namely, first, it must be limited government; secondly, it must be representative government.

First, what is the meaning of limited government? A limited government is one that is permitted to exercise only the powers that have been delegated to it by the people, and no absolute power whatever. In one of John Marshall's decisions, he said of the Congress: "The powers of the legislature are defined and limited; and that these limits may not be mistaken or forgotten, the Constitution is written."

Then there must be a mechanism. The government has got to work. The mechanism is a system of checks and balances, or, by another phrase, a division of powers. No one power is supreme. Each one is complete in itself, and yet no one of them represents the complete power of government. Nor does the complete power of government exist in all

129

three of them together. Above them, limiting them, is the written Constitution.

Who writes the Constitution? The people do that. The people themselves constitute the only sovereign power. They make the law; therefore, they are above the law, limited only by their wisdom, their experience and their use of self-restraint.

We speak very loosely of the sovereignty of the people, as if it meant a definite thing. It means nothing about government. There is a sense in which people are sovereign in any form of government, free or unfree. They may elect a tyrant or proclaim a king, and when he has ruled them badly they may depose or behead him and take another. That is sovereignty of a kind. Suppose they extort from the new king a piece of writing, and he swears to it, that he will govern them in a certain limited way. When he has forgotten the writing or has despised it their only recourse is to violence, and for that moment again they are sovereign. The Roman mob, tearing down one Caesar and raising up another, was sovereign in the sense of having the last word.

So you come to the second great principle implanted in the Constitution—namely, the principle of representative government. This principle presents a problem that can be solved only by a people in a very high state of political development; nor can it be solved once and for all and forgotten. It has to be met and solved again, over and over, else the scheme for reconciling government with liberty will fall.

What is the problem?

Final sovereignty shall reside in the will of the people. That is, to begin with. But how shall this sovereignty itself be restrained? And if it be not restrained, how shall orderly and continuous government be maintained? How shall individual rights and immunities be defended when they happen for a moment to be unpopular?

Though they are sovereign and above the law, though they make the law, still people do not directly govern themselves. They cannot and never did. Either government is imposed upon them or they impose it upon themselves.

There, is, therefore, only one possible answer to the question: Who shall restrain the sovereign power? The sovereign power must be willing to restrain itself.

And that is why the writing of a Constitution is the highest and most reasonable political act so far performed by people. It is people at their best. The Constitution is their character, their conscience, the sum of their wisdom, their appeal from themselves to themselves, their ideal statement of things that are done and things that are not done. It is as if they were giving hostages to reason, justice and equity, knowing beforehand how liable they are in sudden passion to be unreasonable, unjust and impulsive. They establish the fundamental law in laudable brevities. That is their Constitution. They define the kind of government they will have, and confer upon it what they believe to be all the necessary powers—these and no more. The power to make laws is conferred. That is necessary. But all the laws the government makes must conform to that fundamental law of laudable brevity, else they are unconstitutional and beforehand void.

The Constitution not only binds the government; it binds also the sovereign power that has written it. How is this? What binds the sovereign power? The undertaking on its part not to change the supreme rules but by the rule laid down therein. This means—and here is the magnificent act of self-restraint—that the sovereign power, itself above the law, forbids itself to alter the fundamental law except in a mood of conscious deliberation. And so long as it is obedient to this self-imposed restraint, you have limited, representative constitutional government in the American form.

It is a pretty grand house. Not a perfect one. It is easier to conceive a perfect house than to make one: easier still to imagine making one than to imagine people who would make perfect use of it. What the Constitution created was a system of civil liberties unlike any that ever existed, offering sureties for individual rights and guarantees against the rise of despotic government beyond any system hitherto known.

The American mind had long been schooled to think in political principles; such things as the science of government and the sprit of law were topical matters, everywhere discussed, and had that displacement in popular thought that now belongs to economic subjects. The constitutional convention, wherein the sovereign power of the people appears, enacts its will and disappears, was and is distinctly an American institution. It is the town meeting, mature and magnified. The Constitution was American in a profound, original sense. It represented a separation of New World from Old World ideas. For more than one hundred years American ideas were universally held to be the first in the order of advance. The Old World borrowed such of them as it could use and gave credit.

These attitudes have recently been changing. The Old World is reverting to old ideas, and we find ourselves, almost unawares, taking ideas from there and calling them new. The idea of exalting the executive power of government is from there; it could not have arisen in the American tradition. Formerly our debate was on what government should be. More and more we leave that aside and debate what government should do—what it should do in a providential manner for people more than people can do for themselves, how it shall confer upon them welfare, security, happiness—forgetting that though an omnipotent government were able to confer these blessings, it would be obliged at the same time to confer upon people also the status of servility.

Nearly all the current proposals for changing the fundamental law in ways to alter the American form of government contemplate, directly or indirectly, one thing—namely, to give the government increased power to redistribute wealth. There is running here, as elsewhere in the world, and not for the first time, a dark, destructive thought toward wealth. Thus, no one clause of the Constitution, perhaps, has been more maligned than the due-process clause—the one saying no person shall be deprived of property without due process of law, which means compensation. The feeling is that this clause has been often invoked legally to defend the greed and selfishness of wealth.

That is more or less true. It has. But one who admits this is faced with this question: Then shall property rights be placed above human rights? Do you answer yes or no?

It is not a matter of yes or no. The Supreme Court, upholding the due process clause, does not answer yes or no. The question is not what is asked. The question is: On what shall government be founded, phrases or principles? Property versus human rights is an emotional phrase, innocent of any principle. You cannot define it. In the first place, there is no such thing basically as property rights. Property has no rights. But there is a human right to possess property. It is one of the natural rights. The framers of the Constitution regarded it as one of the three great natural rights, as may be understood from the clause as a whole. It occurs in the Bill of Rights, and reads that no person shall be "deprived of life, liberty or property without due process of law."

But leave the argument. It will go too far. Suppose the right to possess property has been abused. Suppose the due-process clause has been invoked to defend abuses of it. Then suppose amending the Constitution to read: "The right to possess property shall be subject to the power of the government to take individual property where it will, from whom it will, without compensation, and do with it what it will in behalf of the general welfare."

That would make it another house in another world.

Or suppose, somewhat with Senator Borah,[3] that those now complaining of the constitutional restraints upon the lawmaking power of the government shall propose an amendment to the Constitution as follows: "The supreme lawmaking power of the land is hereby vested in the Congress of the United States, and legislative power may be delegated to such executive departments of government as may be created from time to time by act of Congress."

These few words, which perhaps no one would dare to

offer as an amendment to the Constitution, would set the government free. In a constitutional manner they would produce that change which the Supreme Court has just said the executive power had sought by usurpation. But at least people would know what they were doing. Never again would any act of Congress or any sudden law imposed upon the country by a system of executive bureaus be declared unconstitutional by the Supreme Court in cold, legalistic words—on principle.

In the spring of 1937, under threat from Roosevelt to "pack" the court, its resistance to the New Deal collapsed. On a case about the minimum wage, it dismissed the doctrine that "due process of law" protects the individual's freedom of contract. On a case about the doctrine of union representation by majority vote, it threw out the literal meaning of the interstate commerce clause and said Congress could regulate anything that "affects" interstate commerce—the same idea Roosevelt had proposed in his press conference. From 1937, the door was open to any economic regulation the national government could think of, and any social regulation on a matter that might "affect" the economy.

In 1995, the court began striking down, with much controversy, non-economic laws—a federal rape law and a federal ban on gun possession near a school—that had been justified by a ritualistic citing of the commerce clause. But the New Deal's grant of complete power to Congress to regulate economic activity has been challenged by only one justice, Clarence Thomas.

In 2001, the court considered a case that would have applied the "sick chicken" decision to strike down the broad powers wielded by the Environmental Protection Agency. The court declined to do it, unanimously upholding federal power.

---

[1]Grover Cleveland.

[2]Fiorello LaGuardia.

[3]William Borah, 1865-1940, "The Lion of Idaho," senator 1906-1940. A progressive Republican and silver-state populist, he supported the income tax and direct election of senators, and opposed U.S. entry into the League of Nations.

CHAPTER NINE:

A New Culture

A Sound No Longer Heard

From "The Lost American," March 28, 1936

One way to learn what people are thinking is to look at what they read, because what they read day by day will represent what they are thinking; and for this you may take the daily press. What is the press saying?

The radical papers are all saying what the voice of government is saying, but with grotesque distortions and with an air of injured authorship, as if now the truth were being plagiarized. Well, that is to be expected. The radical press is tiresomely the same all over the world, employing in every language the same typeworn images and symbols.

Then the megalaphonic press. Comparing the press with what it was ten years ago, you will expect it to reflect a change in the weather of popular feeling. It does. After six years of depression, it would. The tone is cynical. There is a morbid preoccupation with the sore spots. The stock effigy of wealth is not good-humored or ironic, as before, but hateful. More significant than any of the ugly appearances is one notable disappearance. The theme of achievement is missing. Ten years ago that had been the ruling theme; and even though what it celebrated had been materialistic only—material prosperity and material power—nevertheless, there was with it a sense of direction, and that, too, has been lost. A people believing they had found the way to unlimited well-being made a spectacle to thrill the world! But where, now, is any believing?

Turn now to the conservative press. Nothing has happened to the editorials, except, it may be, they are duller. The writing seems tired, the general attitude is defensive and the spirit of challenge is low. And that is all. But increasingly the feature parts of conservative newspapers, such as the literary supplements, the book reviews, the privileged smart columns and the departments of criticism, are written by young men whose facilities are censorious. They have no heroes. They know nothing worshipful, past or present, and scoff at worship. If they are radicals, they plausibly deny it. As reckless idol breakers, they might be respected. But neither for anything they believe against idols nor for robust love of melee would they risk it. They want to be comfortable, and to live with small, sharp teeth inside the institutions they despise and bespatter. Their sneers at success, their envious glances at wealth, their ridicule of simple patriotism and their contempt for the whole American achievement, are like venomous spitballs.

In this vogue of seeing meanly, a writer goes to and fro in his country to make a book. From New England to California and back, through the whole length and breadth of a land in which human well-being has touched the highest point in the history of the human race, he finds nothing good. There is progressive badness in it. There is social and economic anarchy. Greed and selfishness everywhere. People moving in a midst of terror and hatred; people fighting wolfishly over the bones of prosperity.

And when his book appears, the book-review supplements of the conservative newspapers give whole front pages to it with the comment that the public will do well to read it and give heed.

A New Culture

The American of old is nowhere to be found. What has become of what he believed?

The sound of him has been lost. You may search the writing of the past six years, up to the extremely prolific academic sources, and you will find nothing of what you remember. Philosophers, scientists, economists, engineers, pedagogues, singly and in groups, have contributed hundreds of volumes to the world of despond, until it would seem that every possible way of disbelieving in the American achievement had been found and no way at all of believing in it had been imagined. Laissez faire was buried on the mountaintop. There the ways parted. There is no going back. Nothing can ever be again as it was.

Taking it that what people are thinking about themselves, about one another, about their country, is everything that has been written during the past six years—in books, periodicals, newspapers and as propaganda—visitors will note a pathological fact. Whether it be radical, liberal or conservative, all thinking has exhibited one character in common—introversion. People all alike have been thinking as introverts. For six years this has been the weakness of American culture. Where has been any thought of making a new attack on the environment, a new conquest of reality? That would be a dynamic thought, turning outward, in what had been always before the natural American way.

And what else is running in the news? What is the longest and most exciting serial story in the daily press? It is the story of a ceaseless, unseemly struggle at the door of the public treasury, classes and groups of citizens contending there with one another and threatening the Government, all saying they have the right to help themselves because formerly the brigands of the skyscrapers had indirect and subtle access to it. And it is not their word for it. The Government tells them it was so.

Ten years ago, the example nation of the world, the one most to be envied, the one most emulated. Here was power in new magnitude and new meaning. Paramount power in the earth. We had achieved it almost unawares. Wealth is enviable; but what other nations properly marveled at was the wide and progressive distribution of it.

And now! A passion to abase the American achievement. A passion to accuse the American motive, even the national motive in a war to which we contributed life, treasure and victory, and then, when the spoils were on the table, took nothing. A worse passion to strain past evils and corruptions through the public fingers, for love of the stench, or in order that every man may be sure of something as bad about his neighbor as he knows about himself.

New Writing Over Old

From "The Youth Document,"
November 7, 1936

Just as the telephone bell rang, the Old Reporter was trying to think of a word. He was all ready to check out, and he had been gazing down on the lighted city from a high hotel window. The word he was trying to think of was one beginning with p, from the Greek, meaning a manuscript on which there is new writing over old.

That had happened here. New writing over old. A city that he remembered had been erased. He remembered it vividly because it had been his first city. Now in place of it was another, and not such another one as might have been foretold, not merely new writing over old of the same kind, but original writing in signs and characters that never existed before. Steel buildings, floodlighted towers, motor traffic, sky travel, voices without bodies, world news in the air, tame power endlessly performing automatic functions in place of human exertion, people at ease and bored, diminished by the importance of their own external ideas. A modern city. And yet the same place, the same name, the same manuscript.

That was the idea that kept associating itself with the word he was trying to think of. On this very site might have been the grand, four-story gas-lighted hotel with half a block of guest chairs and spittoons on the sidewalk in front, and every little while the excitement of a bus careening up the hill from the union depot, the steel shoes of the horses cutting sparks out of the cobblestone pavement. You could not sit in one of those chairs. If you did, a man immediately came to look you over. If you were fairly well dressed, he would ask: "Are you registered?" If you were not so well dressed, all he said was, "Wiggle!"

It was a hard, unfriendly city. If you were hungry, you would let it go for a long time without asking for anything, for if you asked, you were a bum. The Old Reporter remembered that, too, for he had been hungry there; and he smiled as his memory entertained him with recollections of what he had done about it. He smiled again as he remembered how he left the city, that first time, without a shirt, because the shirt he washed on the river bank and hung on a bush to dry blew into the river while he dreamed. He wondered what it would be like now to go at night into the largest railroad yard in the world—without a shirt, remember—find the place where the next fast freight train east will be made up, then stalk it until the petulant yard engine that makes it up has dropped it and the big road locomotive has picked it up on the outbound track. The difficulties would have changed, of course; the largest railroad yard in the world is now covered by electric floodlights.

He supposed that all the difficulties in the way of youth attacking life would have changed. What if he were now at the age he was then, braving a city for the first time—a city like this? How different would it be? What would he do for an empty stomach? The thought was no good. He kept seeing the old writing through the new, as if the new were not there.

Suddenly he thought of the word. The word "palimpsest." A manuscript on which old writing has made way for new. That was it. And he reached for the telephone.

Downstairs was a young voice saying, "I am a reporter." And could he come up? He came up. His errand was to interview the Old Reporter on what impressions he had formed of the political situation.

They talked. It was presently evident that the young reporter stood rather to the left. He said so; it was personal in every way.

"Why?" asked the Old Reporter.

The answer was not very clear. It took off at random from the general feeling that what the young reporter named the old system had produced intolerable social and economic conditions. It had broken down. There would have to be something very much better—political and social change to make life better, more abundant, more secure, less of a struggle for existence, and so on.

The Old Reporter drew from his visitor these facts— that he was twenty-four, that he had come to the city from a school of journalism in a nearby college, that what he earned was not much, and yet enough to have ruined a cub reporter in a former time; also that the feelings he had been expressing were prevalent. Many of his contemporary associates felt the same way. The Old Reporter might take it that he was speaking for all of them.

"And when you are discussing these things together," the Old Reporter asked, "do you look at the fact that our form of government may be in danger?"

"What's so sacred about a particular form of government?" the young reporter asked. There was a slight asperity in it.

"Only this," said the Old Reporter, "that under our form of government civil liberty has been raised to the highest point that was ever known. It had to be fought for; it can very easily be lost if people, by taking it for granted, forget what it means. Does the word liberty move you at all?"

"We have felt no loss of liberty," he said.

"Not yet, perhaps," said the Old Reporter. "Let us suppose we are speaking of tendencies. You work for what you earn. Would you say it was your right as a free person to receive the whole of what you earn and do with it what you like? Would you say that if that right may be taken away from you, without your consent, you are no longer quite free?"

142

"Perhaps," said the young reporter. "I don't see what you are coming to."

"To this," said the Old Reporter, "that without your consent, a law of compulsory thrift has been imposed upon you by a Government that undertakes to administer a part of your earnings so that you shall not come to want in your old age. Ultimately, each week, whether you like it or not, it will take 3 per cent out of your pay envelope; it will keep it for you, invest it for you in Government bonds, and give it back to you when you are old."

"Oh," said the young reporter. "The new Social Security law. Well, that may be all right. Security is a fine thing."

"If you had to choose between liberty and security, which would it be?" the Old Reporter asked.

"It seems to me," said the young reporter, "that in a land where there is always plenty, people are entitled to economic security. That is beginning now to be provided for, and, as I say, we feel no loss of liberty."

"The new writing," said the Old Reporter to himself.

"What?"

"That was something I was thinking out loud," said the Old Reporter. "Tell me. Were you ever hungry?"

"No."

"What would you do if you were out of a job, without a nickel, without a friend, and hungry in this city today?"

"I suppose I'd apply for relief or a WPA job," said the young reporter.

"What if there was no such thing as unemployment relief? What if there was no such thing as WPA? No bread lines even. Still, would you starve?"

"I'd probably not starve," said the young reporter. "But why do you ask? Are you saying there ought not to be any relief?"

"I'm saying something you don't understand," said the Old Reporter. "Let's come at it another way. In Central Park, in New York City, a few weeks ago, I stood looking at an evening band concert. Three or four thousand people. Many of them—I dare say a majority of them—on relief or on WPA jobs. They were all well-nourished looking, well

143

clothed, and now being entertained at public expense. I think, by the way, it was a WPA band. As I looked at this scene, I said to myself, 'Here is civility of a very high order.' I had a warm feeling about it. In no other country in the world were the unemployed taken care of like this, and never in this one before. But then it occurred to me to project these people into their own future, into the future of the country—these who were saying, each one to himself, 'No matter what happens, I shall be fed and clothed and housed. The Government will see to it.' And then, by way of contrast, to project in like manner another crowd of the same general character, with only the difference that each one is saying to himself, 'This is very nice, but I ought to be thinking of tomorrow. Therefore, I must be thinking of how to take care of it myself.' At the end of twenty years, how will the works of one crowd compare with the works of another? Which will make their country richer? Which will produce the most wealth? Those who possess that comfortable sense of security you speak of, knowing that, if necessary, the Government will support them, or those who should have had that anxious sense of self-responsibility?"

"I see what you mean, of course," said the young reporter. "If people get the idea that the Government is going to support them, it will be bad. But, after all, these people at the band concert are out of work through no fault of their own. Is there not plenty of everything to go around? Well, then, if the private economic system has been unable to distribute this plenty, who shall distribute it, if not the Government?"

"We haven't much time left," said the Old Reporter. "Let's try a short cut. If, as you say, there is plenty of everything to go around, have you any idea how that came to be so?"

"How?"

"Because until now we have lived by the old proverb which says there is no conquering weapon like the necessity to conquer. If you were penniless and hungry in this city today, with no such thing as unemployment relief, no WPA jobs, what would save you from starving? The necessity to

144

eat. Given the necessity to eat and the existence of plenty, will you find a way to feed yourself or shall the Government find your sustenance and give it to you?

"Are you saying," the young reporter asked, "that we should go back to the law of pitiless necessity, root hog or die? In that case, what is the meaning of plenty? Why should a country be rich?"

"That fails," said the Old Reporter. "One more short cut. We change the ground. What is the first problem of democracy? I think I know what it is, but what would you say it was?"

The young reporter went around that question without looking at it. "Democracy," he said, "is not the only way. There are other ways. There are other kinds of government, too, and some that might be better."

"What are they?" the Old Reporter asked.

"That's too much for an offhand answer," said the young reporter, taking his hat. They shook hands and smiled. The young reporter went back to his conservative paper and the Old Reporter checked out.

For a long while he lay awake in his air-conditioned berth, thinking on it. He had not touched the young reporter's mind at all. He was sure of that. And he kept asking himself why. Their education and experiences had been very different, of course, but it was something more. He believed he knew what it was, but he couldn't formulate it. The failure had not been all on one side. The young reporter did not know what the Old Reporter was talking about. But did he know what the young reporter was thinking? Just before going to sleep, it occurred to him to ask himself what he had thought about the form of government when he was that age. The answer was—nothing. When he was that age, one took the form of government as a fact to begin with, like the fact of one's parentage, and did not think about it at all. In any case, he was much too busy at that age thinking of something else—namely, himself and his own problems.

The next day the Old Reporter had an errand to go by motor. Driving alone, he took up from the highway a young man in uniform. The history of this young man was that he had finished high school, that he was twenty-three, that he had tried first one kind of job and then another, and that at last, unable to find another one, he had enlisted in the cavalry. But he was bored and unhappy. He didn't like horses.

They stopped for lunch at the best hotel in a fairly large town. The young man's manners were all right. He came out suddenly that he was getting his discharge from the cavalry.

"Then what?" the Old Reporter asked.

"I'll be looking for a job," said the young man.

"Do you know," said the Old Reporter, "I think you youngsters are all upside down. You are thinking always of a job. Why not stop thinking of a job and think of work? In any direction you look, right in front of you is work."

The young man was silent, politely so, as one who, after all, was eating at another's expense. When it was clear that he was not going to ask what the difference was between a job and work—had no curiosity about it, in fact—the Old Reporter went on:

"I can illustrate the difference between a job and work. On a corner of my farm in South Jersey, by the highway, a great oak tree died and was cut down. A few of the small branches were taken off for firewood, but there lies the hulk, with at least two cords of wood for anybody who will cut it up. Now imagine that a man comes walking through that highway and up to my door, asking for a job. I say I am sorry; I haven't any job; I have all the labor I can use on the farm. So he goes away saying—and saying truthfully—that he has tried to get a job. Then imagine another man walking that same highway, past that same oak-tree hulk, who comes to my door and says, 'Have you got a cross-cut saw and an ax?' I have. But why does he ask for them and who is he? He says, 'I want to cut up that big oak tree down there by the highway.' I say, 'Fine. Take the saw and the ax. In the toolhouse you will also find a sledge and some wedges.' He works a day and a half at it and gets sixteen dollars' worth of cordwood out of a tree hulk that I should, perhaps, have moved away with a tractor. That is work.

And the difference is that I do not pay him for that work. The work pays for itself. He has converted a useless tree hulk into salable cord wood."

The young man went on being silent in a polite way. They finished lunch. As they were parting, the Old Reporter said, "I can guess what you are thinking. You are thinking of one dead tree and that there is work in it for one man for a day and a half, whereas the number of unemployed men is millions."

"Yes," said the young man. "I didn't know it, but I was."

"Remember it only as an illustration," said the Old Reporter, whereupon they parted.

The Old Reporter was saying to himself: "Nor did I touch that young man. I did no more to his mind than one lunch of short ribs of beef will do to his stature." Nevertheless, he added a mental note to one he had made the night before. For the time being he put it aside and went on with his work.

Both episodes were revived in his mind when, on returning to his desk a few weeks later, he found in his mail several letters meant to acquaint him with the American youth point of view. The occasion for them was that the Old Reporter had published some magazine articles on the alarming extension of bureaucratic government.

The letter that interested him most, and one in very nice temper, opened with a modest personal history. The writer was twenty-six. He was graduated from a state college in 1930 with a diploma in science. He got a job at once with a corporation, then lost it. Owing to the depression, there were no more jobs like that—in fact, no jobs at all of his kind—and what saved him was a bureau job with a Government relief agency. As the depression began to abate, he discovered that the big corporations such as he was equipped to work for preferred to take on men "fresh out of college," rather than to take back those in whose lives this interval of unemployment had occurred.

The rest of his letter was this: "I am representative of thousands of American college men with a problem we would like to present for your kind consideration and

mature judgment. How can we combat the tug toward
Socialism in the face of the attitude taken by the businessmen of today? Finding no chance for employment in private
industry, and lacking capital to start a business of our own,
where do we turn to spend the vital energy of American
youth? Rather than be idle, the temptation is strong to support that form of government that will create and set up
bureaus in which employment will be available."

The first answer the Old Reporter wrote was not from
that mature judgment that had been imputed to him. Then
he stopped and tore up his reply. He would fail again, as he
had failed first with the young reporter and then with the
young man in uniform. For the same reason? Yes, for the
same reason. And there he was again trying to formulate
that reason. He read the letter again and dwelt upon the
sentence: "I am representative of thousands of young
American college men with a problem."

The Old Reporter was unable to imagine that thousands
of young college men had "a" problem. He could imagine
only that thousands of young college men would have thousands of problems, and no two of them alike. Then what
was the question? Suddenly he began to see where the
impasse was and why he had been unable to touch these
young minds. His way of thinking was individual. Theirs
was not. The young reporter, for example, could be made to
see that as one resourceful individual he probably wouldn't
starve. But that was not naturally his way of thinking.
Instead, he no sooner imagined himself unemployed than
he began to think of himself not as himself alone but as one
of millions in like circumstances; and, of course, he could
not imagine that millions would not starve. Then the young
man in uniform—his first thought was that the work of
making one tree trunk into cordwood was no solution for
the problem of millions out of work; and that was the problem with which he identified himself. And now the college
man who wrote the letter. He was not stating his own problem; he was using himself to illustrate the problem of a
class to which he belonged, namely, unemployed college
men.

A New Culture

In contrast, the Old Reporter, if he were out of work, would never think of himself as belonging to a class of unemployed old reporters. He couldn't. He would think of himself only as one old reporter out of work.

CHAPTER TEN

The Work of Agriculture

From "The Political Curse on the Farm Problem,"
August 22, 1936

I was born in the Mississippi Valley, handled a team at ten, wore overalls, as all the men did, made by the women out of a striped cotton material called bed ticking. I have been looking at agriculture critically, and writing about it, since a time when automobiles, tractors, motor trucks and combines were unknown, and, except for the steam-engine threshing outfit, the only power was animal power. And now, for the love of it, I live on a farm and operate it.

On my desk is a letter from the county agent telling me how I may get ten dollars an acre from the Government by planting a cover crop in my orchard, as I have always done. It is true that I can afford to ignore his letter on principle. I have an income from writing and operate my farm with tenant labor. But it is also true that my tenant farmer, if he owned the farm and the tools on it, would not really need the money, because there has never been a year when the income from apples, corn and alfalfa was less than enough to pay the taxes and the upkeep, and to provide a family with all the necessary things it could not produce for itself.

Where my sympathies lie may be imagined, but that does not matter. My conviction is that a sentimental treatment of the farm problem is wrong. On the other hand, a realistic assessment of it is difficult, owing to the intensity of human feeling; and for the politician it is impossible. The discussion proceeds from a stultified premise of what ought to be and arrives at a proposal to make it that way by law.

We say, for example, that the farmer ought to participate equally in the increase in modern wealth. The fact is, he doesn't; the fact is that the farmer's share of wealth has relatively fallen, not only here, but all over the world. What do we do with this fact? We treat it as evidence that others have been taking unfair advantage of him, and we propose to seize it from these others and give it back to him. But suppose that the farmer's contribution to the total product of modern wealth is unequal; suppose that the contributions of others have increased more than his. In that case, the problem is how to increase the farmer's contribution. If you do that, the income will redistribute itself. If you cannot do that, then to redistribute the national income by act of Congress will not solve the farm problem. It will degrade the farmer to the status of a minority caste, and it will retard, if not stop, the increase of wealth.

A few weeks ago, in conversation with a group of agricultural-college people in a prairie state, there came, as usual, that place from which there is no place to go. Impasse in every direction. Then one of them said:

"I say, of course, there is no problem that the sow and hen couldn't cure. You know what I mean. I remember how we used to go visiting on Sunday. One farm especially. I see it vividly. The greetings and embracings on arrival. Our women going indoors to help because it is going to be a long table. We drive on to the barn, unhitch the horses and turn them in to the corral. While they stand with their noses in the watering trough, we pull down some hay and bring a few measures of grain. Then we walk slowly toward the house, looking at the pigs, the calf, the two colts. The chickens we do not notice. There are fruit trees and some bees under them. There are berry bushes. There is a vegetable garden with not a weed in it. We are coming to the house. I can see the churn canted toward the sun to sweeten, the lid of it upside down; I can see the apple press and the lye drip from the wood ashes for soap making. I can smell the flowers around the porch. Then I can smell the food. What food! A baked ham from their own smokehouse. Fried chicken. Corn on the cob. Wilted lettuce with sliced hard-boiled eggs. Home-made bread, butter and jellies. Cider up from the cellar. What a life. I only say that if we had more farming like that was, we'd have just so much less of a farm problem."

"One question. Anyone may farm like that today who has the small amount of capital necessary to begin with. It is safe. Nothing possibly can happen to it. But here is the question: Reproduce that farm just as you remember it. Could it support an automobile?"

"Let me think. No. No, it couldn't."

"A motor truck, a tractor, electric refrigeration?"

"No. It could not begin to do it."

"Nor the taxes for concrete roads and modern schoolhouses."

"No."

"Well, then. That world is gone. Shall the farmer belong to a world that is gone or to this one? This world is one in which farmers, as soon as their income begins to rise a little, renew their automobiles before they paint their barns, repair their houses, restore their fences or put a little concrete dam across the gully that is running away with the soil. This you may see now wherever you look. The farm plant as a whole deteriorating and the country roads full of new motorcars."

Impasse again.

So let us not fool ourselves about what the farm problem is. It is a problem of relation. The simple difficulties of sustaining life on the soil have not increased; they have lessened. In twenty-five years, the standard of living on the farm has not fallen; it has risen, incredibly risen, tested by the conveniences, comforts, and satisfactions that were unknown a generation ago. The farmer does not compare his absolute condition with what it was twenty-five years ago; he compares it with what it ought to be now. What he complains of is not that his standard of living is lower; he complains that for others the standard of living has risen more. This is true. And in trying to achieve urban standards of living, he has gone heavily into debt, he has exhausted the increase in the capital value of land, and by intensive cash cropping with a desperate commercial motive, he has distorted agriculture until he has forgotten the art of idyllic farming, even if he were willing to return to it.

Nor is it a recent problem. We keep referring it to the effects of the World War, but if there had been no World War, there would still be a farm problem. It might be only chronic; or it might be again as acute as it was in the 1880s and 1890s, when Mrs. Lease[1] was telling the farmers of Kansas to "raise less corn and more hell," and everywhere alliances, wheels, leagues and secret societies like the granges were rising to carry on the agrarian crusade.

A crusade against what? Against the old political parties that had permitted such intolerable conditions to develop, against Wall Street, against the tyranny of gold money, against the heartless mortgage holders of the East, against the rapacity of the railroad monopoly, and so on, all of which meant simply nothing. The real demon was change—a change that was taking place all over the world.

The apex of that agrarian crusade here was the formation of the Populist Party, declaring for cheap money and plenty of it, Government control of credit, Government ownership of railroads and a subtreasury in every agricultural county to make direct loans to farmers on their stored crops, so that they might withhold them from the wicked Board of Trade speculators in Chicago. In the election of 1892, the Populist Party polled a million votes, elected a few senators and representatives, like Sockless Jerry Simpson of Kansas,[2] and then died. The free-silver movement with Bryan,[3] under the delusion that the plight of the farmer was owing to dear money and a gold conspiracy, succeeded the Populist movement, and that also slowly died.

Why? Because, beginning about 1900, the country overtook its own food supply, whereupon agricultural prices and the value of land began to rise.

The terrible economic depression had been caused by these three facts: First, the very rapid extension of agriculture upon free land of virgin fertility after the Civil War; second, the very rapid development of agricultural implements—multiple plows and cultivators and self-activating horse-drawn machinery, such as mowers, reapers, binders and planters—all tending to increase the productive power of man upon the soil, and, third, a system of transportation that made one measure of grain anywhere in the world competitive with every other measure of grain in the world, so that there was no longer an Ohio price or a Kansas price, not even an American price, but only a world price.

And the recovery was owing to the one simple fact that the abundance and cheapness of food greatly stimulated the growth of cities and the extension of industry, both here and in Europe, so that the urban population increased amazingly while the rural population relatively declined, until there was balance.

After 1900, for nearly twenty years, the fortunes of farming improved, to a point at which the urban population began to talk bitterly of the farmers' monopoly, saying it had the cities by the throat. During the World War, crop acreage was greatly extended to reap the high prices. The price of land was terrifically inflated. That was, perhaps, inevitable; and at its worst it may be regarded as an internal disaster. These are the aggravations only.

For the current agricultural depression, we mistake aggravations for causes and look for causes that do not exist, because the true cause is the one we have not learned how to deal with. We know all the same what it is.

Industry, with its technology, its science and its enterprise, has acted again upon agriculture to transform it. By the tractor, the motor truck, the combine, the automobile, even the airplane for insect and blight control, the productive power of the individual has been so increased that now only one-half of those who continue to be employed in agriculture are really needed there.

In 1870, more than one half of all the people employed were in agriculture. In 1900, it was still two-fifths. But in 1930 it was hardly more than one-fifth, and only one-half of that one-fifth was really needed to produce our commercial crop. Think what that means. And that has happened also to Canada, Australia, South America, South Africa—areas to which American industry had been exporting agricultural machinery. These have arrived at enormous production.

These are not political facts. They are not such facts as may be changed by passing a law. For more than fifty years the Congress has been passing laws to destroy the imaginary dragons devouring the prosperity of agriculture.

Was it the railroad monopoly charging so much to haul the earth's produce to market that there was nothing left for the farmer? A law was passed. Now the Government says what the rates shall be.

Was it the speculator who bought the earth's produce and cornered it? A law was passed. There are no more corners, except beneficent corners conducted by the Government, as in cotton at the present time. The private speculator has a ring in his nose and the Government holds him by it.

Was it the hard country banker? A law was passed, setting up a great system of Federal farm-credit banks.

Was it the mortgage holder, who made mortgage money dear and ordered the sheriff around? A law was passed. More than $2,000,000,000 of farm mortgages have been taken over by the Government at low rates of interest, and there is a great system of Federal Land Banks to provide the farmer with long-term credit at the lowest possible rates. The fallacy that what the farmer needed was more and cheaper credit has exploded itself; the Federal Government has swamped him with credit, and he is now more in debt than ever before.

Was it the necessity of the farmer to sell his crops in the harvest glut? A law was passed to create a Federal Commodity Credit Corporation that at harvest time lends the farmer money up to the market value of his crops, sometimes more, in order that he may hold them for higher prices. If prices go up he wins; if they go down the Government loses, because these are loans without recourse.

Was it, after all, the gold standard? That famous delusion was revived after fifty years. The gold standard must be overthrown; in place of gold-standard money there must be people's money, cheaper and more plentiful. Well, the New Deal did overthrow the gold standard and cheapened the dollar two-fifths to make agricultural prices rise. Besides that, it opened to the farmers a system of cash subsidies, first by taxing the produce of the earth on its way to the consumer and giving the money to the farmer, and then, when that was declared unconstitutional, by taking the money out of the United States Treasury direct and paying the farmer a subsidy to hold 30,000,000 acres of land out of production.

All this with what result?

With the result that when the Democrats and Republicans, respectively, come to that plank in the party platform that must be devoted to agriculture, they lock the door, lean their heads against the nearest hard substance, and groan in chorus, "Now, what shall we say to the farmer?" The sound must be sympathetic, the words must be plausible, and there must be a certain dimness in which to execute strategical maneuvers. In a little while the floor is littered with rejected compositions. After a long while, the triumphant plank appears, suavely planed, free of visible knots. The sound of it says, "We stand for a prosperous and contented agriculture."

In every campaign of the past fifty years, the Republicans and Democrats have written their agricultural planks in that way, competing for the farmer's favor, telling him what he believes, promising him what he expects.

Now from the New Deal he expects subsidies. The Democratic Party platform says: "We favor assistance within Federal authority to enable farmers to adjust and balance production with demand, at a fair profit to the farmers." The Republican Party platform says one of its paramount objects is "to promote policies which will bring about an adjustment of agriculture, to meet the needs of domestic and foreign markets" and , "As an emergency measure, during the agricultural depression, Federal benefit payments or grants in aid . . ."

From the New Deal the farmer expects cash subsidies for conserving the fertility of his soil. In this he shall not be disappointed. The Republican platform favors "such a balance between soil-building and soil-depleting crops as will permanently insure productivity, with reasonable benefits to cooperating farmers . . ." And the Republican plank proposes, besides, one benefit the Democrats left out—namely, to pay an indirect bounty on agricultural exports. The only reason for doing this would be that agricultural commodities are exported at a loss. Well, but to pay the farmer a subsidy to build up the soil and then a bounty out of public funds for exporting the product of that same fertility at a loss is something that can happen among rational people only in a political-party platform.

Neither party has a solution of the farm problem. There is no law that can be passed to solve it. No political party can say what the problem is, for if it did, the idea of solving it by act of Congress would be too absurd.

What are the facts that create the problem? The one most simple statement of them has been resting for two years in the files of the Department of Agriculture. It was made by O.E. Baker, senior agricultural economist of the Bureau of Agricultural Economics in 1934. And it is this:

"Half the farmers produced about 88 percent of the commercial production of farm products in 1929, and could readily produce the remainder."

158

That is to say, of the eleven millions of people now employed in agriculture, one-half could easily produce our
total commercial crops; the other half simply is not needed.

Imagine passing a law about it.

Imagine trying to solve such a problem as this by over-
turning the gold standard and debasing the value of the
dollar to make prices go up.

Imagine trying to solve it by redistributing income in
favor of these who are unable to produce an equivalent on
the soil. They can only consume the income.

What will Federal benefits and grants and aids and subsidies do? These five and one-half millions who are not
needed to produce the commercial crop may be assisted,
but how will that solve the farm problem?

These five and one-half million generally are either tenants and landless or they are heavily in debt. Extreme proposals are to provide them with land and relieve them of
debt. But suppose the Government gave each of them a
farm, debt-free, still how could they support themselves on
the land with only one-eighth of the commercial crop to
produce, and not needed to do that? Shall the other half be
made to produce less in order that these may produce
more?

Now, given the fact that there is not work enough on the
soil to support a modern life for the people who continue to
be engaged there, what is the problem? It defines itself naturally. How to increase productive work in the hands of
agriculture.

No one is without access to this truth. There it stands,
stark and bald. Nevertheless, the Government, the
Department of Agriculture, the AAA, the Congress and the
farmers have been pursuing the incomparable delusion
that the remedy is to enable agriculture to do less work.
Where the trouble is that one-half the people are not needed, the remedy is to retire 30,000,000 acres from production. By the end of this year cash subsidies in the amount
of two thousand millions of dollars will have been distributed by the AAA among farmers to compensate them for
doing less work.

The farm problem has come to have a kind of specious oratorical reality that removes it entirely from the realm of economic reason. It is covered with imaginary political sores. It is like a lost province or a submerged race. Those who talk rationally about it are cast out.

Nevertheless, the problem will be what it is. How to increase the work of agriculture. That is the problem.

The answer is astonishing. The answer is that we have, perhaps, not enough land and certainly not enough labor on the land to do the work that agriculture might be doing.

Our imports of competitive commodities—oils, pork, corn and others—represent the use of 30,000,000 acres of crop land in foreign countries, while paying the American farmer a subsidy out of the public treasury to hold 30,000,000 acres of American crop land out of production. If we produced these commodities instead of buying them, we should need the labor of maybe a million and a half more people on the soil. And the buying power of that $600,000,000 of our own money would be in the pocket of the American farmer.

That alone would not solve the farm problem. But it would be a very helpful beginning. More important, it might begin to change our ways of thinking. We might begin to think what more we could be doing with our own. We might ask ourselves even such questions as these:

What can be the matter with a country possessing a surplus of cotton, a surplus of labor and a surplus of mechanical equipment that plows up its own cotton and buys cotton goods from Japan? Why shouldn't we be sweeping the cotton-textile markets of the world? Our principal competitors are Japan and Great Britain. They do not produce raw cotton: they have to buy it. We produce raw cotton so easily that we have what we call a surplus, and destroy it as worth less than nothing. What has happened to our genius for low-cost manufacture, so that formerly, with the highest standard of living in the world, we were able to beat all competitors in foreign trade?

These are very interesting questions, provided you ask

them in a naive manner and ponder them simply. They suggest what might be possible if industry and agriculture knew how to collaborate.

The internationalists at the State Department who now conduct this country's foreign trade will explain to you again very patiently that unless we buy from foreign countries, we cannot sell to foreign countries, for unless they first receive dollars from us, they will have no dollars to spend with us.

They will be unable to explain to you how American exports rose to first place in world commerce while our foreign trade was in the hands of men who never heard of that nice formula and couldn't have understood it, any more than Japan understands it today. They believed that the way to sell goods in the foreign trade was to make something the foreign customer wanted and offer it to him at a price he could not resist. Where or how he got the dollars to pay with was his business.

What of cotton itself? The economic importance of cotton may be declining. It may be a crop that is going out from under us. Suppose that were true. Before there was such a thing as cotton there was indigo. A lady in Charleston planted some Oriental indigo seeds on the Ashley River in 1741, just to see if they would grow. For fifty years thereafter indigo, worth a dollar a pound in Europe, was a miracle crop, and every indigo planter was rich. Then the chemists showed the dye makers how to dispense with indigo, and all the indigo planters were ruined. Did the Government assist them? That was not even thought of. In a little while they turned to cotton, which was a new thing, and cotton became a valuable crop.

Now the chemists have taught the textile makers how to get a silklike yarn from the cellulose of wood, and the rising rayon industry is a disaster for cotton. But as the South went from indigo to cotton, so it can go from cotton to something else. To what else? Maybe to rayon.

Or to paper. In precisely that part of the South where the cotton problem is most acute, there is enough perpetual pine to make this country self-contained in paper. In this case, the technical difficulties have been solved. This wood pulp of Southern pine has been sent in carloads to Canada and run on the fastest paper mills in the world, and Southern newspapers have then run that paper on their presses, with entire success. With the money the AAA has already distributed to cotton farmers in the way of rentals and benefits for not growing cotton, there might have been created in the South, and be operating there, a paper industry that would keep in this country the $200,000,000 we spend annually in foreign countries for newsprint paper and wood-pulp base.

To this the economic advisers in the Department of Agriculture object, in the words of the State Department, that unless we spend our dollars in foreign countries for wood pulp and paper, they will have no dollars to spend with us. That is, we must buy wood pulp and paper from foreign countries in order to sell our goods there, instead of buying from the South and selling our goods here.

The one agricultural commodity for which we spend the most money in foreign countries is rubber. We consume seven-tenths of all the rubber consumed in the world. We call it a noncompetitive agricultural commodity because we do not produce it. That is not to say we cannot produce it. The fact is we can; the fact is in an experimental way we do. Thomas A. Edison was not the kind of man anyone would have called visionary. The axis on which his imagination turned was: Will it work? Is it practical? His last enthusiasm was to increase the work of agriculture by adding rubber culture. In the midst of his Florida experiments he died. A small bureau in the Department of Agriculture is going on with them.

That many varieties of rubber-yielding plants will grow in this country is well-known. There is one that grows wild on a belt of land one to one hundred miles wide running from Fort Stockton, Texas, to the Tropic of Cancer in Mexico. There are others that can be propagated in Florida, Arizona, New Mexico and California, even on waste land. The principal difficulty is one of cost. Well, suppose to begin with, it did not pay. Suppose that our own rubber should cost us more than British rubber. So, in the beginning did our own manufactures. That is what the first tariff was for—to subsidize American industry in order to create it, else we should, perhaps, never have had this paramount place in modern industry. And how much more rational it would be to subsidize rubber culture, if necessary, than to subsidize farmers to hold land out of production!

But there is one enormous crop that could begin to be added at once. That is the fuel crop.

For several years the idea of blending alcohol with gasoline for motor fuel has been held in suspense by what appears to be a controversy over technical facts. Would it be feasible to do it? Would it pay? And so on. Alcohol is an agricultural product; gasoline is from oil wells. Alcohol is an annual crop and, therefore, perpetual. Petroleum is like coal. Therefore, to blend them for motor fuel would be to give agriculture much new work to do and at the same time conserve our irreplaceable asset of oil in the ground. Yet there has been much propaganda against it, and most people would say offhand that, as a practical matter, it remains to be demonstrated.

As a practical matter, it has been demonstrated, and by an American oil company, but not for the benefit of American agriculture. Those who have been in England recently will remember on filling-station pumps this sign: CLEVELAND DISCOL. What is it and who makes it? It is a motor fuel, one-third alcohol and two-thirds gasoline, and it is produced jointly by a British distillery and a subsidiary of the Standard Oil Company of New Jersey. And this is the way it is advertised to British motorists:

"There are two principal reasons for using alcohol in your car—first of all, its tremendously high antiknock qualities, and, secondly, its remarkably smooth running effect . . . No ordinary car can knock on Discol, and pinking and consequent power loss is simply impossible. Acceleration is just amazing. Instead of easing your pedal down, you can literally step right on it . . . We do not say buy Cleveland Discol because it is blended with British alcohol, but it is

163

worth your knowing that in using Cleveland Discol you are supporting a rapidly growing British product."

Do you suppose the Standard Oil Company of New Jersey is misrepresenting Cleveland Discol to the British motorist? Or do you suppose that what is an ideal motor fuel in England would be an ideal motor fuel here?

Our use of motor fuel is so enormous that to produce the alcohol necessary to make a blend of one-third alcohol would require, it is estimated, 90,000,000 acres of land and employ 6,000,000 people. The oil industry need not be alarmed. At the present rate of use, all the petroleum it knows of is bound to be exhausted; beginning now to add alcohol to the gas will only prolong its life. True, the present cost of alcohol is greater than the cost of gasoline. But cost can be reduced by organized production on a large scale, and, on the other hand, we are once and for all using up our irreplaceable store of petroleum in a perfectly reckless manner because while it lasts it is bonanza cheap.

Can the work of agriculture be increased? That was the question. The answer is that it can be increased, immensely, and in ways so obvious that it seems the question must have been asked in a rhetorical spirit. Then what is it that frustrates a solution to the farm problem? Why do we subsidize agriculture to do less work where we might be assisting it, by subsidy if necessary, to do a great deal more?

There is a political curse on the farm problem. What happened to agriculture was modern industry. Nothing else. In 200 years, industry, by means of science, invention, technology and machines, has multiplied the wealth of the world ten, twenty, maybe thirty fold. It is too prodigious to be estimated. All the material wealth the human race had been able to accumulate through millions of years up to the beginning of the industrial era seems as nothing to what the wealth of the world is today. Industry did this, not agriculture.

Nevertheless, agriculture says: "I feed and clothe the world. I am the immemorial source of all wealth. Therefore, I am entitled to participate equally in this great increase in wealth, and it is not the case."

164

That is nonsense. But for industry, agriculture would be barely able to feed and clothe itself, as was immemorially the case. But for industry, a measure of grain in Kansas would have no commercial value whatever. The family that produced it could only eat it. A bale of cotton in Georgia would have no value but to clothe the family that grew it. The tools with which agriculture now produces a great surplus beyond its own needs and the means whereby this surplus is moved from where it is produced to where it is wanted—these were first imagined and then created by industry.

It was inevitable that industry's share in the new wealth of the world should be greater than agriculture's share, since it was industry that was creating it. Before modern industry, the great fortunes had been in land, and that was something agriculture could understand. Then suddenly the great fortunes began to appear in industry, and to multiply there incredibly, and that was something agriculture could not so easily understand.

However inevitable this may all have been, still it was natural and human for agriculture to feel depressed, and envious, and unbelonging, and to open its mind to a sense of injury. When people are in that state of feeling, their zealots appear and are mistaken for leaders. But the demagogue and the political champion appear also; and these, acting upon the farmer's sense of injury to exploit it, have deepened it until it has become an obsession, possessing almost a racial intensity. They have told him, not why he is losing his world and what he should do to hold his place in the new one, but that those who were creating the new world were doing it at his expense, which was not so. It is true that for a long time they were unmindful of the fact that the farmer was on the wrong side of change. Even that is no longer so. For selfish reasons, it is no longer so. A time has come when industry cannot solve its own unemployment problem until much more new work has been created on the soil.

Yet the political friends of agriculture seem resolved

only to intensify the feelings and passions that frustrate solution. They propose to increase the farmer's buying power by redistributing the national income, and to do it by law, in the beautiful name of social justice, tinged with revenge. It is being done. But the farmer's want of buying power is an effect; the cause of it is agricultural unemployment. Increase the work of agriculture, and the farmer's buying power will increase accordingly.

Garrett was right about cotton being replaced by Southern pine, to be used in the paper industry—and also in lumber and plywood. Alcohol fuel was something else again; it exists today mainly because it is subsidized.

Production controls on American farming lasted until 1996, being replaced by direct payments from the Treasury. At this writing, the subsidies are supposed to end in 2003, though there seems little political will to end them. The most market-distorting programs, in peanuts and sugar, remain.

The share of Americans who make a living in agriculture dropped from 20 percent in the 1930s to less than 3 percent in the 1990s. Of the 3 percent, it may still be true that half of them could do the whole job.

---

[1] "Mary Ellen Lease, also "Mary Yellin' Lease", 1850-1933, was nationally famous in the 1890s for her fiery oratory on behalf of the People's Party. She helped the Populists sweep to power in Kansas in 1890, and in 1896 opposed fusion with the Democratic Party under William Jennings Bryan.

[2] Jeremiah Simpson, 1842-1905, called "Sockless Jerry" because he was a farmer and sometimes didn't wear socks. He organized the People's Party with Mary Lease and Tom Watson, and served as Populist member of Congress from Kansas 1891-1895 and 1897-1899.

[3] William Jennings Bryan, 1860-1925, "the Great Commoner," prairie populist and opponent of the gold standard who was nominated for president by the Democrats in 1896, 1900 and 1908. He served as Wilson's Secretary of State 1913-1915.

CHAPTER ELEVEN:

In the Name of Labor

From "The Labor Weapon," July 17, 1937

Many years ago, during the American Railway Union strike led by Eugene V. Debs,[1] the Chicago switchmen, who were the tough babies, had an artless way of sampling public sentiment. Can you visualize the nut of the bolt that fastens rail ends together? It has eight sharp corners, and one of the old-fashioned kind weighed nearly a pound. The switchmen tied the nut to a leather thong and tied the other end of the thong around the wrist, and then, holding the nut in the hand, ready to throw it, they went up and down Wabash Avenue, saying, "Wid us 'r again us? Say what."

My sympathies at the time were undeveloped. It was a grand shandy all the same, and with a youngster's love of trouble, I had stood on the Fourteenth Street viaduct cheering the strikers as they overturned box cars with their shoulders. Ten or twelve shoulders could do it, by rocking the car a few times and giving one big heave. Yet toward those switchmen with the captive nuts in their hands I was resentful without knowing exactly why. Long afterward I could formulate it. What I resented, firstly, was the affront to my common sense of such an oversimplification of the matter. Secondly, it was the difficulty of maintaining a neutral position, in case I wanted to be neutral.

No change of time or occasion has dulled these two resentments. The second one could only be deepened by the discovery that the difficulty of maintaining a neutral position begins in oneself. There is a bias. One seems to be born with it and there is no more explanation of it than there is help for it. How else one was born has nothing to do with it.

In any considerable body of wage earners, as you might find in a steel mill, a mine or an automobile factory before union organizers get to work on it, there are three definite divisions of the willful human species, and the curious thing is that the proportions are fairly constant. It is one of the few facts labor organizers and personnel managers might agree on. You could take it to be almost a law.

One fifth of the total will be zealots for unionism. That is the material the union organizer seeks to begin with.

Another one fifth will be the extreme opposite. They are not scabs. They are anti-union by temperament, cantankerously free. If it is a matter of telling the boss to go to hell, they do not want a shop steward or the National Labor Relations Board to do it for them. They will do that little thing for themselves, individually, and would not be deprived of the privilege.

The remaining three fifths represent the susceptible middle. If there is a tide, they go with it; if not, they are passive.

The point is that, no matter who or what you are, you belong to one of these three divisions, and the bias natural thereto is a bias natural to you. It colors even your reading of the labor news in the morning paper. To test it, you have only to ask yourself where you would stand. If you belong to the middle three-fifths, you have a bias in favor of going with the movement. If you belong to the one-fifth who are zealots, this is your Roman moment. You have the nut in your hand.

But if you belong to the contrary one-fifth, you exist at your own risk. Anti-unionism now is repugnant to public

168

policy. As an independent wage earner you will be discriminated against. The law discriminates against you. The law says that no employer may discriminate in the least way against a union man on account of his unionism; the law says at the same time that the employer and the union may legally agree to discriminate against you. They may agree to have a closed shop for union workers only, where a nonunion man will be forbidden to work.

It will be noticed that I put some emphasis here, touching the refractory man—the individualist, that is—who imagines he is competent to do his own bargaining with no benefit of union or Government. Therefore, it will be said that I am biased. I have placed myself. That may be so, for what it means. Nevertheless, there is the man in his place. What shall be done with him?

Organized labor disposes of him with one ugly word. He is a scab. The new law of labor disposes of him in two other ways. First, it ignores him. Then it assumes that if he exists, it is because the employer has made him afraid to exercise his natural right to join a union and bargain collectively. Thus the law borrows the first and most important of organized labor's fictions—namely, that all labor has the union spirit, and that all labor would be union if it were not coerced, restrained and intimidated by the boss. Everybody knows better. For why, if that were true, would it be necessary for the American Federation of Labor and the CIO to hire and train thousands of organizers and send them forth to sell unionism to labor, when there is a law that forbids the employer to resist in any way?

It is implicit in the new law of labor that labor is exploited by the employer. It is implicit that the employer cannot be trusted to be fair, and this goes so far that he is not permitted to invoke the National Labor Relations Act, lest he do it with wrong intent. The law recognizes only one kind of coercion—namely, coercion of labor by the employer. The coercion of labor by labor, of the nonunion man by the union, is ignored.

Such are the oversimplifications that confront one's

169

common sense. They may be just as bad on the other side. You may hear an employer say, "Labor is a racket." Do you conclude from this that all employers are economic royalists? That would be as absurd as to take it from him that all labor is a racket. He may be speaking as an economic royalist. It is possible, however, that he is speaking as one who, that afternoon, was locked out of his own plant and is under notice to discuss it, not with his employees, but with a man he has never heard of before.

There is no aspect in which labor is a racket; there are many rackets in the aspect of labor. In the same way of fairness you cannot say that American labor is oppressed and exploited. Not in that unqualified manner. All you can say is that there are notorious cases in which it is true, and that some employers are ruthless. It is still more complicated. What is ruthless? An employer may be ruthless toward labor, which is one thing, or ruthless only toward unionism, which is another thing.

A distinction of that kind would have to be made for the motor industry. It was built on the open-shop principle and hated unionism. Yet it believed in high wages and paid high wages, and, for that reason, was long the despair of the American Federation of Labor, which tried, over and over, to organize the automobile workers on a craft basis, and failed because it had nothing to offer them in exchange for their union dues. Then Lewis[2] did it with his idea of industrial unionism—that is, all the workers, from the assembly line up, to be in one big union. What he held out to them was the glitter of something they could not buy with wages, not if their wages were doubled, and that was power over the boss.

In the General Motors strike,[3] which was the first, wage rates were not in dispute. Recognition was. While that strike was going on, the leaders of it publicly complimented the Chrysler Corporation on the way it treated its employees. Yet scarcely was the ink dry on the General Motors agreement before the same leaders moved against the Chrysler Corporation and locked the owners out. Wage rates there were not in dispute. Neither was collective bargaining, for the Chrysler Corporation was willing to bargain collectively with any group of employees. What the new union demanded was the exclusive right to bargain for all employees, union and nonunion together, which would mean, of course, the closed shop. That was what the strike was about.

It is easy to take sides. All the difficulties are at once resolved. Moreover, it is even possible for one who is emotionally divided to see both sides and hold with one.

I was once a member of the editorial council of *The New York Times*. There was going to be a great Labor Day parade. At council meeting that day Mr. Ochs, the publisher,[4] was very anxious that we should have a fine editorial on it, and he asked Kingsbury to do it because Kingsbury was the finest writer among us.[5] And he asked Kingsbury please to go see the parade instead of writing about it out of his head, as he was most likely to do.

I was in Kingsbury's office that afternoon late when Mr. Ochs came in. He was excited and his eyes were still big. He had seen the parade. He asked Kingsbury if he had. Kingsbury hadn't.

"I'm sorry," said Mr. Ochs.

Kingsbury said, "Well, don't worry about the editorial."

Mr Ochs said, "Oh, it isn't that. I wanted you to see it. It was wonderful. It moved me deeply." He fumbled with a description of it, gave it up, and went on to say what he was feeling. "We talk about the liberty of contract," he said, "and the right of the individual to sell his own labor on his own terms, and that is all right, of course, but there is more to it than that. As I looked at that parade I understood how those men feel about a scab, and why they feel that way. Say what you will, a scab is a man who is willing to take another man's job at a lower wage, or to fill the place of a man who is fighting for a higher wage."

When he had stopped for breath, I said, "Why can't we get a little of that into *The New York Times?*"

Instantly his manner, even his appearance, changed. "No, no," he said. "It isn't as simple as that. It is conflict. They have their side and we have ours. That is necessary.

I may not be able to say why it is so necessary, but I see it and I am sure of it."

The doctrine of free economic conflict. On that ground, Ochs, owner and publisher of the conservative *New York Times,* understood Gompers, president of the American Federation of Labor,[6] and Gompers undertood Ochs. They were on opposite sides of a defined struggle. For many years that worked, fairly well most of the time and very badly some of the time, yet in a way to produce a standard of common living that made American labor the most envied in the whole world. The Kingsbury editorial, which I have entirely forgotten, probably said something like that.

It would have been true. The saying of it, therefore, would give *The Times* a comfortable, sagacious feeling; but on the other side it would produce no feeling at all, or, if any, a feeling of weariness. There you come to a further difficulty.

Suppose you do not wish to take sides. Your aim is to be neutral. You will isolate your bias and put it away: you will hold with the facts and present them in an impartial manner. But this may turn out to be your own oversimplification.

What the intellectual calls the factual approach has certain limitations. To begin with, there are too many facts. Any presentation of them is bound to be selective, and there is no possible selection that may not be quarreled with. Secondly, the facts have to be interpreted. You have to say what they mean. And when you begin to say what the facts mean you are exercising fallible human judgment. Thirdly, it is possible for people to agree only on statistical and objective facts, and these, you will find out, have very little to do with it.

In the room of what I am saying I might be setting down such facts, for example, as that in seventy-five years the buying power of wages has increased threefold, that in the same time the average hours of labor have shortened one fourth, that in twenty years, from 1909 to 1929, wages and salaries increased from 55 percent of the total national

172

income to 65 percent; while the share of owners and investors was falling from 45 to 35 percent; and all this under the free play of a competitive capitalistic system, with no interference by law of Government to alter the terms of division. But when I have set up such facts as these and proved them statistically, what have I done? Labor's proper retort is, "So what?"

If I say these facts to show that, under the doctrine of free economic conflict as men like Ochs and Gompers understood it, we were on our way to achieve a result that no government can guarantee by law, I am uttering an opinion. It is something I believe and cannot prove. On the other hand, if labor says its share in the total product of wealth is not yet enough, what kind of fact is that? It is a fact that labor says it. It is a fact that labor believes it. But whether its share of the total product of wealth is enough or not—that cannot be settled as a matter of actuarial fact. It has to be put to experience, and then it is settled in a provisional way only, because the factors are continually changing. What would have been enough fifty years ago would not be enough today. What is enough today may not be enough tomorrow.

One may read the history of American labor as the story of the rise of the common man. During the first fifty years there was a property qualification for suffrage. Wage earners, as such, were not entitled to vote. Only those who, besides being wage earners, possessed a minimum amount of property were entitled to the ballot. Universal manhood suffrage was not fully established until about 1845. "This," says Commons and Andrews, in *Principles of Labor Legislation,* "was as much as forty to sixty years in advance of other nations, and was, in fact, the first experiment in the world's history of universal admission of the property-less laborer to an equal share in government with the propertied capitalist or employer."

For another fifty years the terms of division between capital and labor were determined in what we now think was a very brutal manner. The price of labor, like the price of pig iron, was subject to the law of supply and demand. Then arose the idea of a living wage as a social imperative. Labor was not to be regarded as a commodity, to be bought and sold at an economic price.

I remember that Judge Gary, chairman of the United States Steel Corporation,[7] once called me to his office to tell me something he thought was news, and yet it was something that could not be printed. He closed his office door and lowered his voice. "My directors may not agree with me," he said, "but I can't help that. I believe our employees are entitled to a living wage."

He had just seized the idea. A little while before it would have been as strange as to speak of a living price for pig iron.

As I staggered forth, I wondered not at the precious lump of liberalism I held in my hands, but at the height of high places. The idea of a living wage was at that time no longer debatable. Labor had gone far beyond that. It had set a new standard, which was a saving wage, or more than enough to live on. And from that it went on to the idea of a progressive wage—the idea that as the production of wealth increases there must be a progressive division of it with labor in order that the standard of common living may rise. Nor is that idea now debatable. It is the accepted idea. It is what you may call the customary law of wages. That is why so often it happens, as in the motor industry, and again in steel, that a strike may not involve the question of wages. It is for something else, like union recognition.

The rise in the estate of American labor in one hundred years is a fact without parallel in the world. And yet the value of it is purely historical. It has no bearing whatever upon the labor problem. For what does it prove? In the language of all labor literature it proves only that the life of the wage earner was once harder than it now is.

During one of the motor industry's strikes a labor leader was telling me of the hardships of working on the assembly line—the terrible monotony of it, the feeling of a man that he is a cog, the nervous strain of keeping up the pace, the petty tyranny of the foreman guarding the company's pre-

cious time. I said to him: "Lets pretend to be rational. You
know what a factory was like thirty years ago and what the
conditions of labor were then. By contrast, the worst
assembly line in Detroit is heaven. These men you talk
about are such as would be digging with shovels and carrying weights on their backs if the assembly line were not
there. Who put the assembly line there? Labor did not put
it there."

"That doesn't interest me in the least," he said. "If the
work of the unskilled wage earner was once harder, does
that make it any easier now? I don't care who put the
assembly line there. It is there, as a fact. That is where we
begin."

One does not criticize the attitude. For purposes of the
labor movement, it is no doubt the right fighting attitude.
Only it is evident that we waste a lot of time making
believe there is some power in facts to settle a labor dispute. Less and less do labor disputes turn on any kind of
fact that may be measured or weighed.

An imaginary grievance, since it has to be built up and
defended, may be even more difficult to deal with than a
real one. But see now what happens to facts. You have only
to excite in labor a feeling of grievance, and although the
grievance may have no basis in fact, nevertheless the feeling becomes itself a fact because it exists.

A labor movement lives on feelings of grievance.
Contented labor is its only despair. Where a sense of injury
is present, it must be intensified; where it is not present, it
must be created. This is the point at which it is said that
labor leadership exploits labor. In that sense it does. There
is a technique for doing it. Two powerful machines now
exist for exploiting the grievances of labor. One is the
American Federation of Labor and the other is John L.
Lewis's Committee for Industrial Organization. They hire
and equip professional organizers and send them forth to
arouse labor; and the C.I.O. having better and more reckless rousers, some of them Communists, who are the most
skillful rousers of all, is forcing the old A.F. of L. to put
more heat on the boss. Such is competition.

175

The organizer is a salesman. He is valued for results. His business is to sign men into the union. You cannot imagine him saying to a labor meeting, "Now let's be fair about this. Let's look at both sides. We have our rights and the boss has his." He begins with the assumption that a man who works on another's premises, with another's tools, for a stated wage, during certain hours, under the eye of a foreman, is a slave—a wage slave—and may be easily moved to a sense of injury and oppression. Often, that is true; and where the boss who owns the premises and the tools is a corporation and the number of employees is many, it is bound to be true of a certain number.

In a free society, a labor movement is not otherwise promoted. If there is a good deal of racket in the selling of it, so there is in the selling of nearly everything else. We understood it. We understood also that a strong labor movement was a good kind of pain for a rich, acquisitive society to have in its middle. If the pain increased, we knew something was wrong. If it became acute, we stopped and did something about it.

Such an attitude, of course, was not socially scientific; it was fit only for a robust society, very sure of its health. The struggle between capital and labor was regarded, not in the ugly light of class conflict, but as an endless economic dispute over division. We said that neither capital alone nor labor alone could be trusted to say how the product of wealth should be divided. One would withhold too much, not only for profit but for the means to yet greater and greater production, forgetting that people must meanwhile enjoy living; labor, on the other hand, would forget the future and consume too much. The terms of division, therefore, were left to be settled by trials of strength between capital and labor—by free economic conflict. The only alternative was for the Government to fix wages and profits, thereby declaring the division, and neither side has ever before wanted that. Only a few years ago the suggestion of it would have been as sincerely rejected by labor as by capital.

176

But in order for this principle of conflict to produce its result—and lest either capital or labor gained undue advantage—it was necessary always for the public and the Government to stand neutral, one to intervene with its sympathies or its common sense, and the other to enforce the law.

Suddenly that has changed. The Government is no longer neutral. It takes the side of labor. With Government on its side, the power of labor is enormously increased. The idea was represented to be one of redress. The Government said capital possessed too much power.

Government in this context means, first, the President, with his tremendously oversimplified theme of the many who are oppressed and the few who oppress them.

It means secondly the Congress, who placed the National Labor Relations Act in the hands of labor, and it is a weapon not unlike the nut in the hand of the Chicago switchman, powerfully persuading the employer to say yes.

It means the National Labor Relations Board, which was created to administer the National Labor Relations Act, and is so partial to labor that its members see no indiscretion in expressing publicly such sentiments as that, "Actually, in so far as successful strikes mean that the workers, who are decidedly the underdogs in our economic scheme of things, are benefited in their purchasing power and their standard of living, the general public and our whole economic structure are gainers."

It means the Post Office Department, when it declines to take parcel-post packages through a picket line to the nonunion men inside a besieged steel plant, on the grounds that the Post Office is not a strike-breaking agency.

It means the Federal Relief Administration, ready to put strikers and their families on public relief, where formerly that burden was on the union's private funds.

It means the Department of Labor, where the philosophy is that a strike is not just another labor dispute but an act in the crusade for social justice. In his *Blue Eagle from Egg to Earth,* Gen. Hugh S. Johnson[8] writes: "Madame Secretary[9] said to me several times that a strike is not an

177

unmixed evil, and to a friend of mine she observed, 'The trouble with Hugh is that he thinks a strike is something to settle.' "

Wherever now there is an important strike, you will find on the ground representatives of the Department of Labor, regarding it not as an unmixed evil; agents from Senator LaFollette's[10] Civil Liberties Committee to mind how strikers may be deprived of their civil liberties; field men from the National Labor Relations Board, with the law in their hands, watching for the employer to step himself into an unfair labor practice. During the sit-down strikes in the motor industry, the National Labor Relations Board had its representatives in Detroit getting the dirt on the motor companies for their espionage among the workers, and the LaFollette Civil Liberties Committee, sitting in Washington, gave it handsome and timely publicity. That was collaboration, with a fine instinct for propaganda.

A ceaseless Government propaganda issues from Washington, all on one side. Some of it is very thoughtfully designed for effect on the mass mentality, the rest of it is spontaneous and emulative. The ingredient of fact is not wanting. But facts in themselves are helpless. They may be employed in a manner to make them more misleading than emotion.

When Senator Wagner was moving the National Labor Relations Act with a speech that was afterward widely circulated, his emotions were always clear. He was for the many against the few, for the poor against the rich, for the wage earner against the powerful corporations. Whether you shared these emotions, you understood them. But naturally, you would accept without questions his statements of statistical fact; most people would accept them uncritically, especially in this case, for the senator was not making a political speech; he was proposing a national labor policy to be embodied in law.

Having indicated in ominous words the rise of American corporations to their great size and power, he made this statement: "As a natural corollary, the wage earner's share

178

in the product created by manufacturing has declined steadily for nearly a century. Standing at 51 per cent in 1849, it fell to 42 per cent in 1919 and to 36 per cent in 1933."

As a statement of uninterpreted statistical fact, this one no doubt is unimpeachable. It so probably is that one need not take the trouble to verify it. Nevertheless, the conclusion any average person would draw from it is wholly false.

What would you conclude from those figures? You would conclude that the wage earner's share in the annual product of industrial wealth had been falling. That is the only conclusion the senator could have expected you to draw from it.

Well, it is not true that the wage earners' share in the annual product of wealth has been falling. It has been rising. It is true—and mark you what a very careful statement that was—that the individual wage earner's share in "the product created by manufacturing" has fallen. What is the explanation? Suppose that one hundred years ago you hired a shoemaker to make shoes. You supplied him with the leather, a bench, needles, thread, wax, knife and a hammer. Suppose, then, in a day he made one pair of shoes and that his share in the product was 50 per cent. What does that shoemaker get for a day's work? He gets the value of one half of one pair of shoes.

But suppose you build a shoe factory and hire shoe workers. Besides the material, as before, you will supply power, automatic machines, conveyor belts and the engineering methods of mass production. Suppose, then, that the total product of your factory equals ten pairs of shoes per worker and that each worker's share in the product is 30 per cent. What does each worker get for his day's work? He gets the value of three pairs of shoes, where the old shoemaker got the value of one half of one pair; it is six times as much, and it is true although the individual wage earner's percentage of the total product has fallen from fifty to thirty.

How much less should the percentage have fallen? How much more should wages have risen? Did the power, the machines, the engineering methods of mass production, whereby the wage earner is enabled to receive the value of three pairs of shoes instead of one-half of one pair, fall out of the sky? If not, where did they come from? What are they worth? What are they worth to labor? If now labor receives 50 per cent of the product, will it be possible to maintain and renew the machinery, to say nothing of continuing to improve it, or shall we have the more abundant life only until it wears out, and then, having eaten it, shall we return to such abundance as the race knew in the age of handicrafts?

The senator does not say. Nobody can say for sure. The Government, with all its wisdom, cannot say. Therefore, such questions are not to be raised. They serve only to befog the idea of social justice.

The senator speaks out of a grand emotion. Wealth must be redivided. If, between 1922 and 1929, profits increased 86 per cent and wages only 10 per cent, it is a scandal. The senator is speaking in 1935. He knows that after 1929 there were frightful losses in place of profits. He knows that billions in wages were paid out of the corporations' reserves—reserves that were built up from the profits that were a scandal. This he does not mention.

What is the nature of profit? Does the senator know? Does profit come out of labor's share? What does it mean that one corporation will make a profit and another will run in the red; competitors, both in the same field, both paying the same wages? What does it mean that in normal times approximately one-third of the entire industrial product is manufactured by corporations that make no profit and pay no dividends?

Again, the senator does not say. Such are more of the questions that are not to be raised. They only complicate matters.

The significance of Senator Wagner is that in labor legislation his is the voice of Government. The voice is saying that life shall be made better for the common man. You might take that to be merely a declaration of what has been implicit in our history from the beginning. If we have not been going toward a better life for the common man, we have been going nowhere. But the voice goes on to say that the common man is entitled to a better life.

Now, "entitled" is a strong word. It means in this case that the wage earner has a rightful claim to something he does not receive. There is a rightful claim to be enforced. A claim to what? To a better life. There is no measure of this better life. It is relative, after all. Nevertheless, better is better. How shall the wage earner's life be made better? By increasing his share in the daily product of wealth. If you ask by how much, that is quibbling.

Take it simply, therefore. Those who work for wages shall receive more. So now it comes to a question of means. How may this be brought about? With one voice, labor and Government say: increase the bargaining power of labor.

That is done. Such is the meaning of the new National Labor Relations Act—whereby the bargaining power of labor is so increased that now it can see for the first time the total unionization of all basic American industry. Under this new law, which defines itself in its first sentence as "An act to diminish the causes of labor disputes," there is an alarming increase of strikes. The law gives labor new power. Labor is exercising that power. There are some employers who still resist it. Hence the strikes. Let the resistance cease and there may be peace. That is the attitude of the Government generally, as of course it must be, for why should the power have been conferred by law if labor was not expected to exercise it?

Labor's demand is for higher wages and shorter hours. From the beginning of modern industry, wages have been rising and hours have been falling, but only so fast as capital and invention were able to diminish the amount of human exertion required to produce the material satisfactions of life. As the productive power of labor is increased by tools, machines, technology and method, the wage earner either may have more things or more leisure. The rise of wages and the shortening of hours have hitherto represented a balance between two conflicting desires. Hours could have been shortened more if people were willing to do with fewer things; things could have been cheapened much more if they had not wanted more leisure.

All of that is forgotten. Is labor asking that capital and invention should do more to increase the productivity of human exertion? No. It demands that wages be increased and hours shortened because it is entitled to more of what is. It has been led to believe that to make the same equal more, it needs only the power to enforce its demand upon industry. But this demanding of industry is a fantasy. It will turn out to be a demand by labor upon itself. Wages—real wages, that is—can be increased only as the productivity of labor is increased. Industry cannot increase it unless labor is willing.

The leaders of labor know this to be true. The Government knows it. The one who does not know it is the man who actually is labor. It seems very simple to him. More dollars in his pay envelope for less work. That is all he can think of. But it is not permitted that the intellectuals who do the Government's thinking on labor, or that a man with the mentality of John L. Lewis, should be so fatuous. They know better. They know that real wages are paid out of production, and that more dollars for less work will not increase them.

Is there, then, some insincerity in their attitudes? Not insincerity. That is not the word. The labor movement is no longer what it was, no longer what it seems. Wages, hours, the principle of collective bargaining—these are hardly more than slogans. They conceal the fact that the struggle now moves on a political plane. For many years, beginning with the starry advent of *The New Republic*, the silken-handed intellectuals who find their self-expression in the labor movement had been trying to impose on American labor the European idea of becoming political. The name of Gompers was anathema to them because he obstinately took the A.F. of L. out of politics.

Well, the time came, and the great temptation, and it happened. Labor embraced politics and the Government embraced labor. The A.F. of L., hindered by the Gompers tradition, was loath to go the whole way, and that was the opportunity for John L. Lewis.

Now the high complications begin. What Lewis wants is power over industry. To unionize labor in order to control it, he needs the Government's aid. But the Government also wants power over industry, and it wants it in its own name. Here are two purposes acting, similar in design yet competitive and, in fact, antagonistic. The difference is that whereas Lewis is thinking only of labor and controlling it in order to gain power over industry, the Government is thinking in terms of a vast social plan; it contemplates power over industry through control of labor as one of the means whereby its authority may be extended over the whole of the nation.

Observe the events. Shortly after the United States Supreme Court had upheld the first Social Security Act and then the National Labor Relations Act, both decisions permitting a far extension of federal authority, and with John L. Lewis going headlong in his purpose, suddenly the Congress receives a message from the President saying the time has come for the Federal Government to regulate hours and wages throughout the nation, and immediately thereafter a pre-written bill authorizing the Government to do this through an agency to be called the Labor Standards Board. The power to fix hours and wages is the ultimate power. It is the power to control production, the power to regulate profits, even to extinguish them—for wages can be made to absorb profits. It is the power to regulate relations between competitive industries.

And all of this is the power John L. Lewis wants in the name of labor. If labor gets it first, the Government will be obliged to either deal with it or to take it by force of law.

This Hours and Wages Bill, so-called, now pending in Congress, was not labor's bill. Labor was not consulted until after it was written. Both John L. Lewis and the president of the A.F. of L. have endorsed it, but in a lukewarm manner and with anxious reservations. They begin to see

183

that what the Government embraces is never again quite free, not even labor.

Such, now, is the labor movement. What formerly was an economic conflict between capital and labor becomes a political struggle for possession of ultimate power. Labor is no longer the wage earner. Labor is a weapon. Who controls the weapon gains the power. What is involved is the next state of society and how it shall be governed. As to that, no one can pretend to be neutral. That one difficulty, therefore, is dissolved. The nut in the switchman's hand was, after all, not a compound evil.

The pro-union tilt of the National Labor Relations Act was modified in 1947 by the Taft-Hartley Act, passed over President Truman's veto by the first Republican Congress since 1930. Sponsored by Sen. Robert A. Taft, R-Ohio, and by a congressman from New Jersey, the act made changes in the law favorable to business. For example, it allowed compulsory union membership only upon a vote of employees. Its Section 14(b) allowed states to outlaw the union shop by passing "right-to-work" laws, which most of the Southern and Mountain states did. But it did not repeal the principle of assigning groups of workers to unions rather than requiring the union to get individual authorization. That principle remains.

---

[1]This was the Pullman Strike of 1894, when Garrett was 16. It began over a wage cut and became a boycott of all Pullman cars by the new American Railway Union. It paralyzed the midwestern railways; there was a federal injunction under the Sherman Antitrust Act and President Cleveland called out federal troops. There was rioting in Chicago, the strike was broken, and the union's founder, Eugene Debs, landed in jail for six months.

[2]John L. Lewis, 1880-1969, flamboyant president of the United Mine Workers 1920-1960. In 1935 he broke away from the A.F. of L. and founded the Committee for Industrial Organization. This became the Congress of Industrial Organizations, a federation of vertical industry-wide unions that was communist-influenced during the 1930s.

[3]A 44-day strike, ending with General Motors' capitulation in February 1937. The workers sat down in the plant, preventing the company from using it. A judge declared the tactic illegal, but the governor of Michigan refused to

enforce the order with armed troops.

[4]Adolph Ochs, 1858-1935. He took control of *The New York Times* in 1896.

[5]Edward M. Kingsbury won the Pulitzer Prize for editorial writing in 1926 for his piece on the Hundred Neediest Cases.

[6]Samuel Gompers, 1850-1924, the British-born cigar maker who became the founding president of the American Federation of Labor in 1886 and led it, except for one year, until his death. He opposed any alignment with socialism.

[7]Elbert Gary, 1846-1927, chairman of US Steel from 1903 until his death at age 80. Called "Judge" because he had been elected a judge in DuPage County, Illinois, from 1884 to 1892, Gary was a corporation lawyer. He helped put together U.S. Steel from the Carnegie and Rockefeller interests, and was asked by financier J.P. Morgan to head it. Gary pushed industrial safety and worker stock ownership, but resisted unionism. In 1920 he broke a 14-month strike over union recognition and the 12-hour day. U.S. Steel recognized the union and adopted the 8-hour day in 1937, the year this article was written.

[8]1882-1942. Johnson helped draft the Selective Service Act in 1917 and served as Army liaison officer to the War Industries Board. He headed the National Recovery Administration 1933-1935, but turned against the New Deal in the late 1930s.

[9]Frances Perkins, 1882-1965, Secretary of Labor 1933-1945. She was a supporter of social welfare benefits and was the first woman in the cabinet.

[10]Robert LaFollette Jr., 1895-1953. A progressive, he was the Republican senator from Wisconsin for 21 years, until Joesph McCarthy beat him in the primary in 1946. LaFollette's more famous father was also a Republican senator from Wisconsin, and ran for president on the Progressive Party ticket in 1924.

CHAPTER TWELVE:

The C.I.O. at Weirton Steel

From "The Crime of Economic Royalism,"
December 4, 1937

Every crime has properly two histories. One is a history of the crime itself; the other is the history of who did it. But to begin with, there must be what the law calls the corpus delicti.

Enter here the Government, bringing a cause entitled, "United States of America before the National Labor Relations Board in the matter of the Weirton Steel Company and the Steel Workers Organizing Committee"—complaining that the crime of economic royalism[1] is manifest in Weirton and that the Weirton Steel Company is guilty of it. The cumbersomeness of the title is owning to the fact that the Government is complainant, prosecutor, jury and judge, all in one.

First, therefore, what is Weirton?

One hour west of Pittsburgh, at a place in the West Virginia hills where the Ohio River rolled over in bed, you will find it, coming on it suddenly. It is not the first Weirton. Tubal-cain[2] and his forge in a blackened forest had the same meaning. That has not changed in thousands

187

of years. It is only that what you are looking at is not the solitary artificer fanning the flame with a goatskin bellows, but the defiant modern process, conducted with such power as to make tremors in the earth, minded night and day by thousands of Tubal-cains, called melters, heaters, rollers, every kind of iron and steel and tin-plate worker; also technicians, machinists, millwrights, chemists and engineers. And all of these, with their families, living in the uproar and smoke and clangor of producing 1,500,000 tons of finished steel products a year, are there because the forge is there. The life of the forge and the life of the people are inseparable. By the changing color of the sky they know what process is taking place. By the density of the haze they know already what appears on the books about the state of the business.

To see it all at once, you will have to stand high on the hillside, level with the tops of the smokestacks. Chromatic clouds of gas molecules, giddy at being free for the first time since the earth was in a molten state, rise until they are chilled, and then die away in the ominous agate haze that lies in the hollow where the river was, filling it to the brim.

If you were at the top of one of the encircling hills, it would seem that you were on the rim of a lake, perceiving objects at the bottom of it, perpendicular things like the smokestacks weaving gently, everything in a state of slight distortion.

For the present you are not at the rim. You are standing on the hillside and are there submerged. The sun overhead is a ball of dull red iron. The weeds underfoot are pale, accommodated to acid.

As you look at them, you feel what they feel. A shudder in the earth, repeated several times. It is from the blooming-mill engine, talking back to the master roller. It happens at the moment when the master roller gags the squeezing rolls on a seven-ton ingot of yellow hot steel. The engine is saying: "I-hope-to-bust, I-hope-to-*bust,* I-hope-to-BUST." Working the levers in his pulpit, the master roller pulls the ingot back again. There is one more tremor, and

188

everything goes smoothly until the seven-ton ingot, turning orange, then red, has been reduced to black steel slabs, each one the size of a common tombstone, and you hear the ring of them piling up.

The blooming mill is the big hammer and anvil. Before it, in the order of happening, are the coke ovens that divide Pennsylvania coal into coke and gas, and the blast furnaces that feed on banks of Minnesota ore and run cataracts of molten metal; after it, in the order of happening, are the finishing mills—the hot strip mill that rolls the thin sheet hot, the cold strip mill that rolls it cold, the tin-plate mill that rolls it thinner still for the tin-plating vat—and it is from these that comes the continuous hum, like the sound of giant gears that may be heard beneath the roar of the ocean surf. All of this, and a sixty-mile private railroad system, you see lying for two miles up and down the gaseous lake. Through the middle runs one long paved street, lined with cafes, saloons, small shops, automobile agencies, filling stations, two banks that never failed, a little chamber of commerce and the company offices.

Beyond, on the steep opposite hillside, running halfway up, are the original Weirton dwellings. That is where the first immigrant labor settled, in houses hastily built, some by the company, some by the immigrants themselves. It is ugly. Even at such a distance and softened by the medium in which it floats, it is ugly. And when you come to walk through it, the effect is depressing. The streets are unpaved and eroded. The churches are blackened. If you touch the fence palings, free black comes off on your fingers. You may notice that the windows are kept hermetically closed.

The earnest young men sent out from Washington to find the dirt on economic royalism are enthusiastic. Here it is. People whose labor produces the wealth, doomed to live in this ugliness! If economic royalism cannot spare the profit to house them better, shall anyone say the Government ought not to do it?

You may ask them if they know what a steel town once

was like. Their answer is to ask what that has to do with it. They are right. That has nothing to do with it; and this is ugly.

You may say to them: "These houses were built before people had automobiles. They had to live close to the works. Where there is a forge there will be smudge!"

They say: "But people do have automobiles now."

That is something to think on. Thinking on it leads to inquiry. Why do these people not have automobiles? If they have, why don't they go out on the hills to live?

Later, when you come to stand again where you are overlooking the works, gazing through the haze at what they call the old town, it is ugly still, but you see it differently. You know something about it. The first generation settled there, and there they are still, growing old. They were Poles, Italians, Greeks, Serbs, Turks, mainly these at first, and a few of nearly every nationality in the world, coming at a time when the company's need for labor was increasing at the rate of 500 to 1000 men a year. They brought their churches with them and took root. They bought houses, but their idea of a house was something to live in with a minimum of actual discomfort, in order to be able to save. Thrift was an Old World habit. When they began, wages were much less than they are now and an eight-hour day was not imagined. As their wages and leisure increased together, they eased their lives a little, dressed better, held more racial festivals and spent more money on their children; but in order still to be able to save, they refused to leave the houses that had been good enough at first.

Now the second generation is coming of age and filling the mills. Its outlook is different. It buys the automobiles and goes out on the hills to live. All the new building is out on the hills. The quality of it is high; the spirit is democratic. On one of the favorite hills—one you cannot see from Weirton, though it is ten minutes away—hundred of new houses have appeared in the last three or four years, and except that it has more ground around it, the house of the president of the company is not remarkable in contrast

190

with that of his nearest neighbor, who is a roller in the mill. No model-village stuff. The company has nothing to do with it.

The interesting fact is that this movement away to the hills owes more than it knows, or much thinks of, to that old town over there. A young man of the second generation, beginning to rise in the mills, takes a wife. He has already an automobile. Now he wants a house on the hills, out of the smoke, where one may keep the windows open and have white curtains. He cannot wait until he has saved the money to build it. So he goes to the bank and asks to borrow the money. The money is there, he is a very good risk, and he gets it. But how does the money happen to be there? Who saved it? The first generation did that. In the savings accounts of the two banks that never failed three-quarters of the money has come from those blackened houses in the old town. The opposite fact is that three-quarters of the money loaned out by the same banks on mortgages is loaned to the young house builders out on the hills, all of whom, naturally, have automobiles. The banks stand in between. Actually what happens is that the first generation, clinging still to the houses that were good enough at first, provides the money that enables the second generation to escape to the hills.

If you are still standing where you were, level with the tops of the smokestacks, the largest building excepting only the company buildings will be a little below you. It is the high school. Directly under you is an athletic field, with boys at exercise. The athletic instructor, seeing you, comes up to talk.

"How many of those boys are from the old town over there?"

"Perhaps a third of them," he says.

"Where will they go from here?"

"Most of them will go into the mills," he says. "Some of them will go to tech school and college, and they will come back to the mills, too, during vacation, to earn their five dollars a day. The company makes room for them in vacation time."

191

He has missed the point which you were going to make—that a steel-mill town must educate its children to hate the environment in which they live. Properly he missed it. He does not see the old town as you see it.

Neither do those boys. It may be said that they do not see it at all. And it may occur to you that there is a way of seeing in which it is not there.

For look. What is permanent here? Remember that only thirty-five years ago there was no Weirton here, no smoke and no sound of industry—in all the view from where you stand, nothing but an apple orchard and some bits of shiftless farming.

Well, everything you now see is still changing and tending to vanish. Permanency is the illusion. The only permanent thing is invisible. What was brought here to begin with was not Weirton, not a steel mill but an idea—namely, the idea of producing divisible wealth. All that is visible proceeds from that idea. What you see with the eye is but the momentary shape of the means and inventions whereby it brings itself to pass. Let the idea continue to act, and let people alone to do what they will with their fair share, and in a little while they will be saying, "Where that new mill is was the old town of Weirton."

How came that idea to what now is Weirton? Who brought it? Here a page turns, and there is a setback in time. History is written that way.

In the year 1901 people went about saying the days of opportunity were numbered. Why were they numbered? Because the trusts were devouring them. The Goliath of trusts had just appeared. That was the United States Steel Corporation, the biggest thing that had ever been imagined in the world—a billion-dollar steel trust. The purpose was laudable. The country's steel and wire and tin-plate industry was in the hands of untamable men who were running it like a battle royal. Their wars of economic frightfulness were very disturbing to the peace of business. The idea of a billion-dollar steel trust was to buy them out, and then impose upon the industry a rule of benign Wall Street dictatorship. That might be very good for the peace of business, but it would mean to limit competition. Who would limit the power of the trusts? What would become of the independent man? Or to the man with small capital? Was the Government itself big enough to control the trusts or were the trusts going to swallow up the Government? Such was the form of the trust question in 1901. Every political-party platform denounced the trusts. Congress enacted laws that were supposed to hinder them. Theodore Roosevelt went forth with a big stick to divide the good ones from the bad ones.

But there was an unknown young man named Ernest T. Weir, and another named J.R. Phillips, working for a wire company that sold out to the United States Steel Corporation. One had $10,000 and the other had $5000, and with this capital they decided to go into competition with Wall Street's billion-dollar steel trust. Even for those days that was ruggedness.

They found a bankrupt local tin-plate mill at Clarksburg, West Virginia, one that the trust would not have looked at, and borrowed enough money to buy it. For thirty years thereafter, they were never free of pressing debt. Now, looking back on it, Weir remembers that the bogey of a sheriff man always about to rise over the horizon with a paper in his hand had an amazing effect on the human faculties, and tells his young executives he almost wishes it was still alive.

They had to rebuild the old tin-plate mill—it was one that bought its sheet steel, rolled it again and dipped it in tin—and the rebuilding of it cost much more than was expected. However, they got started, with a payroll of 150 men. Weir took the manufacturing end and Phillips went out to sell the tin plate. The orders were coming in when one day Phillips was killed in a train wreck. But the tin plate was good and the price was right and the creditors were beginning again to sigh with relief, when one forenoon the superintendent came to the office to say the engine was about to jump off into space. The one thing they had not rebuilt was the engine foundation.

Weir went back to look at it. "She'll hold till the whistle blows," he said. "Then shut her down for good." With that, he went back to the office to think. He thought it was all over. They had had all the trouble they could stand: one more shutdown would be fatal. But by talking about it they thought of a way to prop up the law of gravity and slip under the engine a foundation of concrete and steel rails twenty feet deep, while the bogeyman slept.

They were going again. The tin plate got better all the time, the orders increased, and it seemed too good to be true. The next thing was a nightmare. The billion-dollar steel trust also made tin plate; moreover, it sold to the young men at Clarksburg the sheet metal out of which they made their tin plate. If the trust wanted to put the independent tin-plate mills out of business, it could make a price for tin plate that would break them in three months; or, on the other hand, it could suddenly find it impossible to sell them any more steel. Weir went to talk it over with the chairman of the steel trust. The chairman would not say the steel trust would not decide to make tin plate very cheap indeed, as a matter of policy, if for no other reason than to meet the cry that the trust held prices up; nor would he say the trust would go on forever selling sheet steel to the little Clarksburg mill, especially if they went on increasing their demand for it. It was all very fatherly. The chairman of the steel trust believed in live and let live, and in the golden rule as far as that went, and yet it was a law of Nature that each thing, big and little, had to look out for itself.

So the young men decided they would have to make their own sheet steel; and they might as well go on and build a regular steel mill, to make all kinds of steel. What they needed was a place to put it. In looking for a place, they came to what now is Weirton.

So the idea arrived, one rainy May day, in a buggy. If they had known, themselves, what was to come of it—that in thirty years, here in this empty hollow, they would be meeting a payroll of $20,000,000 a year, they probably would have been scared. What they were thinking of, however, was the exact spot for the steel mill, and how to use the river, and trouble.

Presently there was a Weirton Steel Company and a town of Weirton. The Weirton Steel Company, as it grew, must command its own coal and its own ore, in order to have an integrated operation. But the Weirton Steel Company was hardly big enough to have its own coal mines and ore mines and a fleet of ships to bring the ore down from Minnesota.

Now, at about this time there was a man at Detroit who loved trouble, too. His name was Fink—George R. Fink, a steel salesman, who never could understand why Pennsylvania, Ohio and West Virginia should be making steel for the Michigan motor industry. Why shouldn't the ore coming down from Minnesota stop at Detroit, which was the largest market in the world for steel?

With a way of putting this question, Fink raised enough capital to build a steel mill at Detroit and called it the Great Lakes Steel Corporation; and although he knew what he was about, he did not know that he was beginning on the very edge of a depression. Well, the more trouble the better. All during the depression, paying the highest wages in the industry, he continuously increased his capacity and output. When the motor plants were running with no material in reserve, and wanted steel in a hurry, Fink trucked it to them right off the rolls, often having to turn the hose on it to cool it.

It is a pity to spoil that story by telling it in the margin. The reason for bringing it in at all is to explain that the Weirton Steel Company and the Great Lakes Steel Corporation together with certain coal and ore properties, a fleet of ore boats, terminals, docks and so on, were all brought under one corporate blanket, the National Steel Corporation. Ernest T. Weir, chairman, is the man at the top. Which is all for data.

Now back to the scene of the crime and to Ernest T. Weir, the economic royalist the Government is after. He has a record. There was a first offense; and if you are a student of crime you will realize how important it is to know what that was. Weir's first offense was to take the Blue Eagle to court and to beat it. The particulars are as follows:

In the beginning, Weir's relations with his labor were personal. He started with 150 men, and knew them all by name. The number increased—to 1000, to 5000, to the impersonal number of 10,000—and still he did nothing about it, only to improve working conditions, to pay the highest wages in the industry, and above all, to keep the mills going. During the worst of the depression, the number of unemployed in Weirton at no time exceeded 1 per cent of the population, and this, for a steel town, was exceptional.

In 1933, when the Blue Eagle appeared, the Weirton Steel Company made no difficulty about signing the steel code and accepting the principle of collective bargaining, but its idea of collective bargaining was to have it on the premises, for Weirton employees only. With that idea, Weir began looking around for an employee-representation plan. The best one, he thought, was the one that had been working at the Bethlehem Steel Company. He adapted it to Weirton, offered it to his employees and asked them to vote on it. They accepted it, and it went into effect. All of this was legal, strictly according to the official interpretation of the National Industrial Recovery Act.

However, Section 7(a) of that act was taken by the American Federation of Labor as a mandate to unionize all labor, and it went forth to do it. When it came to Weirton, it found the Employee Representation Plan working so well that it was able to organize but a small minority of workers. With that minority it called a strike, saying the Employee Representation Plan was nothing but a company union and not at all a free instrument for purposes of collective bargaining. The works shut down, but not for long, because a majority of the employees upheld the representation plan by voting for it again, and wanted to go back to work. At the insistence of the old National Labor Board, the Government then said the employees had been intimidated and coerced by the company, that they were afraid of losing their jobs, and that they were, in fact, wage slaves. That was the issue on which Weir went to court with the Blue Eagle. A federal court in Delaware said that clearly on the evidence a large majority of the employees preferred their representation plan over any outside union, preferred it freely, and that it was, in fact, a legal and effective instrument for purposes of collective bargaining.

Shortly thereafter the Blue Eagle expired. The United States Supreme Court killed it. But the Government never forgave Weir for the wound he had inflicted on it.

Then the historic New Deal interregnum, called the breathing spell. The Weirton Steel Company went on making steel. The good sign was that the sky darkened. The pay roll increased; the wage rates rose. The Employee Representation Plan worked better, as amended.

At first, representatives of the company sat with the employees while they deliberated. That was no longer permitted.

At first, it was only an employee who had been for at least one year on the payroll that could be elected by the employees to represent them. The by-laws were amended to read that the employees were free to elect anyone to represent them, provided only that he should be twenty-one and an American citizen.

And one thing more: Weir said it was hurtful to the pride of a man to come to work and find a change of wages posted on a bulletin board. It was too much as if the company were saying: "Take it or leave it." So the by-laws were amended to read: "WAGE CHANGES: The company having agreed to submit all questions of general increase or decrease of wages to the representatives, any action approving such increase or decrease must have a majority of all elected representatives."

Which means that wages shall not be changed but with the consent of the employees.

The Government, meanwhile was neither forgetting nor forgiving, nor was it taking a breathing spell. From the obsequies of the Blue Eagle it turned to write the National Labor Relations Act, declaring it was now become the policy of the Government, not only to legalize collective bargaining but to promote it actively; and to that end the law created the National Labor Relations Board to stand with organized labor and to assist it in its war with economic royalism. Such an opportunity had not occurred before in all the history of the American labor movement. The big man to seize it immediately appeared in the doorway. That was John L. Lewis, with his C.I.O. and every labor leader's dream of a closed-shop nation.

In this country there is one test of a labor leader's prowess. Like the kings of Germany, to any one of whom it was given to be emperor of the Romans and head of the Holy Roman Empire if only he could cross the Alps and fight his way to Rome, so an American labor leader may be king of the mine workers or king of anything else, but to establish an empire he must unionize the steel industry. Could John L. Lewis do that? He thought he could. At any rate, he would be the first to do it with the Government behind him.

Now, the parts of the steel industry are far flung and at peace with one another only by truce. Regarding it as a whole, it consists of one great principality and two independent leagues. The great principality is the United States Steel Corporation, now growing old and mindful of its own comfort. One of the leagues is that group of independents in which Schwab's Bethlehem Steel Company, Tom Girdler's Republic Steel Company and the Youngstown Sheet and Tube Company are the principal three. The second league is the National Steel Corporation, just described, with Weir at the top.

Such were the Alps that John L. Lewis had to cross. As a tactician, he knew the trick of dividing the enemy. He went first to the United States Steel Corporation as a reasonable man in a plausible way. There were several reasons why the United States Steel Corporation should quietly sign a collective-bargaining agreement with the C.I.O. One of them was that the independents would almost certainly refuse to do so, whereupon the C.I.O. would strike them all and shut them down, and when that happened the

The C.I.O. at Weirton Steel

United States Steel Corporation would be in a very favorable position—that is, it would be at peace with labor, running its mills at full capacity, while the mills of its competitors were cold. The great principality signed without notice to the independents. Then John L. Lewis did strike the independents, not all of them at once, but the Bethlehem-Republic-Youngstown league first, thinking it was the more vulnerable. The National Steel Corporation was to come last. The C.I.O. organizers at Weirton, for example, were under orders to prepare the ground and wait. Weir was being saved for the *auto-da-fé,* at which both the C.I.O. and the Government would celebrate the fall of economic royalism in the steel industry.

For all but one flaw, it was a perfect program. The flaw in it was the assumption that the Bethlehem-Republic-Youngstown wage slaves would rise against their oppressors and hail their liberator. They didn't. A large majority of them only wanted to be left alone; they did not even know they were wage slaves. They went so far as to organize themselves against the C.I.O. and then demand that the mills be reopened for men to work. So Lewis lost that first battle in the Alps on the way to Rome.

One more explanatory passage. It is probably the last. You have to know the part the National Labor Relations Board takes. When and where the C.I.O. pitches battle, the National Labor Relations Board stands off to watch. If the C.I.O. wins, that is everything. But if the battle is lost the National Labor Relations Board begins to act. On petition of the C.I.O., it issues a complaint against the economic royalists, brings them into its own court, and there tries them on the charge that in refusing to recognize and bargain collectively with the C.I.O., they have violated the National Labor Relations Act.

From here on, everything happens at Weirton.

At one end of the main street there is an old building with C.I.O. painted on the door in big white letters, the paint running out of them a little at the bottom. This is headquarters for the C.I.O. organizers, who were to prepare the ground and wait. They were not good organizers, not such men as the Weirton steel workers would follow; but they were active, they held meetings and distributed C.I.O. buttons with the face of John L. Lewis on them, and they got some signatures, number unknown, to green cards representing membership in the Steel Workers Organizing Committee of the C.I.O.

Across the street from that building is the meeting place of the Weirton Employees' Security League. This is an organization that issues red cards to employees who say they want to be let alone. The back of the card reads: "I am not a member of, nor will I support in any way, any outside labor organization. If at any time the Weirton Steel Company recognizes any labor organization other than the Employee Representation Plan as a bargaining agency for any group of employees, without first holding an election to determine if the majority of employees want another labor organization, we will protest by whatever means necessary to prevent such recognition."

The Government says this red-card business is an idea of the company imposed upon its employees. And that, of course, is what the C.I.O. people say. The red-card people say it isn't so; it was their own idea. What nobody denies is that the community is bitterly divided. The red-card people and the green-card people give one another dirty looks as they pass, and at night they are tense and watchful, especially the C.I.O. people, for in any casual situation they will be outnumbered, and that is why they avoid the athletic games and the wrestling bouts. The Government is on their side, but the Government is not always there. It is not a policeman. It works in another way.

Observe the Government. When Lewis had lost his battle, it was time for the National Labor Relations Board to do its part. First, the C.I.O. sends a petition to the National Labor Relations Board, saying, "At Weirton we have a labor organization called the Steel Workers Organizing Committee. It is the only bona-fide labor organization there and represents a number of the employees. The only reason it does not represent more is that all the rest are

200

intimidated and terrified by the company. The company refuses to recognize this bona-fide labor organization. What will you do about it?"

The National Labor Relations Board is not surprised. It sends investigators to Weirton to find if there are enough witnesses to swear these things are true to make a case against economic royalism. The Government, in the persons of these investigators, now enters; it takes comfortable rooms at the nearest good hotel. It sends for the C.I.O. organizers, who bring in the witnesses, and in due time the investigators report, saying: "Yes, we can make a case." Thereupon the National Labor Relations Board issues a complaint against the Weirton Steel Company, saying it has evidence to prove that what the C.I.O. organizers allege is true; it appoints the investigators, who have not given up their comfortable rooms, to be Government prosecutors; it appoints a trial examiner to sit as a court; and it notifies the Weirton Steel Company that at a certain place and date, it will be tried. This is the cause, entitled: "The United States of America before the National Labor Relations Board in the matter of the Weirton Steel Company and the Steel Workers Organizing Committee."

And the next day a C.I.O. organizer, who happened to get himself elected constable, is going about Weirton with a big gun in his belt, serving subpoenas for the Government.

What is the charge against the Weirton Steel Company?

The charge is that it has refused to recognize and bargain collectively with a labor organization. What labor organization? Not the Employee Representation Plan, for the Government says that is not a labor organization. There is but one labor organization in Weirton holding itself out to be such. That is the C.I.O. union. Therefore, the offense of the Weirton Steel Company is that it does not embrace the C.I.O.

Weir says this is all nonsense. He says the employees will have any kind of labor organization they want, for anything either he or the Government can do about it. If they want to be represented by the C.I.O. they will be. All they

201

have to do is vote for it. To this the Government retorts derisively. Is it not well known that economic royalists talk like that for effect and that no one of them can be believed under oath?

Employees to the number of 7000 sign their names to a paper, saying they wish to appear before the National Labor Relations Board and swear that what they want is their own Employee Representation Plan, not the C.I.O., and that they are free to elect whom they like to represent them. The Government will not believe 7000 employees for, of course, they are afraid to tell the truth.

The by-laws of the Employee Representation Plan are put in evidence. Under the by-laws they could elect John L. Lewis to represent them, if they wanted him. The Government will not believe the by-laws. Probably they were written by the company. In that case, they do not mean what they say.

Weirton rises in a body, a mile or two of employees marching by mill units, and this is to say again that these, at any rate, want to be let alone; they want the C.I.O., the National Labor Relations Board and the Government all to let them alone. They say it on banners and transparencies, with a good deal of ragging in the words, as you might guess. The Government says this is opera. The company must have staged it.

The company can show as a fact that its employees, bargaining for themselves, receive a higher minimum wage than those for whom John L. Lewis did the bargaining with the United States Steel Corporation. This is a fact the Government severely passes by. As evidence on the record, it could be too easily be misunderstood. Is it now known that economic royalism has two ways of defeating unionism? One way is to intimidate the wage earner; the other way is to bribe him.

But why all this devil whacking? If the pit is there, why not cast him in and chain him down? Is there not one simple question here? The law says the employees may have any kind of representation they like. It says also that a majority shall prevail. There are C.I.O. people here, and there are others who say they want nothing to do with the C.I.O. The question is: What do a majority of the employees want? Therefore, why not put it to a vote and settle it?

Ah, but you do not comprehend these matters. The National Labor Relations Board, of course, could have ordered an election rather than bringing this action. Ultimately it will have to order an election or abandon the case. But to have put it to a vote in the first place would have been unfair. Unfair to whom, and why? Unfair to the C.I.O., and for the reason that the employees cannot be trusted, even with a secret ballot, to vote as they really feel. Not yet. They have been too long in this condition of abject mental and moral servitude. First they must be set free. When they have seen the power of the Government acting, and how the Government can beard economic royalism in its den, then they will begin to believe they are free, and the vote may be very different.

So far from wanting to be counted now, the C.I.O. people anxiously avoid a showdown. Under cross examination they refuse to say again and again how many members they have, and both Government counsel and the court protect them in that position. Clinton S. Golden, regional C.I.O. director, is a witness. He testifies that he kept close watch on the membership drive in Weirton and that all the green cards came to his office. Counsel for the Employee Representation Plan and for the Weirton Steel Company ask him how many there are.

"I will tell you it is a substantial number."

"How many?"

"I won't tell you."

"I want to know."

"Keep on wanting to know."

Counsel insists that the witness shall tell. The Government's lawyers object. The court sustains the objection.

The court—that is, the trial examiner—perfectly understands the Government's problem. Before there shall be a count, the Government must prove that the Employee Representation Plan is an illegal company device, not a labor organization at all, wherefore it cannot be counted against the C.I.O. This is not so easy to prove when the company, by reason of its domination, is able to control a large number of witnesses. Therefore, it is this power of domination that must be proved.

The difficulties multiply. "Domination" is a large word. Therefore, there is a sense in which Weirton is bound to be dominated by the Weirton Steel Company. The only reason for its being is the Weirton Steel Company. Certainly what people live by will influence their thoughts and habits, perhaps even more than they realize. But if you mean more, if you mean deliberate and tyrannical domination, you have the difficulty that the only way you could so dominate a lot of steel workers would be to make their blood run cold, and only some of them then.

Well, the Government says the crime of economic royalism leads to that. It leads to physical crime. In Weirton it has arrived at it. It says the Weirton Steel Company dominates its employees by terror. It says this Ernest T. Weir, whose words are so fair, keeps a secret hatchet gang, and sends it out to chop down C.I.O. people as they go about minding their C.I.O. business.

You see, at last, the dismal stupidity of crime. The head of a $200,000,000 steel corporation, hiring a hatchet gang to terrorize union people, does not realize that he puts himself under the hatchet. True, he might hire a second hatchet gang to chop down the first one when it turns on him, and a third to chop down the second, and so keep ahead of it for a while, but in the end his own hatchet gang will get him, if the Government does not get him first.

Under the ordinary rules of evidence, the Government could not prove the existence of this hatchet gang. The trial examiner understands that moreover, it is the law. The National Labor Relations Act says that in some of these proceedings "the rules of evidence prevailing in courts of law or equity shall not be controlling." Thus, the Government is able to bring witnesses to swear to the existence of the hatchet gang on hearsay and rumor. Everybody has heard of it; nobody has ever seen it. A witness testifies that a certain man was head of the hatchet gang. How does he know that? He heard it. A witness says the hatchet gang meets in a certain place. How does he know? He passed that place and somebody said it was where the hatchet gang met. A witness testifies that members of the hatchet gang stood on his porch one night in the dark; he did not see them, but he could identify their voices. Bring them into court and he will know their voices. What did the voices say to him out of the dark? They were asking where somebody lived, and from the way they asked, he knew they were trying to trap him. A witness testifies that he dreams of the hatchet gang.

Another witness testifies that he was beaten up by men who must have belonged to the hatchet gang, for why else should they want to beat him up? Was this act witnessed by anyone else? Yes indeed; by a lot of people. Does he know the people who saw it? He does. Will he name them? He will not. Why not? Because if he does, their houses will all be "blowed up." By the hatchet gang, of course, which is capable of using dynamite also. And such as this is most solemnly treated as evidence.

It is true that two or three C.I.O. agents were beaten up in the neighborhood of Weirton, and that some wearers of C.I.O. buttons were booed in the mills and chased out, and that in Weirton a C.I.O. organizer does well to mind his step. The Government finds it easier to believe that all this is the work of a hatchet gang, hired by the company, than that steel workers would be unwilling to receive from its hands the gift of freedom, even to the point of resisting.

The fact is that to many of them what the C.I.O. represents is a principle of trouble; and if you know steel workers, as the Government doesn't, and as the C.I.O. is only beginning to know them, a steel town is not a place you take trouble to, unless you are willing to fight for it. One reason why it has always been so hard to unionize the steel industry, and why C.I.O. strikes for unionism only, with no grievances over wages and working conditions, are so unpopular, is that at the top of it you have an aristocracy of labor, making its twenty to forty dollars a day, thanks to nobody but itself.

Here the story stops, for the reason that there is no more of it until it happens. That is to say, it will be continued in the news. Which means that what the reader has, if he has anything, is a little light bearing from behind.

To the Weirton steel workers, if they read this, the writer's thanks for taking him to their games, and then, at the Steubenville hotel, keeping him up most of every night, some of them in dinner jackets, arguing about government, economics, world politics, the physics of iron, and why a ladle crane man, who carries 250 tons of molten steel at a time and pours it gloomily into molds, with the instant life of the place in his hands, is never a civil animal, not even to himself.

The Steel Workers Organizing Committee struck Bethlehem Steel, Inland Steel, the other units of Republic Steel and Youngstown Sheet & Tube, resulting in the bloodiest labor battle since the Homestead Strike in 1892. These companies, collectively called "Little Steel," recognized the United Steelworkers-C.I.O. in 1941. Weirton did not, buoyed by its independent spirit and by the company's willingness to pay workers more than the United Steelworkers' contract rates.

In 1941 the National Labor Relations Board found Weirton guilty of having a company-dominated union, and in 1942 the Employee Representation Plan was disbanded. Employees formed another one, and the labor board struck it down in the late 1940s. In 1951 came an election between the United Steelworkers-C.I.O. and the newly formed Independent Steelworkers' Union. The independent union won by 3-to-1, and remains the representative of the workers fifty years later.

It is still a maverick union. In 1984 it led a worker buyout of Weirton from Republic Steel, through a large pay cut and the world's largest Employee Stock Ownership Plan. In 1989, needing capital, the company went public by selling some of the worker shares on Wall Street. For the elections of 2000, the Independent Steelworkers broke with the AFL-CIO unions and endorsed Patrick Buchanan for president.

---

[1] Roosevelt introduced the term in his acceptance speech at the Democratic convention, June 27, 1936: "Economic royalism carved a new dynasty . . . a new despotism." Control of workers' wages, hours and conditions, he said, "were imposed by this new industrial dictatorship." He said, "The royalty of the economic order have conceded that political freedom was the business of government. But they have maintained that economic slavery was nobody's business . . . These economic royalists complain that we seek to overthrow the institutions of America. What they really complain of is that we seek to take away their power."

[2] A descendant of Cain in the Book of Genesis. He was the instructor of artificers of brass and iron.

CHAPTER THIRTEEN:
Fear

A Dinner in Washington

From "A Washington Errand,"
January 22, 1938

The Old Reporter was having dinner with an accidental group of gloomy men. One was in electric power, two were lawyers whose clients were coal and railroads, one was a public-relations man and one was somebody else. They talked about the Government, not the government in theory or principle, but the Government, and what it was doing to business, and how it had ruined the railroads, and that now it was fixing a social price for coal while at the same time it was itself competing with coal in developing, with public funds, hydroelectric power to be distributed at a social price, and what this would do to the private power companies.

It went on for a long time, with frequent references to the Constitution; and when one of them got too excited, the others looked around to see if he was being overheard, especially the electric-power man, for this was a public dining room, and an administrative officer of the Government might be sitting at the next table.

"Listen, you economic royalists," said the Old Reporter. "I've been listening to you for three hours. Do you realize that everything you have said in that time could have been expressed in one word?"

"What word is that?" the public-relations man asked.

"It's a word," said the Old Reporter, "that I've been trying to think of for three or four days. A single word to define a new fact in the relations between people and Government. The word is 'fear.' You are all afraid of the Government, and that's what you have been saying."

"I'll say we are afraid," said the power man. "I'm afraid to be seen to be talking to a representative of the Government. I'm afraid that if I forget to report it to another representative of the Government—what one I don't know—I'll be breaking the law. You are right. Every man who has anything that can be taken away from him is afraid. Those who don't fear the Government are those to whom the government gives what it takes from the rest of us."

"That's less than I mean, if you mean property," said the Old Reporter. "I haven't any property to lose. What I fear is the loss of something much more important than property."

"I know what you mean," said one of the lawyers. "But isn't it all one thing? An attack upon property is an attack upon common honesty, and that is the same as to attack morals."

"Be careful," said the Old Reporter. "You will be classified as one who sets property rights above human rights."

"Pooh!" said the lawyer.

"And you have been bringing in the Constitution, as if that had anything to do with it," said the Old Reporter.

"What do you mean—'as if that had anything to do with it'?" the lawyer asked.

"This thing we speak of, calling it fear, is new, isn't it?" the Old Reporter continued. "I've been thinking about it a good deal in the last few days. I've been trying to contrast the Washington I'm looking at now with the Washington I first knew. I've brought it down to the attitude of the ordinary citizen toward the Government. How has that changed? When I first came to Washington, the attitude of every man here, of every man who came here on any errand, was that the Government was his Government. He supported it. He had something to say about it because he paid the bill. The ways in which the Government could touch him were definite and limited; he knew what they were and submitted to them in a voluntary manner, and if it tried to touch him in any other way, he knew how to put it in its place. That was fine. At least, I think it was. But that feeling is entirely gone. Where will you find any trace of it left? In place of it is fear. No man is sure what his immunities are. He may be suddenly confronted by a law he knows nothing about. He may be put in jail for violating the rules and regulations issued by a bureau. No man knows how, tomorrow, the Government may touch him or what he can do about it. Isn't that new? Doesn't it suggest to you a great change in the character of Government? Or do you agree?"

"Yes, we agree," they said.

"Well," said the Old Reporter, "has the Constitution changed? Has the Bill of Rights been rewritten?"

"Only violated," said the lawyer.

"You to say that," answered the Old Reporter. "A man of the law. You should say reinterpreted. And observe, reinterpretations of the Constitution by the Supreme Court are constitutional. They become the law of the land. You are fooling yourselves who talk of defending the Constitution as if it were an immutable thing, like the Ark of the Covenant. This change we are looking at has taken place within the grammar of the Constitution. There is no power in phrases written on a piece of skin to stop government. Forget what is written in the document. Defend, instead, the spirit and philosophy that wrote it."

"Why don't you write that?" asked the lawyer.

And that ended the dinner party.

The Sign Ascendant

From "A Washington Errand,"
January 29, 1938

There is a natural law of government, not of any particular government, but a natural law of every government that ever was; and it is like the biological law from which every living thing derives the blind impulse to swell and extend itself to the extreme possibility. A tree would grow to the sky if it could. The living thing is stopped by the resistance of other hostile things and by the limits of the food supply. What a government feeds upon is freedom; the resistance to it is the human motive to defend freedom.

Thomas Jefferson said: "The natural progress of things is for liberty to yield and for government to gain ground." And again: "The spirit of resistance to government is so valuable on certain occasions that I wish it always to be kept alive. It will be often exercised when wrong, but better so than not to be exercised at all."

With this natural law in mind, turn now and look at the principal governments of the world, no matter what they are called or how they name themselves, and you will be struck by their similarities, not by their differences.

All alike, they are extending their powers to the utmost.

All alike, they are limiting the areas of human freedom, for no government can in any way extend its powers over people but to limit freedom.

All alike, they sweat with the conviction of doing to people what is best for them.

All alike, if they do not already possess it, they are pressing for sovereign power, above any law, beyond any restraint.

All alike, they are unmoral, which is to say, whatever they do is right.

All alike, they claim the power to dispose of private wealth, some of them doing it in the name of the state, some in the name of the proletariat, some in the name of social justice. This is extremely important. It is not a mat-

212

ter of what happens to private wealth as such. That is relatively unimportant. But a government, to extend itself, must command money—more and more money. A truth that was learned long ago seems now to be forgotten—namely, that freedom is in the purse. Give the government an unlimited purse and the life of freedom is already pledged. The certain way to limit government is to limit its purse.

And lastly, all alike, they are resolved to dominate economic forces. The reason for this is quite simple. In certain circumstances, as in war or a great depression, the economic sphere is that in which the extension of the powers of government is least resisted, and the one, also, in which the effects are likely to be the most irreversible. Once the government puts forth its hand to touch the economic system, that hand almost cannot be removed. Simple as the explanation may be, there is a history here.

The nineteenth century was that period of modern times in which, taking the world as a whole, there was a minimum of government and a maximum of human freedom. Why was that so? It was so because that was the time during which governments exercised the least control over economic forces. But this was nothing the governments ever intended. The doctrine of laissez faire, or let it alone, was never adopted by governments. What they controlled they never relaxed their hold upon; but what they controlled withered in their hands.

The change was that a new economic world appeared. It was born of science, power and invention. Its growth was amazing and unpredictable. Governments did not understand it, nor the forces and mechanisms it worked with. They were afraid to touch it. That is why they let it alone. So this new economic world was free and went its way. Then the government began to study it. In one hundred years they overtook it. Now they are resolved to control it, even as they controlled the simple economic system that was before this one.

The conclusion is that for all who would defend freedom, government is the enemy, not government of any particular

213

kind or form or name, but government itself in its imme-morial nature.

If government cannot be limited freedom is lost.

To defend the Constitution is not the same as to defend freedom. Under the Constitution, by amendment or inter-pretation, there can be unlimited expansion of Government, even to the point of the absolute. The process is insidious. Let the Government's intent be good. That may be assumed. But the better the intent the worse it is, for the goodness of the intent disarms resistance. For remember, an absolute government, a government that has totally abolished individual freedom, may possess the con-viction that it is doing to the people what is good for them. It brings them security, happiness, the abundant life, equality; in another case it may be the conviction, as in Germany or Italy, that it brings their destiny to pass. And all of that may be so.

Here is no ethical question. It is a question only of what kind of world you want to live in, a world of freedom or one of status.

Such then is the sign that now is ascendant in the polit-ical heavens. Such is the movement that is taking place in the world. Neither the sign nor the movement is new in the world; they are new only in this country, where now, for the first time, it may be that Government will overwhelm free-dom. Certainly it will if the extension of its power be not heroically resisted.

The extension of power was resisted. Middle-class voters were disturbed by the government's toleration of John L. Lewis's sit-down strikes, by Roosevelt's scheme to pack the Supreme Court and by the return of depression in the win-ter of 1937-38. In the midterm elections of November 1938, Republicans gained eight seats in the Senate, including the election of Robert Taft of Ohio, and they nearly doubled their forces in the House. Voters also returned conservative Democrats who had been targeted by Roosevelt. The shift of power was not enough to reverse the New Deal, but it had been checked.

214

CHAPTER FOURTEEN:

Fifth Anniversary

From "Fifth Anniversary N.D.," March 5, 1938

Five years.

On the fifth anniversary is it permitted to ask what there is to show for an increase of two billion dollars a year in the cost of government and fifteen billions in the national debt. What of the goods received? How do they compare with the undertakings?

The undertakings of the New Deal were so many all at once that its laws had to be passed without debate, sometimes unread, just as they came from the White House; and yet that seemed to be all right at the time, because everyone knew how ideal the intentions were and that everything that was done, even though it might have to be done over, would somehow come under one or more of the three Rs, recovery, reform and retribution.

Recovery was the first imperative. There had been four years of frightful economic depression, and it was agreed that, instead of pursuing recovery around the corner, we should have to go the other way and meet it head on. The question is: Did we meet it, did it meet us, or did the New Deal produce it? And if the New Deal produced it, what produced it in every other country at the same time?

The great depression of 1929-1932 was a world-wide

disaster. The recovery likewise was world-wide. Both movements were of tidal character, touching all countries. What might have happened in this country alone, in place of what did happen, is something you can never prove. They may be believed that without what the New Deal did we should have gone down, down, down, with all the rest of the world going up. However, that was not possible. And the fact is that through five years of world-wide recovery this country was a notable laggard, standing all the time in sixth or seventh place.

Taking the world as a whole, industrial production in 1937—the fifth year of universal recovery—was nearly one-third greater than in 1928, which was the peak year of predepression time. In Great Britain alone it was more than one fifth greater. In this country industrial production came to a top in 1937 at approximately the level of 1928. But to have equaled 1928, we should have been producing not the same quantity of things but a greater quantity, because meanwhile the population had increased by nearly ten millions. At the top of the recovery in 1937 our total production of things was less per capita than in 1928. At the very best in 1937 there was relatively less to be divided than in 1928, and at the end of 1937 there was actually much less, because production by that time had fallen in a headlong manner and there was a new depression, not a world-wide depression this time, but one of our own.

All through the rise in American production, even when it was at the top in 1937, there was a sign of weakness in it. The high output was of such things as the economist calls nondurable goods, meaning the things we make today and consume tomorrow. Of durable goods, meaning such things as machinery, power plants, industrial buildings and houses, the great deficit that had accrued in the depression years 1929-1932 was never made up. This means that in order to reach again the level of 1928 in the production of nondurable goods, we were using very largely the equipment we already had, and wearing it out. As far as we did that, we were eating up our tools. Through five years of recovery, ending suddenly in another depression, it

216

is doubtful the total wealth of the country was increased at all.

Considering what our wealth and resources are, considering our famous superiority in mechanical power, to have held sixth or seventh place in world-wide recovery was to have made the worst showing of all. The only one of the principal countries to have made a worse statistical showing was France, and for what it is worth, the fact may be noted that France was the only one that tried to copy the New Deal.[1]

We speak of recovery. It may be that what we are talking about is revival. It may be that we have had no recovery at all, only revival. The difference is to be explained. Merely to make today all the things we may consume tomorrow is not enough to employ our full man power. It takes, it may be, only two thirds of our power to do that. What, then, of the surplus third? The use of that third is to bring the future to pass, if we have a future. Its use is to create the further means to further plenty. Otherwise, being content with what we already have, we propose to limit our exertions, thin down the work, share it around, and embrace the static life. That would mean a standard of living that would rise no more and would tend always to decline.

What we have not recovered—what we seem to have lost for the first time in our history—is a reckless passion for the future. Hitherto we had lived in a world we were overtaking. To the future we sacrificed the present. If now we begin to live more in the world we have, it is the future that must be sacrificed, and the new political delusions will be such as arise from ideas of ever-normal plenty, balanced abundance, planned economy, maximum rewards for minimum exertions, social security, stability—all the ideas of a finished world.

Some will say the New Deal's recovery program was interfered with. One of its principal instruments was the National Recovery Administration, and the Supreme Court destroyed it. The answer to that is that the total recovery from the low of 1932 and the high of 1937 took place before and after the NRA. The NRA period was the one flat spot in those five years. It began in the middle of 1933 and ended in the first third of 1935. When it ended, all production, in mining, manufacturing and agriculture, was lower than when it began. Not only was it lower; it was declining.

Next in the order of the Rs was reform. That is, it was next when it was not first. There were times when the enthusiasm for reform was so high that if a little recovery had to be sacrificed for it, so much the worse for the wicked.

Reform had many aspects, because in a capitalistic society there were so many evils to be abolished. To abolish them all at once, first capitalism had to be tamed and shaved, clothed with social-mindedness and taught to think of people before profit; and then the entire economic life of the country had to be made over. But to do it the Government had to have more power; besides not to be afraid, and so, as the President said, there had to be "drastic changes in the methods and forms of the functions of Government."

Fighting a fight with one hand while making weapons with the other. You can see what a job it was. And what was to come of it?

The causes of depression were to be removed forever. The annual production of wealth was never again to be divided by the blind ferocities of competition, but hereafter by a benign, just, far-seeing intelligence. Supply and demand were to be brought into perfect balance; no more ruinous overproduction, nor ever again scarcity, but always exactly plenty, and the money in everyone's hand to buy it with. The comprehensive word for all this was "stability." There would be stability of money, stability of prices, stability of production and distribution, stability of employment, stability of purchasing power, once that had been apportioned according to a just social plan, and so, altogether a stability of economic happiness.

Well, stability turned out to be only something the chart makers at Washington had made a drawing of. In the last third of the fifth year, just while the floor of minimum

218

wages and the ceiling of maximum hours were about to be added to the temple, suddenly—

The stock market crashed.

Industrial production collapsed.

Purchasing power declined.

The number of unemployed began to rise by millions.

The most startling fact about this unexpected convulsion was that never in the history of free competitive capitalism had there been one of equal severity, not even in the year of the great panic, 1929. In twelve weeks more than one-third of the total average value of New York Stock Exchange securities was wiped out. From the high point of the year, steel production fell 80 per cent. The buying of motorcars declined by one-half. The rise in unemployment during the last two months was faster than in the corresponding worst two months of 1929.

At first the temple builders refused to believe it. When in early December, at a White House press conference, a correspondent asked what was to be done about the recession, the President said, "It is an assumption." At another press conference he charged the newspapers with spreading fear in the country. When asked what the newspapers would gain by doing that, the President said: "That is what I have been wondering."

Where was that far-seeing intelligence? It no more knew than any other that these things were going to happen; nor did it know why they happened.

Nevertheless, Secretary Ickes[2] and Assistant Attorney General Jackson[3] were sent to the radio to tell the people that the wicked rich, the monopolists, the corporate earls, the first sixty families of economic royalism, had done this thing to them again. These enemies of the New Deal had made away with the New Deal's prosperity. In their insatiable greed for profit, they had devoured the feast the New Deal had spread for the people; they were engaged in a conspiracy to destroy profit and ruin the country, themselves included, in order to wreck the New Deal.

The people knew better. Their reaction to these gross absurdities was disagreeable. Was that all the New Deal knew about its own stuff? How could the economic royalists have done it again, if they were following, not leading, as was to have been the new way of things?

And they were more confused by what followed. The economic royalists denounced by Ickes and Jackson began the next week to be called to the temple to discuss ways of mending prosperity in collaboration with the Government. The temple minds were thinking frantically. That was announced each day in the newspapers. But the news of what they were thinking became each day more bewildering.

The General Motors Corporation had laid off 30,000 employees. A Senate Committee on Unemployment sent for the head of the company to ask why he had done it. He said it was because people had stopped buying motorcars. The Senate committee asked him why he didn't cut the price so that people could buy more. Ha! Why hadn't he thought of that simple thing?

A few hours later the President was saying to the representatives of the motor industry and to the correspondents that the motor industry had been selling cars too fast, by the installment method, under high-pressure salesmanship, thereby using up the buying power the New Deal had distributed among the people.

That was a strange point of view. Never had high-pressure salesmanship been carried further than by the New Deal itself when it was putting posters in every post office urging people to buy electric ice boxes, oil burners, new wall paper, plumbing, anything they wanted for their houses, on credit, and the Government would guarantee their accounts at the bank. The New Deal, in fact, went into the installment finance business itself, directly, and is in it still, with a Federal corporation to finance the installment buying of "electric apparatus, equipment and appliances." That is the Electric Home and Farm Authority, capital $850,000, incorporated under the laws of the District of Columbia, entirely owned by the Federal Government.

Along with everything else in this strange debacle went agriculture. There the New Deal had guaranteed stability.

Now comes the Secretary of Agriculture, saying: "We are faced with an urgent necessity for expanding rural relief. The demand for Federal aid is being augmented daily by . . . an impending drought in certain areas, sagging farm prices, the rapid mechanization of agriculture and the industrial recession. Distress is growing rapidly and neither local nor Federal agencies have the means to cope with it."

Stability, exit!

The third R was for retribution. Retribution was for economic royalists, those brigands of the skyscrapers, whose greed and stupidity had been responsible for our 1929 "descent into economic hell." (Line from Fireside Chats.) They were to be cast out. No place was reserved for them in the temple. Indeed, they were forbidden to enter the premises. If they knew how to be good, or they were willing to learn, they would be permitted to follow. Never again should they lead. "They must either follow," the President said, "or shut up shop."

But when Secretary Ickes and Assistant Attorney General Jackson were sent to tell the people the wicked rich had done it to them again, they were obliged to admit the total failure of retribution.

Mr. Jackson said: "Certain groups of big business have now seized upon a recession in our prosperity to liquidate the New Deal . . . The blunt truth is that today we have in command of big business, by and large, the same Bourbons who were in command of the defeat of 1929, and who since then have learned nothing and forgotten nothing. When the Government through the RFC saved the capital structures of big business from going through the wringer it also saved many incompetent managements."

Mr. Ickes said: "Out of their divinely claimed genius as managers of private enterprise, the sixty families led the American people into the worst peace-time catastrophe ever known. Then the disillusioned people changed the Government. The new Government bailed the sixty families out of the consequences of their own mesmeric miscal-

221

culations . . . It preserved the corporate structures in which their capital was invested from going through the wringer . . . And what happened? . . . First the sixty families . . . proved to have learned nothing nor to have forgotten nothing since 1929 . . . Second, the sixty families . . . make . . . a threat that they will refuse to do business at all unless the President and the Congress and the people will repeal all that we have gained in the last five years . . ."

The truth is even more. Not only did the New Deal save the economic royalists and restore to them their capital and their profits; it suspended the one law that makes free competitive capitalism work to the greatest good, the law that obliges it to sacrifice its own economic royalists, the remorseless law that makes it pay for its own mistakes. What is that law? It is an implicit law, saying that those who take the profit shall also take the loss. Every capitalist knows that painful law, and that if it does not act, the consequences will be much worse than if it did. Yet knowing it, the individual capitalist is seldom willing himself to embrace it. Only necessity can make him do it. What the New Deal did was to annul that necessity.

Take the obvious case. In his book *On Our Way,* the President writes: "It is no exaggeration when I say that if the economic conditions of the winter of 1932-1933 had continued, practically every railroad in the United States would have been in the hands of a receiver in a short time."

Therefore, the Government intervened and loaned enormous sums of public credit to the railroads to save their capital structures.

In the first place, the economic conditions of that winter were not going to continue. The tide had already turned in the whole world. In the second place, suppose that every railroad that was insolvent had been let go into receivership. Where would the loss have fallen? Not upon the savings banks and the insurance companies and the private investors who owned the bonds; they were the creditors, they had been receiving interest, not profit, and in the end they should have been all not only safe but better off, because the railroads were easily worth their bonds. The loss would have fallen where it belonged—that is, upon the stockholders. They took that position by choice, because they wanted the profit—not interest, but dividends. They had had their profit, and having had their profit they were obliged to take the loss. No railroad would have stopped running. But a great deal of old and profitless capital would have been rubbed out and new capital would have come in for the sake of profit again, and the railroad situation today would not be the nightmare it is. Exactly this had happened again and again in our railroad history. At one time more than three quarters of our total railroad mileage was in receivership, and all of it came out, with no benefit of public credit. The loss was private.

The general situation in the winter of 1932-33 was that after four years of terrific and necessary deflation a great mass of obsolete, inflated and imaginary capital was about to be wiped out. It should have been wiped out. The entire economic body would have been hardier and healthier afterward.

But the New Deal was obsessed with the idea of using its new and magical money power to restore all prices and all values in one theatrical stroke.

The President writes that at this time he had in mind a picture—"showing two columns, one representing what the United States was worth in terms of dollars and the other representing what the United States owed in terms of dollars. The figures covered all property and all debts, public, corporate and individual. In 1929, the total of the assets in terms of dollars was much larger than the total of the debts. But by the spring of 1933, though the total of debts was still just as great, the total of the assets had shrunk to below that of the debts. Two courses were open: To cut down the debts through bankruptcies and foreclosures to such a point that they would be below property values; or else, to increase the property values until they were greater than the debts."

That is to say—one way was to write down the debts; the other way was to write up the assets.

The New Deal resolved to write up the dollar value of

223

the assets. The way to do that was to cheapen the dollar in which the assets were valued. Hence, debasement of the currency, called dollar devaluation, and then credit inflation, called reflation. Devaluation involved repudiation of the word of the United States Government engraved upon its bonds.

The New Deal, to be sure, was thinking of the little man. The difficulty was that you could not give the little man a sixty-cent dollar in which to price his assets, thereby easing him out of debt, and at the same time keep a dear dollar for the economic royalists. That simply would not work. All assets, big and little, had to be written up in terms of the sixty-cent dollar. Thus all capital structures were saved—that of the farmer along with that of the economic royalist.

Well, since the debts the United States owed it owed all to itself, and since it was all writing anyhow, what difference did it make whether you wrote down the debts or wrote up the assets? The difference is important. By writing up the assets the New Deal saved intact that great mass of obsolete, inflated and imaginary capital that was about to be wiped out and ought to have been wiped out—and we carry it still. It is all there on our backs. This alone would have been enough to limit recovery.

For the devout and the faithful, the roll of disappointments is heavy. Something must have been wrong from the beginning. Was there something wrong, perhaps, with the design of the temple?

In Fireside Chats the President gave a graphic description of it in the process of building. He spoke of the pillars, especially four.

The first was the pillar of relief. The nature of relief was such as had never been imagined before. There was unemployment relief, of course, amounting at length to an obligation on the part of the Government to provide a job for every person who wanted one and couldn't find it. Debtors came next; but as debtors were relieved, so also were the creditors. Mortgagor and mortgagee were both relieved.

224

One could pay his mortgage; the other could get his money. The Government itself took over farm mortgages. Banks were relieved of their frozen assets. The railroads were relieved. Home owners were relieved. No one was forgotten, or if one had been, he was to telegraph the Government about it. "I make the further request," said the President in Fireside Chat No. 4, "that if there is any family in the United States about to lose its home or about to lose its chattels, that family should telegraph at once either to the Farm Credit Administration or to the Home Owners Loan Corporation in Washington, requesting their help." And along with everyone else, the economic royalists were relieved, for otherwise, as the New Deal itself now says, they would have had to go through the wringer.

But this relief pillar was not to be permanent. It was for the duration of the emergency only. It was nothing more than a great prop. When the temple was finished, it could be kicked away. However, on the fifth anniversary it is still there. It has turned out, in fact, to be the most durable pillar of all. No one seems now able to imagine the absence of it—the absence, that is to say, of Federal relief in all hard situations.

The other three principal pillars, as the President described them, were the money pillar, the AAA pillar and the NRA pillar.

The money pillar is still there, supporting all the capital structures that were saved at the time, the good ones and the bad ones together. What else it supports is not easy to say. The belief that it was supporting stability and constancy of purchasing power has just been rudely shaken. One has almost forgotten that when it was erected it was supposed to support our foreign trade. That was absurd; nobody mentions it any more. It could not support reflated domestic prices and at the same time uphold our foreign trade.

The AAA pillar is both there and not there. It has a curious history. The Supreme Court ordered the first one out because it was not in right constitutional style. It was taken out, but another one very much like it was immedi-

225

ately substituted, and it was to support the same thing—
namely, the purchasing power of the farmer. And yet is has
never been quite right. No one has been satisfied with it,
neither the farmers nor the builders.

The NRA pillar was leaning badly and would perhaps
have fallen if the Supreme Court had not knocked it down.
The builders were both angry and relieved at that. They
had been having a lot of trouble with it and although they
hated to see it knocked down, still they never tried to make
a substitute for it. They made instead several small pillars
in the same design, as, for example, the little NRA for bitu-
minous coal.

Now there was one peculiarity about all of these pillars,
and it was that each one had a separate principle or purpose. Furthermore, their purposes were in conflict. It was
as if several groups of craftsmen were working separately,
each group intent upon its own pillar. The President had
some glimpse of this. In Fireside Chat No. 4, he said:
"Though for a moment the progress of one column may dis-
turb the progress on the pillar next to it, the work on all of
them must proceed without let or hindrance." But it is evident he was thinking only of interference on the job, not of
interference in principle.

What was the idea of the money pillar? It was to restore
all prices and values to somewhere near the predepression
level, or to write up the assets instead of writing down the
debts. The effects would be horizontal; all relations would
be restored to what they were before.

But what was the AAA pillar? The idea there was to
alter relations by producing a vertical price effect.
Specifically, the idea was to redistribute the national
income to give farmers a much larger share. It was to be
transferred to them in a wholesale manner, by restricting
production, raising prices and by paying cash subsidies out
of the United States Treasury. Transferred by whom and
from whom? By the hand of the New Deal and from that
part of the population that is urban and industrial. But you
cannot increase the total buying power of the nation by
taking income from one class and giving it to another, nor

226

can you transfer buying power from the industrial population to the agricultural part without a great row.

You may think that was a problem. It was no problem at all. Those who said it was a problem were the wicked scoffers who, as the President said, could shed crocodile tears over the destruction of little pigs. There was a fourth pillar coming. It was just arriving. It was the NRA.

What was the idea there? The idea there was to raise wages throughout industry, so that the industrial class could afford to buy the food the AAA was raising the price of, and to shorten the hours of labor, so that more people would have to be employed. Certainly this would raise the cost of manufacture. But that was all right. In another Fireside Chat the President said: "The proposition is simply this: If all employers will act together to shorten hours and raise wages we can put people back to work. No employer will suffer, because the relative level of competitive cost will advance by the same amount for all."

True, in that case, the industrial employer would not be hurt. But what about the farmers? Everything the farmer buys from industry will go up and the advantage he has been guaranteed by the AAA will be annulled. The NRA was undoing the work of the AAA.

You have, therefore, in the money pillar the idea of producing a horizontal price effect with the intent to restore all economic relations to what they were in predepression time; in the AAA pillar the idea of producing a special vertical price effect touching only agricultural commodities; and in the NRA pillar the idea of producing a compensating effect touching industrial prices only.

The construction was intellectual. Brains and theory did it. No journeyman hand could have done it. The hand would know better.

Yet with all these contradictions, the temple might have stood, as many temples do, askew, out of plumb, held together by the grace of good intention. What wrecked it was the only consistent thing about it, and that was an original economic fallacy rising to the proportions and power of a great popular delusion. A demon was imagined.

The name of it was production. Let go and running free, production devoured first its own wage slaves and then itself, but not itself entirely until it had wantonly ruined the paper wage structure from which we derive our sustenance, the paper price structure that supports our prosperity, and the paper capital structure that keeps us rich. To save these precious structures, to save people from want in the midst of plenty, to save, it may be, civilization itself, chain production down! The only concession to common sense was that the word *over* was often written before the name of the demon, thus: over-production.

The consequences of this delusion defeated true recovery. After four years of depression there was by 1933 an enormous deficit of things, every kind of thing. Yet a surplus measure of grain, a surplus pig, a surplus ton of steel or a surplus bolt of cloth was regarded as a social calamity. You can hardly think of an economic law enacted by the New Deal that did not intend, directly or indirectly, to limit the competitive production of the things that satisfy human wants. Why? Because it might hurt wages or prices.

Through the AAA the Government paid farmers to destroy the existing surplus and thereafter to limit production, and this was to raise the cost of food, while the Government at the same time was borrowing money to feed the unemployed.

In the NRA scheme, the antitrust laws were suspended in order that producers might legally enter into agreements with the Government and with one another to limit competition and limit production. The hours of labor were limited. The speed of wheels was limited. Even the hours of day a machine could work were limited. Additions to productive capacity were limited. Then all producers had to raise wages alike and raise prices alike in order to pay the higher wages, and price cutting was forbidden. Big industries were cracked down upon for breaking faith. A little tailor in Jersey City was put in jail for pressing a pair of pants at less than the fixed price.

Two very serious consequences were unnoticed at the time. One was that every existing plant, factory or store became a potential monopoly, because competition could not increase. The other was that all the weak, marginal, high-cost producers were sustained, which meant that industry and business were frozen on a high-cost plane; never could the cost of production have fallen if the Blue Eagle had continued to rule.

Well, but that was the ring in the demon's nose. High wages, high costs, high prices, limited competition and controlled production—that was the formula for recovery. The President himself expounded it.

In a speech at the Jefferson Day dinner at the National Democratic Club in New York, he said: "Other individuals are never satisfied. One of these, for example, belongs to a newly organized brain trust—not mine. He says that the only way to get full recovery is to lower prices by cheapening the costs of production. Let us reduce that to plain English. You can cheapen the costs of industrial production by two methods. One is by the development of new machinery and new technique and by increasing employee efficiency. We do not discourage that. But do not dodge the fact that this means fewer men employed and more men unemployed. The other way to reduce the costs of industrial production is to establish longer hours for the same pay or to reduce the pay for the same number of hours. If you lengthen hours you will need fewer workers. If you choose lower wages for the same number of hours, you cut the dollars in the pay envelope and automatically cut down the purchasing power of the worker himself. Reduction of costs in manufacture does not mean more purchasing power and more goods consumed. It means the opposite."

This was perhaps the most illuminating single statement ever made on the subject of New Deal doctrine. It reduces our economic history to the terms of a riddle.

Only ten years ago our European competitors were sending commissions to this country to see why it was that with the highest standard of common living in the world, we could compete in foreign markets against low-wage countries. They found out why. By technology, by method, by a prodigal use of mechanical power, we were continually reducing the costs of manufacture and at the same time raising wages. In seventy-five years the buying power of wages had increased threefold. Wages were high by comparison with anywhere else, and yet the actual labor cost was low because productivity was so much higher.

If this be not true, then the 25,000,000 motor cars you see in the highways are not there; it is all an illusion. The concrete highways are not there. We are still going about with the horse and buggy on dirt roads.

But the perfect answer was unexpected. It came from the President himself. When at last the New Deal faced the fact of a new depression, one of its own this time, the President thought of a national rehousing program to be sponsored by the Government. He unfolded the plan serially at White House press conferences, and came always to the one great obstacle. The cost of building was too high. That was it. Not only were building-material prices too high; wage rates in the building trades were too high. Prices must come down. If they did not come down obediently, the Government would drive them down; and it would be well for labor to see that if wage rates were reduced, there would be more work, and larger total earnings, for labor.

But why—if "reduction of costs of manufacture does not mean more purchasing power and more goods consumed"? Why—if "it means just the opposite"?

Here it might seem that what had been the only consistent thing about the temple—that unlimited production was a social curse—was beginning to give way. It was probable, however, that an inconsistency occurred only where the President was thinking of a new pillar. Elsewhere it seemed to be holding.

One special product of the delusion was the idea that there was too much saving and not enough spending. Little people going to the savings bank with their money—that was perhaps all right, except that if they had the social security to which they were entitled, they wouldn't need to do it. But when the great corporations practiced saving, by withholding their profits instead of paying them out in dividends, that was economically and socially wrong, because everyday purchasing power was thereby reduced.

And what did such great corporations do with their undistributed profits? One of two things. Either they built up enormous idle reserves, which gave them too much financial power, or they used them to build more plant and equipment, the effect of which was both to nullify their profits and to cause excess production.

"The use of undistributed profits must be controlled," said one of the brain trust. "Any system of planning would have not only to hedge them about with restrictions, but to direct their uses—if by that time it had not been made impossible for them to be accumulated."

In his message to Congress, January 3, 1934, the President himself referred to "the unnecessary expansion of industrial plant" as wasteful and antisocial, and said, "We must make sure that as we reconstruct our life there be no soil in which such weeds can grow again."

Industrial plant expansion meant more production and lower costs; it meant also the destruction somewhere of obsolete capital producing at higher costs. The demon again!

Whereon it was that after NRA had failed, the famous law taxing undistributed profits was enacted. A corporation that did not pay out its profits in dividends was obliged to hand as much as one-third of them over to the Government. There was revenue from this tax, to be sure, but besides the revenue from it there was the calculated effect that it put a new ring in the nose of the demon. This heavily handicapped what the President had called "the unnecessary expansion of industrial plant" out of profits.

There are two ways in which industrial capacity may be expanded. One way is with new capital; the other way is to do it with profits, and for the last way American industry was famous. Expanding the means of further production out of the profits of past production is a certain way to reduce the cost of manufacture, because on the profits you put back in your business you have to pay neither interest nor dividends. In a rough guess, one quarter of the industrial capacity of the country was so created. And it is enough more to say of the principle of a punitive tax on undistributed profits that it would make another Ford impossible, who did it out of profits; it would make another Chrysler impossible, who crashed into the motor industry with a shoestring of capital and rose to third place in it by putting back more profit than he took out; it would make another Fink impossible, who during the depression created the Federal Steel Company, or another E. T. Weir who years ago started out to compete with United States Steel with a capital of only $15,000 and built the Weirton Steel Company. And again like the NRA, the undistributed-profits tax tended to create monopoly by discouraging new competition.

In these ways the New Deal has crippled the free competitive system that was working in this country, and working, with all its faults, better than any other system that was ever known. In these ways it has been destroying what was unique in the American economic system. Either it did not know what it was doing, or did not know what else to do, and borrowed at random from the Old World systems, social security and unemployment insurance from one, planning from another, parts of a corporate-state principle from another, and so on.

For five years there has been no American system. What we have been watching is the experiment of trying to make captive capitalism work, conducted by a Government that only half believes in it and yet has not the daring to destroy it.

There is modern backing for much of Garrett's analysis. In "New Deal Policies and the Persistence of the Great Depression," a paper published Jan. 2000 by the Federal Reserve Bank of Minneapolis, economists Harold L. Cole and Lee E. Ohanian argue that employment should have returned to its historical trend by 1936 with wages below trend until 1939. But by 1939 unemployment was still high, real output was 25% below trend, and real wages in manufacturing were 20% above trend. Ohanian told an interviewer in April 2000 that using his model, the New Deal's high-wage policy accounted for about 60% of the economy's shortfall in the late 1930s.

In "Regime Uncertainty: Why the Great Depression Lasted So Long and Why Prosperity Resumed After the War," (The Independent Review, *Spring 1997) economist Robert Higgs offers a modern version of the argument from "business confidence." Higgs uses intriguing data—a Fortune Magazine poll, historical accounts and the yield curve on bonds —to argue that fear for the political safety of capital retarded long-term investment from 1935 to 1941*

---

[1]The statistics for industrial production in 1937, with 1929=100, are:

France	82.8
Poland	85.3
Netherlands	90.9
United States	92.2
Belgium	93.6
Czechoslovakia	96.3
Canada	99.5
Italy	99.6
Austria	106.0
Germany	117.2
United Kingdom	124.0
Norway	127.6
Chile	131.6
Romania	131.7
Denmark	134.0
Hungary	137.3
Estonia	138.7
Sweden	149.0
Finland	149.2
Latvia	155.9
Japan	170.8

(Source: Gary Dean Best, *Pride, Prejudice and Politics*)

France endured a 25% deflation, 1931-1936, then elected a "popular front" government that included Communists and Socialists, which began following left-wing labor policies.

[2]Harold Ickes, 1874-1952, Roosevelt's Secretary of the Interior, 1933-1946, and head of the Public Works Administration, 1933-1939. One of the most combative New Dealers, Ickes resigned in 1946 in protest over President Truman's appointment of an oil man to a Navy post. His son, also Harold Ickes, was deputy Chief of Staff, 1994-1996, for President Clinton.

[3]Robert H. Jackson, 1892-1954, general counsel to the IRS, 1934-1936, assistant U.S. attorney general, 1936-1938, U.S. solicitor general, 1938-1939, U.S. attorney general, 1940-1941. Jackson was an fervent New Dealer, and testified in Congress in favor of Roosevelt's court packing plan. Roosevelt appointed him to the Supreme Court in 1941. Jackson supported the New Deal laws, but balked in 1952 when President Truman's seized the steel mills without Congressional authorization, and joined the majority in declaring Truman's act unconstitutional.

CHAPTER FIFTEEN:

The Perfect Closed-Shop Town

As labor rose in power, the question was: Power for what? To create a new social system? Or to make labor more powerful within the existing one? In 1919, when Seattle was convulsed by the nation's first general strike—an emotional seizure by socialists, Wobblies and more traditional labor, following along—young Dave Beck advised his laundry workers' union to keep working. Beck was a practical man. He had no use for "fuzzy-headed" Bolsheviks.

In the 1930s, Beck battled for control of Seattle labor with Harry Bridges, the communist boss of the International Longshoremen's and Warehousemen's Union. With the uneasy backing of the local establishment, Beck won the most turf. Garrett visited him at the height of his power.

From "Labor at the Golden Gate," March 18, 1939

Seattle is the perfect closed-shop town. The power is in the hand of one man. His name is Beck. He derives the power originally from the teamsters. But you may have a very dim notion of who the teamsters are.

Long ago the International Brotherhood of Teamsters

became the most formidable union in the American Federation of Labor. That was owing partly to the nature of teamsters and the superiority of guerrilla over mass tactics for their purposes, but much more to the fact that they controlled both the first mile and the last mile of nearly all transportation. Always, therefore, a strike of the teamsters was a public evil to be avoided at any reasonable cost. Then teamsters became truck drivers and their stature was many times magnified. In the modern case, the power to let or hinder deliveries is the power to paralyze a city. The teamsters of Seattle have it; upon it has been built the union structure that makes Seattle the ideal union town.

And still you do not know who the teamsters are. In the whole city you might be unable to find a teamster who drives a team. The meaning of the word has been forgotten. Truck drivers, bus drivers, taxicab drivers, brewery drivers, laundry drivers, milk drivers, bakery drivers, they are all teamsters, as you would suppose; but by adoption and affiliation, so are longshoremen, warehousemen, retail clerks, barbers, hairdressers, waiters and waitresses, cooks, elevator men, bellhops, dyers and cleaners, tailors, laundry and brewery workers, bakers, bookkeepers, garage mechanics, even automobile salesmen. Members of the Newspaper Guild were teamsters for a while. But after the teamsters had seen them through a strike, they went C.I.O., which taught the Teamsters hereafter to stick to a kind of people they know more about.

With that exception, all organized wage earners may become teamsters by sharing the teamsters' tent and accepting the rule of Beck, who, besides being boss of the teamsters, is the No. 1 American Federation of Labor organizer on the West Coast. He rules with a hard hand. Perhaps nowhere else is labor so sternly disciplined for its own good and for the uses of unionism. Service is commanded. If it is not forthcoming, there is a penalty to be paid in cash, as, for example, a fine for failure to attend meetings or failure to take one's place in picket lines and labor parades. There is grumbling, naturally. The governed must be permitted to grumble. Those who really complain,

236

however, are the few who in every situation prefer free competition because they can always stay on top. They are leveled down. But the lot of mediocrity is made better, and mediocrity is the great middle. If you ask what it is in return that Beck does for labor, it is that and much more. Not only does he mind its wages and hours and conditions; not only does he think for it. Standing between labor and business, he governs a closed-shop town.

There is nothing oblique about it. Given the premise of a closed-shop town, it is reasonable. He has no feud with business. He believes in it and understands it. He demands only that it shall reconcile itself to the facts. In that case he will be helpful. He will do things for business that business cannot do for itself.

The hotel men of Seattle were fearful of a strike that might do to them what a strike was doing to the hotels of San Francisco. They appealed to Beck. He made all hotel employees teamsters—in separate unions, of course—then he fixed wages at what the hotels could afford to pay, which was just at the point of ouch; appointed hours and conditions, imposed discipline. There was no strike. The hotel men, half hating him, all trusting him, were properly grateful.

The department stores of Seattle asked him to organize their employees; they were afraid the C.I.O. was going to do it, and they preferred the A.F. of L. and Beck. The grounds of that preference are well known. The A. F. of L. has a better tradition of discipline and contract keeping; moreover, whatever else may be said about Beck, it is common testimony that his word is good. So again he was helpful and business was grateful for what it may have considered the lesser of two evils.

There was milk trouble. One day the Seattle milk-processing industry—condensed milk, powdered milk, cheese, ice cream, and so on—came to Beck saying the farmers were spilling one another's milk out on the highways. Could he do anything about it? He said he would look into it. Until then his only interest in milk had been that the city milk-route drivers were teamsters. The situation he

237

looked into was this: There were two prices for milk—one for milk that went into bottles on a city's milk routes, and a much lower price for what was called dump milk, meaning milk that went for the processing industry; and there was of this such a surplus that the price of it had fallen very low. The farmers had been trying to help themselves. They had got up an organization in which it was agreed that each member should take only his allotted share of the profitable bottled-milk trade and sell his remainder at the dump price, for if they went on competing with one another at the milk dealer's door, they were likely all to be ruined.

But there were independent farmers who insisted on their right to take all the bottled-milk trade they could get, and theirs was the milk the organized farmers were spilling. The first thing Beck did was to determine at what price everybody could hope to make a little money. To the price of bottled milk he added half a cent a quart; the price of dump milk, which had gone much too low, was doubled. Then he announced that a farmer bringing milk to Seattle could sell only his quota to the bottled-milk trade, and no more; the rest he could sell at the common dump price, or take it home. And that was for all farmers. So it was settled in that fair manner.

But do you see why that settled it? Beck's power had been substituted for the inferior power of the organized farmers. Before that, the independent farmer who could fight his way through the organization and get his milk to the city could sell it there at any price he liked. But after Beck came into it, he couldn't. Why not? Because no milk dealer in Seattle would buy it at any price. And why? Because no teamster would touch it.

That was an act of government. No law had to be passed. The AAA might envy the simplicity and neatness of it.

Detroit used to send its cars to Seattle by the caravan method. That is, it found men who wanted to go West and let them drive the new cars out in a string, instead of shipping them by freight. Beck looked at this and thought it bad. One day he stopped a caravan at the city line and found that among all the drivers there was less than two dollars cash. What were they going to do when they had delivered the cars? How were they going to live? They didn't know. Some would go on relief; some would be looking for jobs in a closed-shop town. So he stopped it. And how simple that was. He had only to say so, and no teamster garage mechanic would touch a car that had arrived by caravan; no teamster automobile salesman would sell one. Another act of government. No law required.

Going to and fro in his dominion he saw an odd thing. California was sending oranges to Seattle by truck, and the cost was but the oil and gas; the same trucks then loaded fish for the return and charged enough to make the round trip pay. That made an unfair exchange of oranges for fish, because the fish had to pay for its own haul and the oranges too. He stopped it. How did he stop it? By word to the teamsters.

One of the acute difficulties of intelligent government is to make people see what is good for them. The laundry workers wanted an increase of five dollars a week, and asked Beck to get it for them. He said he would see. Then he did what he frequently does in such matters. With his own accountants he went into the books of the laundry business. With what he found there he faced the laundry workers, who were expecting him to bring them their increase—else what was a teamster boss for?—and said to them that he was against it. His was a voice like a small nasal siren instructing them in elementary economic sense, saying the laundry business was in a slump because women were doing their own washing, that a teamster couldn't make his own wife send the wash to the laundry if she didn't want to, and that if they got their pay raised and that were added to the prices on the laundry slip, still more women would do their own washing and there would be fewer laundry jobs. Which would they have? More pay with fewer jobs, or let bad enough alone? They voted to keep their jobs.

A similar case had another kind of sequel. His brewery

239

teamsters wanted more pay. He went into the books of the brewing industry and was persuaded that it could not afford to raise wages. He told his teamsters so. "We can get it," he said. "We have that power. But remember, the brewing industry has to make a profit, too. If it can't make a profit, there will be fewer brewery drivers." The teamsters were very reasonable about it. Not long after that, one of the breweries cut the price of beer. He went back in anger, saying: "So this is the industry that couldn't afford to raise wages. All right. Make any price for beer you like, but now we take for the teamsters that increase we waived a while ago." The price cut was canceled. More than that, the Seattle brewing industry was saved from a price war. And all the brewers but one were grateful.

As it works, so it works. Business, on the whole, is resigned, both with and without secret and bitter reservations. Comprehend that a closed-shop town is a conquered town. The fight has been fought and labor has established its monopoly. Then, if everybody will accept the facts in a reasonable way, and provided there is room in one head for both the sense of much power and a little wisdom, it can be made to work, at least a while, and not without compensations as to make some parts of business embrace it.

Those are the terms on which the business of Seattle collaborates with Beck. He does what he says he will do. When prices are fixed, they stay fixed. The policing of them goes to the point that the tags on garments hanging in the shops of dyers and cleaners are inspected. That is not to protect labor. It is to do something for the dyers and cleaners that they cannot do for themselves. They could not police their own prices.

Simply, labor is concerned to maintain a wage structure; business is concerned to limit competition. This is the compound monopoly.

Seattle, as you might guess, is a dear city. Prices are high, wages are high, and yet not beyond reason; and the weight of prices is so distributed that, for example, milk is not too dear, nor is bread, but taxicab fares are high enough

to make walking a spiteful pleasure. Taxicab teamsters are guaranteed five dollars a day. You may say that if fares were lower, more people would ride and there would be more taxicab jobs, but if that is to be argued, let it pass.

You are coming to the teamsters' tent. At a glance you might take it to be the administration building of a large business, and so, in fact, it is, for labor now is big business. When you come to the center of a live web, there is a certain feeling of it. That feeling is here. There is activity of many kinds, stir of coming and going, pressure of errands beginning and ending, the ant-like business of business— business of the teamsters, business of the affiliated unions, business of making and keeping records, business of accounting and bookkeeping by a bank method, business with business, and a great deal of that, if you could see it. The walls are paneled with pickled walnut.

Mr. Dave Beck is on the second floor. If there is anyone with him, you will hear him before you see him. He sits in a corner with his back to the widows; on the desk in front of him, besides telephones, is the voice box for effortless intercommunication. He is short and thick, with hard edges, very tight in his skin, redheaded complexion, blue eyes and blond eyelashes. One of the human-terrier breed, daring but cautious, quick to take and to give offense, friendly otherwise, very fond of combat, but not a killer.

His thoughts are the very shape of himself and have fist in them. He is communicative. His ideas are clear; and what a teamster tongue can do with a clear idea is to be envied. Thinking apparatus and motor mechanism are enmeshed, so that he has to move to think. His first asset is an intense, unencumbered, natural intelligence, the unaccountable gift, and few who know him, or who have bargained with him, will make the mistake to underrate it. He keeps the world in simple view. Such terms as "fair" and "reasonable" are as definite as numerical signs. Thus, if you should say to him, "With what you are doing here you are bound to have some philosophy of competition," he would say, "I believe in competition. Certainly. Only I say it must be fair and reasonable." And that settles it entirely.

On his wrist he wears a costly watch engraved with words of gratitude from the hotel men of Seattle for his helpfulness to them; he exhibits this token in the act of complaining that business does not publicly acknowledge the truth about the benefits of collaboration. Doesn't it bring its problems to him, its own problems? Doesn't it sit in that chair where you are sitting, asking him to do things it cannot do for itself? And doesn't he do them? He is for business; he is for the profit system. The conviction to which he refers everything else is that business must make a profit or else nobody will have a job. Only, of course, it must be a reasonable profit. When he is hammering a union on the head to make it reasonable, he says, "If you want to talk about Russia or settle anything in Spain, get out. This is unionism." And his idea of unionism is that it shall concern itself with wages, hours and conditions of labor. He does not believe in a labor party. Unionism and politics make a bad mix. Many things are wrong. You cannot make them right by shock. Reform must take a reasonable time. Even such a thing as the pecan industry, paying ten cents an hour, cannot be reformed by shock.

If you should say to him, "This is power you are playing with—unelected, arbitrary power," he would wait to see if you were going to make some more sense. Then, if you should go on and ask, "How many labor leaders on the Pacific Coast would you be personally willing to trust with the power you exercise?" he would answer: "I think about it. Labor ought not to have absolute power. For its own sake. What it ought to have is the balance of power to trade with."

You might go a good deal farther, and say to him: "Suppose then it works. Suppose that after this Dave Beck there will be another and still another. Wages are right, prices are right, everybody makes reasonable profits. Therefore, peace and stability. But are you sure that under such happy conditions Seattle would not decay at the roots? What incentive would there be for a man to improve his methods, to risk his capital in new machinery to cheapen the cost of producing the satisfactions of life in order

242

that people may enjoy more of them? What is to save you from becoming a static community, entirely at rest, then presently obsolete?" To that he would say, "I have thought of all that. I don't know the answer. It hasn't happened yet. If it does, we'll have to think of a way to deal with it."

Beck remained a power in the city through the 1940s and went on to become international president of the Teamsters in 1952. He was brought down by an income-tax investigation during the Eisenhower administration with the help of young Robert F. Kennedy. From 1962 to 1964 Beck was imprisoned in the federal penitentiary on McNeil Island. He died in 1993.

Downtown Seattle looked like 1929 until the 1960s. Historian Roger Sale wrote in Seattle: Past to Present *(1976) of Beck's no-chiseling policy: "This made labor costs high, rewarded existing businesses, but discouraged everyone else." At the opening of the 21st century, Seattle remains a union town relative to most American cities, but unions have nothing like the power Beck wielded. So far, unions have had little headway in organizing such New Economy enterprises as Microsoft, Starbucks and Amazon.com.*

CHAPTER SIXTEEN:
Pharaohs

Garrett had no use for the Tennessee Valley Authority, the New Deal's first experiment in public power. In "Explorations in Our First Federal Province," May 28, 1938, he wrote, "TVA is above control. People cannot vote either for it or against it. When it fixes power rates, they are fixed; no state utilities commission can touch them." He would have said the same about the Bonneville Power Administration, which markets the power from the Columbia River dams. But the dams themselves were bold efforts to conquer nature. The hydropower they provided would animate millions of machines, contradicting the NRA, which had sought to subdue the machine. In this piece, Garrett sets aside political questions and extols the engineers and their work.

From "Great Works"
April 8, 1939

When there is a surplus of food, labor, materials and money, the conditions are present under which Solomon builds his temple, the Pharaohs make their eternal tombs and the Greeks freeze Athens in her immortal beauty; and the great builders have always seemed to be in haste with it, as if they were afraid something was going to happen.

Those conditions are now present with us, and we arrive in the appointed way at the monumental phase of our culture. We are building the things we shall leave behind us.

It is not unlikely that those who come after us will be much less impressed by our functional works, for in these a pure grandeur of form is appearing, unlike any form that was in the world before. It occurs in a manner so incidental to the purpose, and we are so preoccupied with size and power and what the thing is for, that we see it very dimly. In the litter and process of creation are magnificent vanishing forms, never to be seen anywhere again; and there are forms of yet a third kind, which are unpredictable compositions of scene and movement that have the quality of aesthetic events; but if a photographer happens to fix one of them in black and white, it is only to illustrate progress.

In a picture textbook on the building of Grand Coulee dam, produced by the Department of the Interior, there is a shot of the work going on in the dark. It is the incredible midnight carnival of the engineers. In a canyon lighted like a stage they are rolling the Columbia River first to one side and then the other, getting ready to lift it; the purpose of lifting it is to break it over an artificial precipice twice as high as Niagara. It is not necessary to know what they are doing. The sense of its drama, music and operatic quality may be stronger for not knowing; more than that it is man acting upon his environment to alter it, under some idea of economic necessity so very urgent that he cannot wait for daylight. You may wonder where God is standing to look and what He is thinking about it. The caption beneath this picture in the book reads: "Under powerful lights covering an area three miles long, work on the base of the dam went on night and day without interruption."

Why?

The engineers themselves see the amazing beauty of it only in moments of abstraction. Their minds are absorbed in the action; their chief excitement is in beating time. To move a mountain is nothing. You could move a mountain with pick and shovel if you took the time. But to move it a mile and dump it upside down in a vacant canyon at the rate of two or three tons a minute, day and night continuously, that is something that speaks of tools and methods, and is suitable for an article in the engineering journals.

The popular theme is bigness. Here is the biggest thing on earth in the way of a man-made structure. It is so big you cannot see it. Can the ant see the elephant? The young man who makes the lecture twice a day at the grandstand on the edge of the canyon, where the tourists come to look, has a nest of little *papier-mâché* models: the first one showing how it looked around here when the engineers came; the next one how it was when they had made themselves room and got down to bedrock; the next one, what you see now, with the dam half finished; then the last one as it will be when it is done, with a highway along the top. On the highway the man places an object half the size of a peanut and says, "That's the biggest automobile of any kind you are driving."

He tells you the concrete in the dam will weigh twice as much as all the people in the United States. He means that if you stood all the people in the United States on one end of a seesaw and dropped Grand Coulee dam on the other, the people would fly off in an arc through the sky. He says the dam will occupy more space than all the people in the United States, by which he probably means that if they were all liquefied and poured into a mold the size of the dam, they wouldn't fill it. He says the lake behind the dam, 151 miles long, will contain 10,000,000 acre-feet of water, which would be 2000 gallons for each human being on earth.

But is it wonderful that we should be building the biggest thing in the world, something bigger than the Egyptians or the Chinese were able to build before the coming of Christ, with hand labor, with no power tools? If that were the feat, we might do better modestly to take it for granted. Magnitude as a physical fact is simple. There is no argument about it. You can measure it. But magnitude is also a relative fact, involved with time.

247

As you look at the colossal works of the past, you ask, "How long did it take?" That is more of a question than you think. It is to ask how long it took in their way to bring to bear upon this task the amount of energy required to perform it. Herodotus says it took the energy of 100,000 men working twenty years to build the Great Pyramid. With the same Egyptian tools and 100,000 men we might be able to build a dam as big as Grand Coulee in forty years, but it would not be worth doing. Rich as we are, we could not afford it. We should be wasting our time. Our time is dear. Egyptian time was slave time and very cheap.

For magnitude in a time dimension, Grand Coulee is so much bigger than any ancient colossus that one would hardly know how to make the comparison. There is no formula for it. To turn the Columbia River lion over on his side and tie him there, as a preliminary, was no engineering miracle; to do it in ninety days was. To mold in the form of concrete the biggest single stone mass in the world need be a matter only of patient accretion, but to do it against a stop watch at the rate of two tons every five and a half seconds is marvelous.

Take the energy of 100,000 Egyptians to equal 10,000 horsepower. How is that amount of energy brought to bear on Grand Coulee dam? Instead of taking 100,000 men to work forty years in the Columbia River canyon, or 10,000 horses that couldn't be worked there at all, the engineer now carries a wire across the desert and dangles it in the canyon. Here, then, is the first wonder—the concentration and transmission of energy.

Now, what does the engineer do with the energy to be plucked from the end of his wire? First he sets up a light circuit in order to be able to work at night. Time of night is thereby added to time of day. Then he ties the wire to a motor and the motor drives an articulated automatic tool that may already be a mile long and is extensible. This tool is a mechanical serpent that, for all we know, may become mythical thousands of years hence. The head of it attacks a conglomerate mountain and devours it in a continuous stream; the internal organs of it crush the conglomerate, wash it clean, and divide it into several streams, one of sand, one of three-quarter-inch stone, one of one-and-one-half-inch stone, and so on up to three-inch size; and then, through a long intestinal tract, it delivers all this digested material in the exact quantities desired to the concrete mixer on the dam site.

You have now the second wonder, which is the mechanical slave—this one but one of many—called the belt-conveyor system.

None of this would be possible without another set of very delicate mechanisms acting over all as a nervous system. This you do not see, or, seeing it, you will not understand it unless you possess technical knowledge of it, and even then you will be able to say only how it works, and no more why it works than you know why your own nervous system works as it does.

Somewhere sits a man in a green eyeshade, gazing at dials, tubes, a panel of winking lights, the zigzag marks made by a pen all of itself on a moving piece of paper. He cannot see the work on the face of the dam; it is too far away. Yet by the readings before him he knows every minute what the state of it is and what materials are wanted. He cannot see the mechanical serpent either: he only controls it. By pushing a button or moving a level he causes it to deliver sand and crushed stone in certain quantities and proportions, and as it does so its response is recorded by nerve reflexes on his instrument board. To make concrete, you add water and cement to sand and crushed stone, and mix them thoroughly. Where is the cement? It is a manufactured product and comes by rail to the opposite side of the canyon and is stored there in a great silo. From the silo to the tail of the mechanical serpent is a pipe more than a mile long across the canyon. The man in the green eyeshade on this side makes a light signal to the man at the cement silo on the other side; the man over there moves a lever, a compressed-air machine blowing into the pipe says, "P-o-o-h," and the cement arrives at the mixing machine. The man in the green eyeshade touches another lever. The mixing machine, in a series of solitary convulsions, opens its mouth, swallows water, cement, sand and crushed stone, churns the mix and spews it into enormous buckets standing on a train of flatcars; when the buckets are full, the train moves out on the steel trestle over the face of the dam, the buckets are swung down by crane and cable, and presently another concrete brick has been molded in place, each brick having the area of a city building lot, five feet thick. And this is the third wonder, named control. Remote magnetic control of all that energy leaping in thousands of horsepower from the end of a wire, and all of the automatic tools it drives.

The three articles of wonder are in the order named—transmission, automatism, control. A fourth one follows, which is the nonchalant audacity with which now we push Nature around, as you will see the engineers doing at Grand Coulee. More than to push her around, we play low tricks upon her. The Grand Coulee idea is an astonishing trick.

Fed by ice and snow, the Columbia River rises in British Columbia, enters the United States by the northeastern corner of the state of Washington and cuts its way through the mountains to the Pacific Ocean. Of the fast rivers it is the largest on the continent; it is second in point of flow only to the slow Mississippi.

After millions of years it had made itself a nice comfortable canyon bed 1000 feet deep in lava rock and solid granite. Then came a glacier out of the north and poked its nose into the canyon, stopping it up at just where the Department of Interior would some day wish to build the largest dam in the world. What the glacier did was to lift the river up and out of bed. It rolled out over the rim of the canyon onto a high plateau, and there, in a gnashing rage, went about making another bed for itself, digging it in some places 1000 feet deep and grinding into silt an amount of earth material which, if it were heaped up in a pile, would be forty miles square and forty miles high. It was a very mighty river then. At one place up there on the plateau it made a waterfall one hundred times bigger than Niagara.

But it never liked this high bed, and when the glacier went away, it returned to its old one down below, leaving the high one dry. Now, in that high, abandoned dry bed, besides the spectacle that is called the dry falls, are the many weird and awful effects of free erosion before there was any AAA to forbid it. That forty cubic miles of earth gouged out and ground up by the river was deposited in the form of silt over a large, fairly flat area, and that area now is fertile, or would be if it had any water. We found it there and named it the Big Bend country, at a time, unfortunately, when rainfall was more than normal. The railroads made a land boom on it. Thousands of settlers rushed in to plant bonanza wheat. Many of the forsaken farmhouses are still there, falling down. Ever since then the Northwest empire builders have been dreaming of ways to lead water to the Big Bend Country by canals. They could think of many ways, but they were all too costly—that is, the cost of the water would have been more than irrigated agriculture could afford to pay—until the Government got the idea of the multiple-purpose dam, which is a dam to control the floods, to aid navigation, to provide water for irrigation, and to produce cheap hydroelectric power for the people, all in one time, with the argument that profits from the power business will make it possible to provide water for irrigation at a price that agriculture can afford to pay; besides, that by the same stroke the wicked power trust will be cut off at the pocket.

With this idea to work on, the engineers went again to look. Physically it would be possible to lift the river so high that it would flow again into the high dry bed it didn't like, and from there it could be led by canals to the fertile Big Bend country. Practically that thought was no good, because if the dam were that high, the lake behind it would back up into British Columbia, besides flooding many towns and cities, even Spokane.

"No," said the engineers, "but since only about one seventh of the river is needed to irrigate the Big Bend country,

251

this is what we can do. Say the total lift from where the river is to where it was is 635 feet. Well, with a dam down here in the canyon, we can safely raise it 355 feet, and then we can make it lift one seventh of itself another 285 feet for nothing. How? With such a dam we can produce hydroelectric energy equal to 2,500,000 horsepower. Then we can go up there in the old dry bed and stop one of the gorges at both ends to make a reservoir. With only a part of our horsepower we can pump water into the reservoir up there, and from the reservoir we can take the water by canal to more than 1,000,000 acres of that fertile land."

And that is the trick. First to dam the river and force it through turbine wheels to produce 2,500,000 horsepower of energy; then to make it lift one seventh of itself to irrigate maybe 30,000 farms.

But after it has done all this, after it has been obliged to split off one seventh of itself and give it to economic slavery, what is left to go over the top of the dam will represent 32,000,000 horsepower. It may be thinking that that much of itself will still be free to take revenge. It does not know. These 32,000,000 horsepower will be caught in a silly concrete trap called a surge bucket at the base of the dam, and all thought of revenge will be churned out. If then the river thinks that anyhow the worst has happened, it is wrong again, for in a little while it will come to Bonneville dam. It is intended that there should be ten dams between Grand Coulee and the Pacific Ocean.

Such pumps as will lift one seventh of the Columbia River over the rim of the canyon have never been built in the world. No one worries over a trifle like that. No one doubts that they can be built and that they will work. The lift will be more than 250 feet through rock tunnels, each thirteen feet in diameter. The capacity of the pumps will be 16,000 second-feet. A second-foot means one cubic foot of water passing a point in one second. A flow of 16,000 second-feet would cover an acre of ground with water one foot deep in less than three seconds. And yet to drive such pumps, less than one-half the hydroelectric power produced at the dam will be required.

Bonneville dam, now finished, is in the lower Columbia River, 140 miles from its mouth at tidewater. Ocean-going vessels are expected to navigate the river beyond this point. How shall an ocean-going vessel get over a seventy-foot dam? For this purpose the highest lock in the world is provided. A ship lock is a chamber—this one 500 feet long by 76 feet wide—with gates at the ends. Suppose a vessel is coming upstream. The upper gate is closed to hold back a seventy-foot wall of water while the lock is emptied until the water is down to the level of the river below. The lower gate is opened, the vessel moves in, the gate is closed behind it, water from above is admitted until the water in the lock is again level with the river ahead. Then the upper gate is opened and the vessel goes on.

Here the refinements of remote control are carried to a high point. What you see gives you a hollow, dispensed-with feeling in your middle. You are standing at the lower end of the lock and a vessel is coming upstream to go through. The lock is full; the level of the water in it is higher than the smokestack of the approaching vessel. Looking down on the outside of the gate, you see the water at river level, a dizzy seventy feet below. Suddenly, down there, begins a roaring agitation as the great valves beneath the gate are opened to let the water out of the lock. You see the water in the lock falling, When it has fallen to the lower river level, the roaring stops. Then the gate, which is in two leaves like a double door, begins to swing open, until they stand wide open for the vessel to come in.

All of this has taken place as if it were a natural event, like the time come in and going out, with no visible human intervention. The gate is 102 feet high; each of its two halves weighs 525 tons. For all you can see, it has silently closed and opened itself in an effortless manner. That is control. The man in the control station does not witness the effects. He could be fifty miles away. He has before him a battery of switches and push buttons and a panel of winking lights.

In the powerhouse near by, turbine wheels and generators weighing hundreds of tons revolve like singing tops, each unit on a vertical steel shaft larger than the trunk of an old oak tree, each unit converting the energy of falling water into 60,000 horsepower of the cheap electric current that will improve the lives of the people by casting out human drudgery. Here again you have the appearance of machines minding themselves by their own intelligence.

With a great primary engine that must not stop, you associate the figure of a man whose relation to it is one of moody, pessimistic vigilance, watching, listening, touching it here and there to make sure it is running cool and free of pain. This veterinary, acting by his senses and intuition upon a dumb mechanical power, now is dispensed with. That way is no longer scientific and, moreover, the machine is no longer dumb. These prime movers talk. Their language is precisely translated. Speeds, pressures, temperatures, frictions, soreness, even the state of the lubricating fluid in their joints, are all recorded upon sensitive instruments in a distant control room. If anything goes wrong, there is an alarm. If nothing is done about it, there is a more urgent alarm. If still nothing is done about it, the machines will stop themselves. That ought never to happen, of course; it would happen only if the man in the control room should happen to fall asleep, but even this contingency is thought of, for if he falls asleep, that fact will be automatically recorded and there will be an alarm of another kind.

Remote control is a new science, coming suddenly. Concerning its inventions there is a curious fact that we cannot realize them as objects. Thus it seems probable that if we leave them behind us they will be lost. We have tried to think of them as mechanical men, calling them robots, but that is silly. What is it we see? Only the effects. It is as if an invisible hand were acting, but when you come to the hand, it has no form that can be seized or defined as an image; and to aesthetic perception it is lost for the further reason that the meaning is apart from it, existing only in the effects. What is it? A tube, a coil of wire, a photoelectric cell, or two pieces of thin metal making a bridge in a little glass box. A man controlling one wild horse may be represented in a painting or sculpture in a way to give us a feeling of the race imposing its will upon Nature to conquer and tame it. But there is as yet no art form whereby to evoke that feeling in the figure of a man sitting at ease before a panel of pushbuttons controlling a million horsepower of Nature's wild energy.

We may be rough and domineering with rivers, thinking they have neither instinct nor vital principle. Not so with life; in this case, fish life. The Columbia is the great salmon river of the world. Each year the salmon that have matured in the vast deep return to the river to cast again the thread of life. Instinct compels them to find the place where they were born, the female there to deposit her eggs and the male to fertilize them. Coming now to fight their way through the Cascade Rapids, memory of which has been in their cells since they went down the river as fingerlings, they find instead a seventy-foot dam, of which they have no memory at all. To get an ocean-going vessel over a seventy-foot dam you have only to build the highest ship lock in the world. But how shall you get a salmon over it? For this purpose the engineers have built around each end of the dam what they call fish ladders.

Simply, they are a series of small concrete pools in easy stairway steps under a regulated flow of water; and besides these stairways, for salmon that might not take to them, are elevators like small ship locks. The salmon swims into the lock, a gate closes, the water rises to the level of the river above the dam and a gate opens in front of him, so that he may swim out. Lest he be confused, a wooden platform rises beneath him to push him out.

You may wonder what a salmon thinks. The Department of the Interior already knows. "The returning hordes of salmon," it says, "welcome the fish ladders as a decided improvement over the roaring Cascade Rapids, now buried under seventy feet of water."

The trouble with Nature has always been that it made

life too hard, even fish life. "Bonneville Dam," says the Department of the Interior, "is making life easy for salmon coming home to spawn"; and, by means of the lifts, making it easier still for the lazy ones. It is no longer necessary for the salmon to waste their strength in the rapids, and if you think their effortless passage, assisted by public funds, might soften them, you have to learn again that Nature is often wrong. The Department of the Interior reports that salmon now caught above the dam "have much firmer flesh" than their ancestors.

The dams did not make life easier for the salmon. Sixty years later, they have nearly wiped out the salmon, a result also caused by farming and forestry practices that have degraded spawning habitat. As power generation, though, the dams were wonderful investments. Today they provide the cheapest power in the United States.

CHAPTER SEVENTEEN:

A World That Was

Garrett had written about Henry Ford for years. In the 1930s he watched as Ford held out against the NRA and then against the United Auto Workers. In this piece, written as the nation is about to exit the New Deal and enter World War II, he tells a story that could be read as a warning to the New Economy enterprises of 60 years later.

From "A World that Was," June 8, 1940

On their own unpopular premises, and not too happy there, Laissez Faire and Rugged Individualism would ask a question. They are looking at the American motorcar industry. The question is this: If the conditions that now exist had been present forty years ago, could it have happened?

Why was it Detroit that became the world home of the motorcar? It did not invent the automobile, it had no monopoly on technical skill or ingenuity, nor any physical advantage of site.

Place seems often to be an eccentricity of the event. Any idea that makes great change in the world must somewhere produce its wonder piece, and there will be a place where that occurs in the room of all else that might have happened, or nothing. For many reasons running together, Detroit was the place where American genius for the free competitive system, knowing neither what was impossible nor any extreme, was bound to put forth its prodigy.

If you call that system capitalism, and if you take the motorcar industry to be the magnificent dramatization of its principles and works, then you may imagine that capitalism will stand or fall by Detroit. It is on the defensive there. There, as everywhere, it is defending the world it created against those who represent the forces of social frustration and revolt, and to whom capitalism is the modern satanism.

It is a long way back. The sense of time has been so altered by experience and change that when we think of life forty years ago, it is dim, like a race memory. Yet one-quarter of the people now living were born in the horse-and-buggy days, before automobiles. How can that be imagined?

And as you look at the motor industry today—at the miles of machines that see and feel and react to stimuli as if by instinct, and in fact possess nearly all the attributes of the human animal save willfulness, self-consciousness and political folly; at its amazing research laboratories where thousands of trained scientists are continually exploring the further nature and behavior of automobile matter; at the functional wonder of its assembly lines where the idea of an automobile takes form as a thing; at all this triumph of man's hand and cunning and faculty for organization—looking at it now, you almost cannot believe that in the beginning there was neither engineer nor scientist in it.

They were mechanics, grand tinkers and nuts. Not only did they make the first automobiles with their own hands; they thought with their hands, for they belonged to a hand-minded civilization. Many of them are still living. Henry Ford has under the bench in his private shop the first car he made that would go and come back; it resembles a horseless baby carriage. He yanks it forth to show it, amuses himself to identify the bits of scrap out of which it was built up, and then, kicking it back, he says: "It would still run, only somebody has been taking souvenirs off."

Ask those who did it with their hands what made the motorcar industry. They will not think of what they did. They will not see the industry as you see it. The science, the engineering, the invention, the technology, the evolution of tools, the synchronization of movement—all of that resulted. They take it for granted. None of that made the motorcar industry. What made it, then? They will tell you. It was that the world of economic adventure had no more boundaries than a dream. Men were free to gamble there on their visions for great sweepstakes. If they won, it was theirs. The odds might be a million to one.

What a gamble it was!

They had no capital to start with. Bankers would not touch them. The only security they could offer was what they saw in the sky. Those who put money with Ford—and it was less altogether than fifty thousand—were a coal dealer, his clerk, a confectioner, two owners of a little machine shop, two bookkeepers with a dream, a carpenter and two lawyers. All the capital after that came out of earnings; and when Ford at length bought out his original stockholders in order to have entire control, they were all rich.

General Motors, the largest and most profitable manufacturing corporation in the history of the world, was reared on a heap of broken adventures. By that time, however, a few private capitalists, notably the du Ponts, were beginning to see what the original visionaries had put on the sky; and as they went in at their own risk, Wall Street began gingerly to follow. Then when at length the bankers were in and the industry was one that was apparently closed to individual attack, requiring not thousands but millions at the taw line—and this would have been in the early 20s—a man named Walter P. Chrysler and an engineer named Fred M. Zeder went up and down Wall Street peddling a high-compression engine around which they proposed to build a new competitive automobile. The bankers said there were too many cars already. If production continued to increase, the time would soon come when they couldn't be sold in ten-cent stores. Chrysler and his engineer were crazy, as all motor makers had been from the beginning, but in this case they were crazy too late. Nevertheless, with a gambler's mite, a car that had to be sold before it was made, Chrysler crashed the industry's gate and in a few years was the third whale there. That was tall adventure.

And so it was that the phenomenal, unpredictable American motorcar industry did bring itself to pass, out of the void. Largely, it made its own capital as it went along; and until it had proved its vision, that was entirely so. No industry ever before put back so much profit; consequently, no industry ever before grew so fast by a process analogous to biological proliferation.

But the large key is still missing. It is not the American automobile as a thing that gives the industry its famous character. All people of skill, even the Japanese, make motorcars. European cars may be as fine as ours, some of them perhaps superior. It is possible to make the very finest automobile by hand, one at a time, but the cost of it would be such that only the rich could buy it.

What those early fantasts saw in the sky was not a fine automobile. In their nature as mechanics and grand tinkers they would have been thrilled by that, of course; but they were dreamers, too, and as dreamers they saw this day to come. That is to day, they saw the motorcar as a common utility, which meant that the way of making it was the great problem.

With this thought in mind, if you will look again at the motorcar industry, you will realize that what is wonderful about it, is not the motorcar, but the way of making it; a technic of mass production whereby the cost of one car is cheapened to the point where even an unskilled worker may possess his private means of transportation. In the early days of the industry the wage workers in it came to the shops by trolley car and on bicycles, as they still do in

Europe; but now the American automobile worker comes and goes in his own automobile, and it is the same kind of car the boss drives.

It seems to have been in the mind of Henry Ford that the idea of the universal motorcar first crystallized. After much trial and error of big and little cars, he settled on the mechanical shay that was named the Model T, which was the most astonishing vehicle ever created in the world. The cost of it was cheapened to the price of a good horse and buggy and the complaining gutturals of it unfailing exertions became as familiar to the American ear as the sounds of Nature.

But the idea was implicit in the genius of the industry. An automobile as a luxury for the rich was a limited thought. After all, when you begin to count the rich, they are really few. But an automobile for the common man was a thought to dazzle the imagination, besides presenting original difficulties to the nth power of incentive. All the fame and greatness of the American motorcar industry, and all the profit, too, came from that one idea. An automobile for the common man. One for every family. The motive was profit, to be sure. A small profit per car on millions of cars would be vastly greater than any amount of profit you could calculate on the number of cars it would be possible to sell to the rich alone.

And when they had done it—when it was that a poor man's car could hold the road against a rich man's car, and when, furthermore, the low-priced car, year after year, was so improved in quality, performance and looks that at a little distance all cars looked alike and the rich themselves in common sense began to buy the low-priced car, then you might have supposed that the industry had produced a social effect of extreme importance. You might have said, and it was said, that the serpent of envy had lost a fang. That view was too optimistic, as it turned out; nevertheless, it was interesting and may yet be important.

Many reasoned predictions went wrong. It was only the phantasy that came wholly true. There was never a plan, more than finding a way to do a thing today that had not been imagined yesterday. In a planned economy the American motorcar industry could not have happened at all. The idea of making motorcars by the million, of ticking them off at the end of an assembly line as minutes on the clock—how could that have been planned before there was any way of doing it? The idea was a seed. Everything had to grow, and what it would be nobody could tell until it had appeared.

The growth was uncontrollable and seemed always tending toward disaster. When Ford had to abandon the Model T because his competitors were passing him with a better low-priced car, his entire fortune was at hazard. After Model T had been scrapped and before Model A had appeared, it is doubtful if he could have sold the largest, finest motorcar plant in the world at ten cents on the dollar in Wall Street. Everything was at stake on the quality and cost of the new car. Could he do it?

He did it. And then, after a few millions of the Model A, that, too, was abandoned because again his competitors were overtaking him, and he did it all over again with the V-8.

I remember sitting with him one day looking at the Model A. It was finished and ready to start down the assembly line. Although he was satisfied with it, he kept saying there had been nothing the matter with the old Model T except that people were tired of seeing it.

"This is a much better car," I said. "Take it to be the best car there is for the price. But what are you going to say about it that your competitors will not be saying about theirs at the same price? They are all good."

"Let the advertising people worry about that," he said. "It is the car at last that has to sell itself."

"At any rate," I said, "you will be making all the Model A's you can and General Motors will be making all the Chevrolets it can, and so Chrysler with the Plymouth, all good cars, and the market will scream. Why can't you make a reasonable statistical calculation of the total number of cars that can be sold in the low-priced field, divide it among you and regulate production accordingly?"

He said, "You would take all the fun out of it."

It was an unexpected answer. The meaning came to me later. Profit was the motive, yes; but the deep psychic rewards were from the excitement of overcoming, of success and triumph, of grand play with physical forces.

I said, "No. I am trying to interest you in the possibility of bringing some kind of stability to the motor industry."

"Stability," he said. "Do you know what that is? Stability is a dead fish floating downstream. The only stability we know around here is change."

It was change that saved the industry from breaking on that imaginary point of saturation which seemed always to be standing there just ahead and yet always went away when they came to it.

Such a thing as a good motorcar really wearing out is seldom seen. What happens is that long before it wears out, it goes out of date. That is not to say merely that it goes out of style. It becomes obsolete in a practical sense and had better be thrown away for a cheaper and better car. For example, in the year 1920 the cost of operating a popular size of the four-passenger car, including depreciation, was nearly seven and one-half cents a mile. This has fallen steadily until now it is about two and one-half cents a mile, owing to more efficient engines, better materials, better carburetors and lower first cost. The self-starter, the four-wheeled hydraulic brakes, the welded-steel body—such were improvements which made every existing car obsolete. There need be no end to it, or, at any rate, there has been no end to it yet, and that, of course, is what the engineering and science laboratories are for.

Enough of how it happened. What is it—this American motorcar industry?

Last year the Federal Trade Commission published a volume of 1077 pages on what it is. In the number of wage earners employed, the amount of wages paid, cost of raw materials consumed, value added by manufacture and value of finished product, it is the No. 1 industry in the country, which is to say, in the whole world. There is nothing remotely like it anywhere else.

What is industry for, after all? To produce wealth is not enough. The wealth must be distributed. Nor is profit the end. Profit is incentive and reward, and yet, if industry should keep for its owners the whole of what appears on its books to be profit, it would defeat itself and also defeat the meaning of the capitalistic system, which is that the cost of human satisfactions should be progressively cheapened.

Thus, industry is obliged to share its profit with both the consumer and with labor. You have, therefore, to ask yourself how the motorcar industry has acquitted itself toward the consumer, toward labor, and then toward what you might call the economic welfare of society in the whole.

Firstly, the cost of an automobile has been steadily falling. It is at least one-half less than it was twenty years ago, besides such improvement that the low-priced car today is a better one than you could have bought at any price twenty, fifteen, even ten years ago.

Secondly, the wages of automobile workers have been rising. In forty years the average annual money earnings of the automobile worker has increased threefold. Or take it for the last ten years. Since 1929 the price of an automobile per pound has fallen from 28 cents to 21 cents, or one fourth, while at the same time the wage rate per hour in the automobile factory has increased nearly one third.

Thirdly, though machines made this all possible, no labor has been dispensed with. Employment per car, too, has been rising. The number of man-hours required to produce a car now is higher than it was in 1929. As fast as labor has been released by machines and methods, it has been reabsorbed in the manufacture of improvements added to the car, as you may comprehend from the one fact that, whereas a standard model of car fifteen years ago contained 4500 parts, it has now 16,000 parts. As more value was added to the car, labor's share in what the Census calls value added by manufacture—meaning the value added by both machines and labor to the materials—labor's share of that value has been increasing. In 1929 it was less than 37 per cent. Today it is more than 50 per cent.

Fourthly, the hours of labor have been shortened to forty a week and the conditions of labor have been improved beyond recognition.

Lastly, the profit. The industry's net profits per car, before Federal income taxes, was $55 in the year 1929. In the next ten years it fell to $29 per car.

Ford was the first big profit maker. During thirty-four and one-half years, says the Federal Trade Commission, the Ford Motor Company made 27,000,000 cars and the profit was $978,900,000. But $610,000,000 of that profit was put back into the works. Then General Motors was the big profit maker. During twenty-nine years, its profit, after taxes, was $2,610,885,556. But of this, $558,980,000 was returned to the property. Out of profits of $310,317,944 in thirteen years, the Chrysler Corporation returned one-third to the property. The motor industry became the rich province it is because it plowed back its profits by the hundreds of millions.

Formerly it was free to do what it liked with its profit. Having had a good year, it could and did write away entire plants as obsolete, tear them down and build new ones, charging it all to profit. The industry is no longer free to do that. No industry is. Why not?

In the first place, more than one-half of the motor industry's profit may be devoured by taxation.

The tax bill of the General Motors Corporation last year amounted to 55.6 percent of its net earnings. More striking still, it amounted to $523 per employee, or to more than one fourth of the total pay roll. For each $100 of wages and salaries paid, the tax collector got $28.

That, however, is simple partition. There is more to it.

In its great need for tax revenue to support itself, the Federal Government is fearful that corporations will conceal their profits by plowing back their net earnings, and do this to beat the tax collector. So it is written in the Federal tax law that there shall be deducted from pre-tax earnings only a "reasonable allowance" for depreciation and obsolescence, and nothing for new property. Who shall say what a reasonable allowance is? Who shall say where obsolescence ends and new property begins? The motor industry is no longer permitted to say. The Internal Revenue Service at Washington decides; and if more net earnings are plowed back than it thinks is reasonable, supposing it were itself running the motor industry, then those net earnings are taxed as if they were profit, so that it costs the corporation more to reinvest its own money in its own works than if it went out and borrowed the capital at interest.

Given the Government's necessities, the law, perhaps, is what it must be, for it is true that many corporations would conceal their earnings in the manner suspected; nevertheless the result is this: The head of an automobile corporation takes you to a window that overlooks a large division of the plant and says: "Look. From that corner right there to the end of those buildings you see in the distance, everything is obsolete from our way of thinking. We know how to do it much better. If we could do as we used to do with our profits, we could be tearing that all down in order to build it over and pay for it out of one year's untaxed net earnings. But what we could have done in one year before, we must take six or eight years to do, because the Government tells us how fast we wear out, what our rate of obsolescence is and how much we may write off each year of our earnings."

It is certain that if the "reasonable allowance" for obsolescence now permitted by the Government to be deducted from untaxed earnings had been the motor industry's rule from the beginning, with nothing at all out of untaxed profits for new property, the industry would have been much less self-financed and its debt would be much greater, with the result not only that its career would have been different but that there now would be much less profit for the Government to tax, if any.

So you may see that the motor industry is losing control of its profits. But all of this refers to losing control of them after they are made. On the opposite side, it is beginning to lose control of them before they are made.

Suddenly it has lost control of labor. For that reason its control of labor costs is weakening. And if labor wins one point more, which is the right to say what the standard speed of production shall be, it will have lost control of production—and of all matters, as a motor maker thinks, that would be the crucial one.

Until the CIO, in the year 1937, made its conquest of the motorcar industry by methods of aggression which included taking physical possession of the plants and running the boss out, Detroit was an open-shop town. Unions did not thrive there. Fewer than one-tenth of the automobile industry's employees were organized at all, and these were skilled craftsmen belonging to unions of the old-fashioned AFL type. Note that at least 90 per cent of automobile factory workers are unskilled and semi-skilled. More than one fourth of all the jobs require no previous training whatever; nine-tenths of them require less than one year's experience.

Needing so little skill and experience, a labor force is easily recruited, especially at times when there is a surplus of labor; and such are the conditions under which, historically, the wage earner has been exploited. Nevertheless, the motorcar industry could sincerely say that it never did exploit labor to cheapen it, and that its treatment of the wage earner had been generous. It could believe, and it was true, that its long immunity from labor troubles was owing largely to the fact that unionism, wherein it concerned itself with wages and hours and working conditions, had little to offer these workers, because their wages were higher than in any other industry for comparable work, even unionized industry; the length of the work day was shortening itself, and the physical conditions under which labor was performed were superior.

At the same time the industry did control its labor, and not with a soft hand. It fixed the wage, it fixed the tempo of human exertion, it made all the terms; the individual was free only to take them or leave them, and the boss was feared.

It is to be remembered here that the men who made the motorcar industry had themselves come the hard way. They knew the meaning of work, and they were drivers, but they drove themselves too. They had among them one saying, which was, "Get it done!" And two obsessions— namely, time and production. Production had to be moved through time faster and faster.

Beyond this, they were generous and personally fair. They believed in high wages and fine shops to work in— wages so much higher and conditions so much better than anything they had known when they were themselves wage earners that they could not see what men had to complain of. They believed, too, that wages and profits could rise together, which is true in the American scheme, provided only you keep increasing the productive power of the individual by putting behind him better machines and more scientific technic. They did not believe in altruism. It would not occur to them.

There is a way of seeing it by contrast and history.

No member of the motorcar industry was more inflexible with labor than Henry Ford. Yet when the industry was still young, hardly fifteen years old, he electrified the country by announcing a minimum wage of five dollars a day. Those who are not old enough to remember cannot imagine what a commotion this produced in the world of industry. There were many who said he must have lost his mind; many others thought he must have had a sinister motive, and who believed, in any case, that he was likely to ruin industry. I went to Detroit to see. That was the first time I met Ford.

Before seeing him I went about Detroit, asking people what they thought. The Board of Commerce was in a panic. Smaller manufacturers, outside of the motorcar industry, had been serving notice that they were leaving Detroit, and several of them did. The owner of the barber shop at the hotel told me he would have to go out of business; even barbers would be wanting five dollars a day. And at the new

Highland Park Ford plant there was a strange scene. From all over the region, from the hills of Tennessee, from Chicago and other cities, the rush of men to seek five-dollar-a-day jobs led to an uncontrollable situation at the gates, and the fire hose was turned on them.

Then I saw Ford. He said: "It's perfectly simple. A man who is keen about his job can save me five dollars a day by picking up small tools off the floor instead of sweeping them out."

We went through the plant together. I knew the difference in rhythm between a piece-rate factory and a day-wage factory. Never had I heard a rhythm so fast in a piece-rate factory—and this was day wage. If we started down a corridor and a man was coming with a material truck, he wouldn't hesitate even for Ford. It was the boss himself who had to jump. Labor there was certainly on its toes. And what was the result? The labor cost per car declined.

I said to Ford, "But do you never have any labor trouble?"

He said: "They brought me word one morning that when the tool makers came on the job they were going to strike." There he stopped.

I asked: "What did you do?"

He said: "I told them to pull the switch in the tool room." And stopped again. When the tool makers arrived, they had no power, no jobs, nothing to strike, and there was no strike.

I asked: "Then what did you do?"

"Oh," he said, "we looked into them and took all but two or three of them back."

Yet with no benefit of unionism the motorcar industry was thereafter established on a high-wage plane, paying more for unskilled and semi-skilled labor than any other. Today the wage with Ford averages $7.25 for an eight-hour day, and rises to more than $10.00. A window washer or a floor sweeper gets $6.00 a day. But this is not Ford alone. The average pay for unskilled and semi-skilled labor for the entire motorcar industry is 91 1/2 cents per hour, or $7.32 per eight-hour day.

So now the contrast.

Three years ago John L. Lewis sat at a conference table there, settling the first Chrysler strike. Suddenly one of the Chrysler men said, "Do you think this is fair? First you strike General Motors alone and let Chrysler and Ford make the cars. Having settled with General Motors, now you strike Chrysler alone and let others make the cars."

Lewis answered, "That may not be fair. I sympathize with your point, gentlemen. I dare say it is the first valid point you have made in the whole course of these negotiations. If you hold to it, suppose we make it fair all around. Suppose tomorrow we close you all up."

You may take that to be the moment at which the motorcar industry lost control of labor.

The industry thinks that the sudden triumph of unionism was made possible by the National Labor Relations Act. That may be so. The act declares the intent of Congress, as a matter of public policy, to promote the organization of labor for purposes of collective bargaining, on the ground that the refusal of an employer to recognize unionism and bargain collectively tends to obstruct interstate commerce. The law to begin with, the National Labor Relations Board which is the law's instrument, and all the blessings of the national Administration, were behind the organizers when they went forth to capture Detroit.

At the peak of the struggle between the CIO and the motorcar industry, it happened that the Administration at Washington was in the heat of its attack upon the conservative principle surviving in the United States Supreme Court, and there was at least the appearance of collaboration when the strikers who were in unlawful possession of the automobile factories and daring the courts of Michigan to enforce their injunctions held monster mass meetings in the streets of Detroit and denounced "nine old men" as enemies of the people.

Nevertheless, when its sky began to fall, the motorcar industry was shocked to find that it had overcounted its credit with labor; and more than that, its understanding was baffled. It was not enough to say that during all those

270

years of open shop it had paid high wages, for wages seemed not to be the crucial matter. True, the strikers demanded still higher wages—always that—but everyone knew that no possible wage increase would bring the peace. Nor did it help to mention the fact that the physical surroundings under which automobiles were made had been improved to the point of excellence.

Then what was it labor wanted? An impossible thing? No, not an impossible thing, nor a new thing, only that it seemed strange in this environment.

In the old philosophy of the American labor movement the struggle with capital was over a division of the product—that is to say, it was an economic dispute, not complicated by ideologies of class warfare. It is no longer so simple. What now has to be faced, what is taking place in fact, is a struggle over division of power.

It is industry's power over labor that is challenged. The aim of labor's crusade is to break that power, and in the breaking of it to gain power for itself over industry.

This evangel goes deeper than the pocket. It goes to the roots of the man's ego and produces violent emotions. And it has created in the mentality of labor, mass labor especially, a spirit of revolt.

A revolt against what?

From its literature and propaganda, you might take it to be a revolt against anything a wage earner could think to complain of—against the mechanization of life, the humiliation of being a number, fear of losing one's job, profit for a few while there are yet any who want bare plenty, what the boss gets, and so on. Superficially, it is all of that. Yet for all such unreasoned expressions of it and for such banner cries as "wage slavery" and "economic freedom," there is one constant translation. At heart it is a revolt against the capitalistic system of production that gives industry power over labor. There is Communism in it, acting deviously. There is extreme radicalism in it. But there is much more that needs to be thoughtfully accounted for.

One of the very significant aspects of the conflict as it comes to a head in Detroit is the militant attitude of the

271

Catholic Church. It is believed that more than one-half of the wage earners in the Detroit region are Catholic. In order to train them to take an active part in the labor movement, there was created the Archdiocesan Labor Institute, with schools in forty parishes, where, said the archbishop, "a large number of workmen, under the direction of an interested and informed priest and the helpers he gathers about him, will be equipped to sift the good from the bad in labor proposals and to be the defenders of sound, constructive union activity against the inroads of communistic agitation."

There was then organized the Association of Catholic Trade Unionists, and there is a definite and powerful Catholic labor movement, guided by the interpretations of the famous encyclicals, especially that of Pope Pius XI, entitled *Quadragesimo Anno*, on reconstructing the social order, and that of Pope Leo XIII, *On the Condition of the Working Classes.*

The association publishes a paper, named *The Michigan Labor Leader.* On its first page, Nov. 3, 1939, it printed an Open Letter to Catholic Employers, saying: "Dear Sirs and Brothers in Christ: . . . The seemingly radical trend of the Association of Catholic Trade Unionists, and the Catholic labor movement in general, has no doubt disturbed you deeply. We'll try to explain . . . When we condemn the spirit of capitalism as un-Christian and unjust, when we blast the modern economic system and call it heartless, cruel and relentless, we do not mean to apply those terms to you personally. We know that most of you are good guys, and even the worst among you is as bad as the system. What, then, do we expect of you? Briefly, we expect you to recognize the cruelty and immorality of the system, of which all of us are a part, and we expect you to join with the working class in efforts to better it."

At the head of the Catholic press in the Detroit diocese is *The Michigan Catholic,* a weekly paper. During the second Chrysler strike last year, it printed on the first page a two-column editorial in which it took its position squarely behind the strikers. It said: "In this dispute there has been a request by the workers for a voice in the determination of production standards, which, when no agreement could be reached, was modified into a demand for arbitration of grievances. Both these demands are justified in the light of Catholic principles . . . The closed-shop issue was dropped by the union two weeks ago. Even if it were still an issue, it would be a justified demand, according to Catholic principles."

Seldom may one be so sure of anything to come as that between organized labor and the motorcar industry there will be no peace—only a working truce—until labor definitely has won or lost the two principles—namely, first, the closed shop; second, the right to act on the standards of production speed.

The industry's most dogged resistance will be made to the second principle. Why should it resist? Labor's argument is very plausible. If what wage a man shall receive for a day's work is a bargainable matter, then why is not the amount of work he shall perform for that wage also a bargainable matter?

Here occurs an impasse of mind. Industry is not labor-minded; labor is not industry-minded. Passing more and more production through a given quantity of time is the very magic of the motorcar industry. You could, of course, have a motorcar industry at any tempo, even at the old tempo of carriage making, but it would not be this motorcar industry.

What the industry believes is that if labor, having already gained the power to price itself higher, gained furthermore the power to say how much work a man shall perform for a day's pay, it would act upon production never to speed it up, but always to slow it down. Slowing it down would increase the cost of making an automobile, and in the end would be found to limit employment.

Until now, the industry has been able by invention to keep the price of an automobile falling, with wages at the same time rising, and with actually no technological unemployment. This has been almost its finest achievement. But

273

there is a price for labor—no one can say beforehand what it is—but a price, nevertheless, at which either the increased labor cost would have to be added to the price of the car or machines would have to be employed purposely to reduce the amount of labor required to make it. Then you would have for the first time in this industry the true problem of technological unemployment. The margin is already very thin.

Not a very optimistic view. Yet optimism in the motor-car industry is a powerful habit. It need not be reasoned. It may, and now does, take the expression: "All we know is that we will go on beating it as long as we can." The attitude of labor is to say: "We'll take it while we can."

The Michigan Labor Leader, the Catholic paper, quoted from a speech by the president of General Motors the statement that there was no objection to shorter hours and higher pay so long as shop efficiency continued to increase, so that the total cost of making an automobile did not go up. To this, the retort was made in italics: "He'd give us more pay if it didn't cost anything. What a system!"

But it isn't the motorcar industry nor any corporation that pays the increased cost of a car. The buyer does that.

So lastly the question returns that was set up in the beginning.

If the social and political conditions that now limit the will and the freedom and creative anarchy of individual enterprise had existed forty years ago, could this motor industry or anything like it have happened at Detroit? You might guess the answer would be divided. But those who made the industry and still do largely control it answer all alike. The answer is no.

If they are right, and you cannot imagine going back, then that amazing, too-free world in which it happened is on the way to becoming a legend.

Garrett once called General Motors a confederacy, Chrysler a democracy and Ford a monarchy. Besieged by forces strange to him, Henry Ford turned to his bodyguard,

Harry Bennett, "a sailor and very handy with his fists," to head the company's internal police. "In a few years," Garrett wrote, "Bennett began to behave as if he were Ford's private Gestapo, as in fact he was; and there came to exist between them a singular intimacy."

Bennett's tactics left a stain on Henry Ford's legacy and have become iconic in the history as told by the unions. And Bennett was not able to save Ford. After a bitter strike, Ford recognized the United Automobile Workers-C.I.O. in 1941. In The Wild Wheel, *a book that expanded on the themes in this article, Garrett said:*

Ford was the most implacable of the Big Three and for that reason was the last to be attacked. He was then seventy-five. His defeat was without solace. The union won more than it asked for, and after that the Ford Motor Company was a closed shop; only union members could work there, and Ford became the collector of the members' compulsory union dues, acting for the union treasury.

What he had lost was not just a battle with labor. He had lost his world. Never again would the wheels be wild in a Ford shop. The union would attend to that.

The significance of this change was deeper than anybody knew at the time. Although Ford never expressed it in rational terms, he must have known it intuitively.

CHAPTER EIGHTEEN

To Work

This was written in July 1940, a few weeks after the fall of France, which left Britain alone against the German Luftwaffe. Russia was fighting Finland; it had just seized Latvia, Lithuania, Estonia and the Romanian province of Bessarabia, and had a non-aggression pact with Germany. Roosevelt had committed the United States to helping Britain by all means "short of war," and had declared a national emergency.

This is an unsigned Saturday Evening Post *editorial. By then, Garrett was the editorial writer in chief, and this is clearly his work.*

"Work," August 10, 1940

It is Saturday morning in Indiana. The two owners of a machine shop are at the drawing board designing parts for heavy turret lathes. They have many urgent orders. The machine parts they make are needed for the national defense. But the shop is silent. Why? Because the men have already worked their statutory forty hours for the week, and anything more than that would be overtime at penalty wages.

Legally and artfully we have lightened the yoke; yet it may be that God's second arrangement with Adam shall not be so easily broken.

France was in flight from the curse of work. The hours of labor were foreshortened by law, wages were raised by law, the workers controlled the speed of production, and disputes about it were settled sometimes by locking the boss in until he gave up and sometimes by locking him out. Now France is a slave nation.

In Great Britain the rise of labor to political eminence as a self-regarding class was one of the magnificent social gains of the century. Now Great Britain is fighting for her life.

In Russia, where labor was puppet king, the hours of toil have been lengthened by decree. Why? In order that a proletarian state, like any other aggressor, may increase its military exertions for purposes of conquest.

In the moment of going to war, Mr. Mussolini's swollen adrenal glands caused him to betray all the silly ideologies in which the aggressors had clothed their intentions. The war, he said, was a war between the lean and hungry nations that had got the power, and the rich, soft nations that had lost it; and now the lean and hungry ones were going to take what they wanted.

How did they get the power—the lean and hungry ones? Their natural resources were inferior.

Look back at what was taking place in the world. The principal great powers were eight. Three were richer than the other five together. They had higher standards of living, a softer culture, more than two thirds of the world's material wealth, not to speak of their social gains, but they were all in flight from work. These three were the United States, Great Britain and France, now commonly called the democracies.

The five were the lean and hungry ones. And what were they doing? While the three were limiting and reducing their hours of labor, the five were extending theirs. While the three were saying the machine was to relieve man of toil and if only they could think of a law to distribute in a social manner the plenty the machine had made possible, everybody could have more with less and less work, what were the five saying? They were saying the machine was to enable people to perform more work, not less. It was their means to power.

The first consequences were economic. The five, especially Germany on one side and Japan on the other, working harder and consuming less, pressed cheaper goods on all the markets of the world. The three were unwilling to meet this competition. To protect their higher standards of living and their social gains, they put tariff barriers against those cheaper goods. The American tariff was specifically designed to equalize differences in the cost of production, for of course it was unfair that goods produced by people working sixty to seventy hours a week at low wages should be permitted to compete with goods produced by people working forty hours a week at high wages.

But the lean and hungry nations, especially Germany, worked all the harder and consumed still less and sold goods over all tariff barriers; and they did it because they had to buy the materials they needed for the war machines they were building.

What follows is the dire consequence. Tariff walls are an economic protection but of no military value whatever. What a pleasant world it would be if you could stop the aggressor with a prohibitive tariff, or by a tariff law equalize a disparity of military power!

Work inherits the earth. The power of the aggressor is an idea externalized by work. What the dictator commands is labor. Note where it was where the social malady of unemployment became chronic. Not in the lean and hungry countries. It was the problem of the three rich countries, and most acute in the richest of all, our own. Only a rich country can afford unemployment.

In his annual message to Congress, January 4, 1939, President Roosevelt said: "The first duty of our statesmanship today is to bring capital and man power together. Dictatorships do this by main force . . . However we abhor their methods, we are compelled to admit that they have obtained substantial utilization of all their material and human resources. Like it or not, they have solved, for a time at least, the problem of idle men and idle capital."

We are looking at it, but in an oblique manner, not seeing it for what it was. We kept thinking and writing about it as Nazism, Communism, an philosophy of state, or what else, whereas it was a very old thing. Those who will intelligently and purposefully perform the most work will possess the world. Either they will dominate it economically or they will take it by force, and there is no help for it. But we made no such deduction. Neither did Great Britain or France.

We went on slowing down our industrial machine, killing our surplus, limiting the hours of labor, dividing the work, subsidizing youth to keep it in school and off the labor market, giving pensions to the elders in order to retire them sooner from the labor market at the other end of the scale, spending more than a billion a year in unemployment relief—and then, when all of this notwithstanding, the more abundant life with still less work did not appear, the brilliant little doctors at Washington began to write and lecture on the strange case of a young country that was prematurely and suddenly old. We were arriving at what they called a static economy. Never again would there be work enough for everybody. That was the best thing they could do who did not know what they were doing. The Government did not know. The people did not care too much to know, because the evangel of an easier life, everyone who had not had enough now to have more by less exertion, was extremely attractive.

For a free people it is the law of necessity that acts in the place of a dictator. But it is a very hard law, and it is human to rebel against it. Here was a Government saying there was an easier way, saying there was already plenty and surplus if only it were properly divided. Leave that to the Government. It would plan the economic scheme and administer it. On borrowed money, and it may be on borrowed time, it undertook first to restore old values and then stabilize them, to regulate production, to support the wage structure, the price structure and the capital structure, all at one time. For purposes of this balanced economy there was apparently a surplus of labor. That was said to mean only that the wage earner had been working too hard to support the private-profit motive. The thing to do, therefore, was to shorten the hours of labor; less work for the same pay, and everybody to have more than before.

First, the revolt against necessity, the phantasy of producing less and consuming more, the surrender of self-responsibility to a Government that said it knew this magic—and then the flight from work.

We have always been a very hard-working people, and for that reason we have been able to accumulate an enormous surplus of wealth. The existence of that surplus and the free distribution of it by the Government, downward through the social structure, created for a time the delusion that the magic was true. But it could last only until we had devoured, used up, worn out, our surplus wealth.

We were coming to the end of it. Our standard of living was beginning to fall, simply for the reason that we were not performing enough work to maintain it, and thoughtful minds were already in a state of acute anxiety as to the sequel, when suddenly the country was faced with the unexpected necessity to prepare a national defense beyond anything hitherto imaginable.

The emergency is one that involves our destiny; it may be our survival as a free people; it calls for us to work harder, perhaps, than we have ever worked before. Yet almost the first thing the President said was: "There is nothing in our present emergency to justify making the workers of our nation toil at longer hours than those limited by statute." And he has been saying it ever since. The statutory hours of labor are now the lowest point we have ever known. That is the position the Government takes; it becomes naturally the fixed position of organized labor.

Billions for national defense. We vote them—like that! Billions to any number for the American destiny. But no harder work. No increase in the hours of labor. Not that.

Would that it were so. Would also that it were a world without war or aggressor in it. The reality is bitter.

We cannot buy defense. There is nobody to buy it from.

We cannot spend these billions we are voting unless by our own labor we produce the ships and planes and guns and machine equipment they are for; and to produce them in time, or at all, we shall have to work harder.

We cannot prepare an adequate national defense and at the same time afford our present standard of living unless we enormously increase the production of all things.

We cannot increase it by voting billions. It can be increased only by more work.

Above any law that we can make, there is a jealous law of work. It was passed at the gate of the Garden of Eden, with man on his way out. Man's entire history since then has been the story of his struggle to overcome it. He has had the cunning to invent for himself a race of mechanical slaves and still he cannot beat it.

The war brought plenty of work for his fellow Americans. But at age 64, Garrett, who had worked at the Saturday Evening Post *through the entire Depression, was out of a job. He offered his services to the government as a reporter, a writer and PR man. No takers. In October 1942 he gave up waiting for a government job and went to work in a shipyard.*

Other Libertarian titles from
CAXTON PRESS:

ANTHEM
by Ayn Rand
ISBN 0-87004-124-x
Hardcover $12.95

WHAT SOCIAL CLASSES OWE EACH OTHER
by William Graham Sumner
ISBN 0-87004-165-5
Paperback $6.95

THE ART OF CONTRARY THINKING
by Humphrey B. Neill
ISBN 0-87004-110-x
$17.95

CAXTON PRESS
312 Main Street
Caldwell, Idaho 836705

www.caxtonpress.com